THE BAKER
COMPACT
DICTIONARY
═══ OF ═══
THEOLOGICAL
TERMS

THE BAKER
COMPACT
DICTIONARY
OF
THEOLOGICAL
TERMS

GREGG R. ALLISON

BakerBooks
a division of Baker Publishing Group
Grand Rapids, Michigan

© 2016 by Gregg R. Allison

Published by Baker Books
a division of Baker Publishing Group
P.O. Box 6287, Grand Rapids, MI 49516-6287
www.bakerbooks.com

Printed in the United States of America

Library of Congress Cataloging-in-Publication Data is on file at the Library of
Congress, Washington, DC.

ISBN 978-0-8010-1576-2

16   17   18   19   20   21   22   7   6   5   4   3   2   1

This *Compact Dictionary* is dedicated to my grandchildren. I pray that as you learn the basic theology defined in it, your childlike trust in Jesus Christ will grow to become a mature and settled faith. I hope that this book will help foster a deep love for our Triune God and a sacrificial commitment to missional endeavors for the sake of the kingdom.

Contents

Introduction

The Baker Compact Dictionary of Theological Terms is designed for people who seek a concise understanding of the most significant words at the heart of the Christian faith.

When God reveals himself, a key means of his self-disclosure is through words. When God called Abraham, he commanded this pagan to leave his country and family and to settle in an unknown land. Then God promised to make Abraham a blessing to the whole world (Gen. 12:1–3). God spoke in human words, and Abraham obeyed and trusted him. When Jesus called Peter and Andrew, he told them, "Follow me, and I will make you fishers of men." God the Son spoke in human words, and these men followed and were transformed into Jesus's first disciples (Matt. 4:19–20). Of course, the pinnacle of worded revelation—Scripture—is the Word of God in human words.

Similarly, words are vital to the church as it constructs its theology. The essential beliefs about the Christian faith cover many areas: God, Scripture, humanity, Jesus Christ, sin, salvation, the Holy Spirit, the church, last things. Each of these theological topics has its own specific terms: Trinity, inspiration, the image of God, hypostatic union, concupiscence, justification, sanctification, baptism, the millennium. For ease in understanding the most significant theological terms at the heart of the Christian faith, this dictionary was written.

This is a compact dictionary: it contains about six hundred terms, each of which is defined in roughly one hundred words. Its concise nature means that many terms had to be left out. Still, the six hundred that are included are the most important terms, those that readers of theology books and other theological resources will come upon over and over again. Its concise nature also means that each definition is very tight, sticking to essential matters. Much more could be written, but each term's succinct definition avoids extraneous ideas and nuanced discussion.

This dictionary has a specific use. My hope is that readers, when reading a theology book, listening to a lecture about some theological topic, or hearing a sermon on a Christian doctrine, will consult this dictionary for the definition of terms that are not explained. For example: What is meant by the *eternal generation* of the Son in discussions about the *ontological Trinity*? Or what is the difference between *total depravity* and *total inability* in debates about *original sin*? Still again, what is the distinction between *transubstantiation*, *consubstantiation*, *memorial view*, and *spiritual presence* with regard to the presence of Christ in the celebration of the *Lord's Supper*? Simple navigation of the alphabetical ordering of terms is all that is required to find the definition of these terms and to be able to answer these important questions that people have about theological matters.

The theological terms included in this *Compact Dictionary* are of a few general types: doctrines (e.g., the atonement, the church), biblical terms that are important for theology (e.g., Messiah, Son of Man), church practices (e.g., anointing of the sick, immersion), philosophical terms that are important for theology (e.g., *a posteriori*, *a priori*, compatibilism), persons (e.g., John Wesley, Thomas Aquinas), councils (e.g., Councils of Nicea I and II, Council of Trent), movements (e.g., Protestantism, Pentecostalism), and documents (e.g., the Chalcedonian Creed, Chicago Statement on Biblical Inerrancy).

Every book is written from a certain perspective, so this dictionary reflects my theological outlook. Most broadly, I am a Christian, championing the general theological consensus or tradition that has been handed down from Jesus and his apostles through the early church to today. More particularly, I am a Protestant, following the legacy of Martin Luther, John Calvin, and their successors. More specifically yet, I am an evangelical, standing in the heritage of this expansive movement that is centered on the evangel, or gospel, of Jesus Christ. Accordingly, this dictionary's theological terms are defined from an evangelical perspective.

A few features of this book need a brief explanation:

- *Cross-references*: After each term, I provide a list of other key theological terms that are related to it. For a fuller grasp of its definition, readers should consult these additional terms.

- *Word origins*: In many cases, I provide the etymology, or origin, of a theological term. Even readers who are unfamiliar with Latin, Greek, and Hebrew will be helped by this feature as they gain a sense of where these terms originated.

- *Translations*: In the appendix, I have listed three hundred of the most important theological terms and have provided, with the help of native speakers, the equivalent for them in French, German, and Korean. Only the theological term, not its definition, is translated. This feature is designed to help English speakers who, for research purposes, are learning French and German. It is also designed to help the many Korean students enrolled in North American and British universities and seminaries as they take courses in theology and need some help to master these terms in English.

All books are a collaborative undertaking, and I would like to express appreciation to my acquisitions editor, Brian Vos. He first proposed the idea of this dictionary, championed the proposal, and provided encouragement and counsel during the writing process. I also want to thank Baker Books for the opportunity to design and write this dictionary and other projects on which I am working. A special nod goes to Justin Holcomb for making this dictionary better. Finally, I am very thankful to François Turcotte, Lars Kierspel, and Byoungjim Kim for their translation work in French, German, and Korean, respectively.

The Baker Compact Dictionary of Theological Terms is dedicated to my grandchildren, who at the time of its writing are Caleb, Alia, Zoe, and Ethan Schneringer, and Annelie, Hudson Roy, and Vaughan Schuetz. I anticipate that more will be added to this list. To all of you born and still to come, I love you and am so thankful that I can be your Doc.

A

A POSTERIORI / A PRIORI 启文 妖文 With respect to the doctrine of God, two types of arguments for God's existence. *A posteriori* (Lat., "from what comes after") knowledge is based on experience, and *a priori* (Lat., "from what comes before" or "prior to") knowledge is prior to or independent of experience. Ontological arguments for God's existence are *a priori* arguments, reasoning from the concept of God's being. Cosmological, teleological, and moral arguments are *a posteriori* arguments, reasoning from observations of the world, its purpose/design, and moral experience.

ABRAHAMIC COVENANT   The structured relationship that God established with Abraham (Gen. 12–17), consisting of typical covenantal features. This covenant (1) was unilateral, initiated by God, who passed between the pieces of animals while Abraham slept; (2) created a structured relationship between God and his partners, Abraham and his future innumerable offspring; (3) featured binding obligations, including the divine purpose to make of Abraham a great nation (with its own promised land), to bless him, and to make him a blessing or a curse to others; and (4) involved the sign of circumcision for all boys when they were eight days old. *See also* circumcision; covenant.

ACCOMMODATION   God's act of condescending to human capacity in his revelation of himself. Though affirmed earlier in history, this doctrine is especially associated with John Calvin. He underscored the appropriateness of God, who is infinitely exalted, accommodating himself to human weakness so that his adjusted revelation would be intelligible to its recipients. Indeed, God stoops like a parent communicating with a child. This accommodation is especially seen in Scripture: it is the Word of God written in limited human languages for sinful human beings with limited capacity to understand it, yet it does not participate in human error.

ADAMIC COVENANT   The structured relationship that God established with Adam and the creation (Gen. 1–3), consisting of typical covenantal features. This covenant (1) was unilateral, initiated by God, the Creator of the creation in general and of human beings in particular; (2) created a structured relationship between God and his partners, both the creation and Adam and Eve; (3) featured binding obligations, including the cultural mandate for human beings in relation to the creation, and the prohibition of eating the tree of the knowledge of good and evil; (4) did not involve signs or oaths because of the absence of sin. *See also* covenant; federal headship; natural headship of Adam; original sin; Reformed theology; representative headship of Adam; sin.

ADIAPHORA   "Indifferent matters" (Gk. *adiaphora*) are activities that are neither moral nor immoral. Moral activities (e.g., loving one's neighbor) are in accordance with God's law. Immoral activities (e.g., murder) violate it. Activities that fall in neither category are *adiaphora*, or indifferent before God; people may choose to engage in or abstain from them. Examples include eating meat sacrificed to idols and celebrating special days like Christmas and Easter. Christian conduct in these matters is ruled by two considerations: stronger Christians should not cause their weaker counterparts to stumble, and weaker Christians are not to condemn their stronger counterparts for engaging in these activities (Rom. 14).

ADOPTION   In regard to the application of salvation, the mighty work of God to take sinful people—enemies who are alienated and separated from him—and embrace them as beloved children into his family forever. Redemption through the Son of God results in their adoption as sons and daughters, together with the reception of the Spirit of adoption, by whom God is called "Abba! Father!" (Rom. 8:14–16; Gal. 4:4–7). Adoption as children into the family of God means further that Christians are brothers and sisters, united with one another (Gal. 3:26–28) and fellow heirs with their brother Christ (Rom. 8:17).

ADOPTIONISM/ADOPTIANISM   With respect to Christology, the denial of the deity of Jesus Christ. Adoptionism is also called Dynamic Monarchianism, and it bears a few similarities with Ebionism. Major tenets: (1) Jesus was an ordinary, though unusually holy, man on whom the "Christ" (the power and presence of God, in a dove-like form) came at his baptism. (2) At that point, God "adopted" Jesus as his son, conferring on him supernatural powers. The Council of Nicea I (325) rejected adoptionism by its affirmation that Jesus Christ is the eternal Son of God incarnate, consisting of a fully divine and a fully human nature. *See also* Council of Nicea (I, II); Ebionism; hypostatic union; Jesus Christ, deity of; Monarchianism.

ADVENT   The coming of Jesus Christ, and the church's celebration of it. In the first sense, *advent* refers to the two appearances of Christ. At his first advent two thousand years ago, Christ came in humility and suffering, dying "to bear the sins of many" (Heb. 9:28). At his second advent in the future, Christ will come in glory and triumph, "not to deal with sin but to save those who are eagerly waiting for him" (Heb. 9:28). In the second sense, Advent is the period of four Sundays before Christmas in which the church celebrates Christ's first and second comings. *See also* second coming.

AFFUSION   *See* pouring.

AGE OF ACCOUNTABILITY   With respect to soteriology, the time at which people become moral agents and thus responsible for their actions and for responding to the gospel. Biblical support includes affirmations that children "have no knowledge of good or evil" (Deut. 1:39; cf. Isa. 7:15–16). Accordingly, children are not under divine condemnation and, because of either their innocence or an extraordinary application of Christ's death to them, children who die are saved. Objections include the weakness of biblical support for such an age and the absence of biblical affirmation of an extraordinary work of grace apart from personal faith in Christ.

不可知论

AGNOSTICISM In regard to the doctrine of God, the position that one cannot know if God exists. From the Greek (*a-*, "no"; *gnōsis*, "knowledge"), *agnosticism* refers to "the view that human reason is incapable of providing sufficient rational grounds to justify either the belief that God exists or the belief that God does not exist" (William Rowe).* While it may be the case that God does exist, nothing within the realm of human reason can count for or against that case. Strong agnosticism holds that God's existence is unknowable, while weak agnosticism maintains that God's existence is unknown but not unknowable. *See also* atheism; theism.

ALEXANDRIAN SCHOOL With respect to biblical interpretation, an approach that developed in the early church (e.g., Origen in Alexandria, Egypt) and that focused on an allegorical, rather than literal, interpretation of Scripture. For Origen, Scripture contains several meanings, including a literal sense and several spiritual senses. For example, with respect to Old Testament burnt offerings and sacrifices, according to the literal sense, these were actual sacrifices; according to a deeper sense, they pointed to Christ's sacrifice; according to the spiritual sense, they symbolized the spiritual sacrifices that Christians should offer. The Alexandrian School stood in contrast with the Antiochene School. *See also* allegory; Antiochene School; hermeneutics.

ALLEGORY With respect to biblical interpretation, a specific approach emphasizing that the biblical text is a symbol of, or pointer

---

* William Rowe, "Agnosticism," in *Concise Routledge Encyclopedia of Philosophy*, ed. E. Craig (London: Routledge, 2000), 17.

to, deeper spiritual meanings. While the literal sense (the meaning of the actual words) of a text is considered, the allegorical sense (focusing on the things to which the words point) is more important. This deeper sense could have reference to Jesus Christ, to the salvation that he brings, to moral behavior for Christians to engage in or exemplify, to the church and its ministries, or to some future fulfillment. Allegory stands in contrast to a literal interpretation of Scripture. *See also* Alexandrian School; Antiochene School; hermeneutics.

AMILLENNIALISM With respect to eschatology, the position that there is no (*a-*) millennium, or no future thousand-year period of Christ's reign on the earth. Developed in the fifth century, it superseded (historic) premillennialism. Key to this position is its nonliteral interpretation of Revelation 20:1–6: Satan's binding is God's current restraint of him, enabling the gospel to advance everywhere. Saints who rule are Christians who have died and are now with Christ in heaven. At the end of this present age, Christ will defeat a loosed Satan, ushering in the last judgment, the resurrection, and the new heaven and earth. *See also* dispensational premillennialism; historic premillennialism; postmillennialism.

ANABAPTISM A movement that was identified as the "radical" Reformation (in distinction from the "magisterial" Reformation) in the sixteenth century. From the Greek (*ana-*, "new/again"; *baptizō*, "to baptize"), *anabaptism* signifies "new baptism" or "rebaptism." *Anabaptism* was applied to this movement because of its repudiation of infant baptism—that of both Roman Catholicism (baptismal regeneration) and Protestantism (covenant incorporation)—and its insistence on baptism of believers. Anabaptism also broke from the centuries-old church-state relation, insisting instead that churches be free of state influence and control. Other Anabaptist emphases included regeneration, nonviolence, discipleship, separation from the world, and care for the poor. *See also* baptism; baptismal regeneration; infant baptism; magisterial Reformation; radical Reformation.

ANALOGY OF BEING (*ANALOGIA ENTIS*) The idea of correspondence between God and creation, especially human beings. There is an analogy of being between God and the world such that the visible creation reveals the invisible God's nature. Moreover, there is an analogy of being between God, who is characterized by love, goodness, and justice, and his image bearers, who are similarly distinguished by love, goodness, and justice. Accordingly, observation of the created order provides a glimpse of God's attributes (e.g., Rom. 1:20). Many Protestants consider the analogy of being to be wrong because its starting point is humanity rather than God.

ANALOGY OF FAITH (*ANALOGIA FIDEI*) With regard to the interpretation of Scripture, the principle that (1) less clear passages should be interpreted in light of clearer passages, and (2) all Scripture should be interpreted in light of the historic Christian faith (the body of sound doctrine). Taken from Paul's expression "the proportion [Gk. *analogia*] of faith" (Rom. 12:6 KJV), the principle is grounded in the Spirit, who inspired all Scripture such that its many parts form a unity of self-consistent truth. Application of this principle prompts interpreters to disallow contradictions between passages and to dismiss interpretations that contradict sound doctrine. *See also* hermeneutics.

ANGELS The category of creatures that have been created as immaterial (without a body) beings. Whereas humans are created beings consisting of both an immaterial aspect (a soul or spirit) and a material aspect (a body), angels are only immaterial beings (though they can appear in physical, even human, form). They are highly intelligent, moral creatures who wield significant power and authority, and they both worship and serve God, especially providing help for believers (Heb. 1:14). Though all angels were originally created good, some rebelled against God, lost their original goodness, and now seek to oppose God and his work. *See also* archangel; demons; Satan.

ANGLICANISM A theological and ecclesiastical movement that developed in the seventeenth century out of the earlier English Reformation. As a *via media* championed by Queen Elizabeth and her successors, Anglicanism includes elements of Protestant theology and historical catholic faith. Anglicanism (from Lat. *Anglicana*, "English") is the state religion of England. Major features include (1) the Thirty-Nine Articles; (2) the Book of Common Prayer; (3) episcopalianism that locates ultimate authority in church matters with the bishop (Gk. *episkopos*, "overseer"), with the archbishop of Canterbury as head; (4) threefold order of ministry (bishop, priest, deacon); and (5) membership with Anglican churches worldwide through the Anglican Communion. *See also* bishop; episcopalianism; Thirty-Nine Articles.

ANHYPOSTASIS *See* hypostatic union.

ANNIHILATIONISM With respect to eschatology, the position that after death, the wicked will be destroyed as punishment for their sin. Support for this position includes (1) the expression "eternal destruction" (2 Thess. 1:9) in relation to the destiny of the wicked; (2) the imagery of fire—a destructive element—in association with hell; and (3) the principle that, because the punishment must match the crime, eternal punishment would be cruel and unjust, so the wicked will ultimately be destroyed, perhaps after limited punishment. The church's historic position—the wicked will experience eternal conscious punishment in hell—has always included a denunciation of annihilationism. *See also* condemnation; conditional immortality; eternal conscious punishment; hell; universalism.

ANOINTING OF THE SICK One of the seven sacraments of the Catholic Church that, as a sacrament of healing, provides grace for those who are sick, frail because of old age, facing an operation, or about to die. The sacrament is administered with the sacrament of penance and the Eucharist and features the priest laying hands on the recipients and anointing them with oil. While Protestantism denies that anointing is a sacrament, many churches practice prayer for the sick. Pastors anoint the sick with oil in Jesus's name, urge confession of sin, and pray in faith for healing (James 5:13–16). *See also* laying on of hands; prayer.

ANTHROPOLOGY, THEOLOGICAL One of the topics of systematic theology, being the doctrine of humanity (Gk. *anthrōpos*). It treats humanity's origin (creation in the image of God), human nature (traditionally, either dichotomy—human nature is two-fold: body and soul/spirit; or trichotomy—it is threefold: body, soul, and spirit), and the origin of the soul (traditionally, either creationism—God creates the soul; or traducianism—it is passed down from parents to their offspring). Contemporary discussion focuses on dualism (human nature is complex, being both material and immaterial) versus monism (it is simple, usually material only) and treats gender, embodiment, sexuality, and more. *See also* creationism; dichotomy; dualism; embodiment; gender; monism; sex/sexuality; traducianism; trichotomy.

ANTHROPOMORPHIC LANGUAGE With respect to the doctrine of God, a way of speaking about God in human terms. Anthropomorphic (from Gk. *anthrōpos*, "humanity"; *morphē*, "form") language is found in biblical affirmations: God has "eyes," "ears," "nostrils," and "an outstretched arm" (e.g., Exod. 6:6). The use of such language acknowledges the limitations of human speech to describe God and his ways. At the same time, the fact that divine revelation uses anthropomorphic language encourages people to embrace the adequacy and truthfulness of such speech and to see in such use of common language God's commitment to communicate clearly to ordinary people. *See also* hermeneutics.

ANTICHRIST The one final manifestation of all that opposes Christ, who will appear before Christ's second coming. Although Christ and his people have been continuously opposed by many enemies, at the culmination of this age, one ultimate antichrist will be revealed (1 John 2:18). He is "the son of destruction, who opposes and exalts himself against every so-called god or object of worship, so that he takes his seat in the temple of God, proclaiming himself to be God" (2 Thess. 2:3–4). After the tribulation provoked by the antichrist's rebellion, Christ will return and will publicly destroy him (2 Thess. 2:8). *See also* Great Tribulation; second coming.

反律法主义

ANTINOMIANISM <u>Lawlessness.</u> From the Greek (*anti-*, "against"; *nomos*, "law"), *antinomianism* refers to a rejection of any role for the law. A common Catholic accusation against the Protestant doctrine of justification is that it leads to antinomianism: if people are saved by faith alone apart from works of the law and guaranteed salvation, then they have no motivation for obeying the law and fall into antinomianism. The Protestant response underscores that while justification is not by the law, Christians are motivated to fulfill the law by the forgiveness of sins, Christ's imputed righteousness, the new birth, and the indwelling Holy Spirit. Some heretical theologies and movements embrace antinomianism.

ANTIOCHENE SCHOOL With respect to biblical interpretation, an approach that developed in the early church (e.g., Theodore of Antioch, in modern-day Turkey) and that employed both <u>a literal interpretation of Scripture and typology</u>. In contrast with the Alexandrian School's emphasis on allegorical interpretation, the Antiochene School insisted on the literal meaning, and thus historical reality, of texts. Its typological interpretation underscored the idea that the people (e.g., Moses), institutions (e.g., the temple), and events (e.g., the bronze serpent) in the Old Testament are types that prefigured the people (e.g., Christ), institutions (e.g., the church), and events (e.g., Christ's crucifixion) of the New Testament. *See also* Alexandrian School; hermeneutics; typology.

预示预定的

APOCALYPTIC A genre of Scripture that is characterized by mysterious symbols, bizarre dreams, and exotic visions (often given by angels) of blessing and judgment awaiting future fulfillment. The apocalyptic (from Gk. *apokalypsis*, "revelation") genre is found

21

in Ezekiel, Zechariah, Daniel, and Revelation but was also common in Jewish literature in the intertestamental period. Common apocalyptic themes include the sequence of forthcoming events, divine sovereignty in the midst of coming chaos, God's providence to keep his faithful people, the intensification of the battle between good and evil, and the ultimate defeat of evil and the triumph of the kingdom of God. *See also* hermeneutics.

APOCRYPHA Seven additional writings, and several additional sections of two books, contained in the Catholic, but not Protestant, Old Testament: Tobit, Judith, Wisdom of Solomon, Ecclesiasticus (or Wisdom of Sirach), Baruch, 1 and 2 Maccabees, six additional sections in Esther, and three additional chapters in Daniel. These writings were never part of the Hebrew Bible. Written in Greek, they were added to the Septuagint, the Greek translation of Hebrew Scripture. The early church rejected the Apocrypha as canonical writings, but Augustine (fifth century) insisted they be included in the Latin Vulgate. The Reformers removed the Apocrypha from the Bible. Eastern Orthodoxy's Old Testament includes the Apocrypha along with 1 Esdras, Psalm 151, the Prayer of Manasseh and 3 Maccabees (which also appear in the Septuagint). *See also* canon of Scripture.

APOLLINARIANISM With respect to Christology, the denial of the full humanity of the incarnate Son. Major tenets: (1) In taking on human nature, the Word of God only became united with "flesh" (John 1:14). (2) Christ's human nature consisted of only a human body but not a human soul, which was replaced by the divine Word. The church objected that if Jesus was not a fully human being, then he could not save ordinary human beings. The Council of Constantinople I (381), in its Nicene-Constantinopolitan Creed, and the Council of Chalcedon (451), in its Chalcedonian Creed, condemned Apollinarianism as heresy. *See also* Chalcedonian Creed; hypostatic union; Jesus Christ, humanity of; Nicene-Constantinopolitan Creed.

APOLOGETICS 打扰公草 The discipline that offers an apology, or defense, of Christianity. Apologetics (from Gk. *apologia*, "defense") both defends the Christian faith from its detractors and clarifies misunderstandings of it. In the early church, the apologists wrote to Roman leaders who were persecuting the church and argued the case that Christians should not be punished or killed, because they were doing nothing wrong. They also clarified misunderstandings such as charges that Christians were atheists, cannibals, and committers of incest. Apologetics deals with arguments for the existence of God, the reliability of Scripture, evidence for the resurrection, the problem of evil, and more.

APOPHATIC THEOLOGY 否定神学 With reference to the doctrine of God, an approach emphasizing the limitations of human language to talk about God. Also called the *via negativa* ("negative way"), this theological method insists that God is beyond definition and focuses on expressing what he is not. Even many words used to describe God are negations: God is *im*mortal (*not* able to die), *in*visible (*not* able to be seen), *in*finite (*not* limited), *im*mutable (*not* able to change), and *in*dependent (*not* dependent on anything else). Apophatic theology stands in contrast with kataphatic theology, which emphasizes the ability to talk about God based on revelation. *See also* incomprehensible; kataphatic theology; noetic effect; theological method.

APOSTASY 背教 An ultimate falling away from the faith. Apostasy (from Lat. *apostasia*, "abandonment") can be a general apathy that increases until one abandons the faith, or it can consist of open rebellion or doubt that festers until one renounces the faith. A key debate is whether genuine believers can commit apostasy. According to Reformed theology, though genuine Christians may temporarily slide into worldliness, God will renew and restore them to love and good deeds. Thus, apostasy is not possible. According to Arminian theology, genuine believers may sin heinously and persistently, fall away from the faith, and lose their salvation. *See also* Arminian theology; perseverance; Reformed theology.

23

APOSTLE   Apostles are the disciples chosen by Jesus to be the foundation of his church. Foremost among these leaders were the original apostles—"the Twelve"—whom Jesus called to follow him. They were Spirit-empowered eyewitnesses of his life, death, and resurrection. Additionally, *apostle* (Gk. *apostolos*, "messenger") is used to refer to a few other leaders—Paul, Barnabas, and James. The apostles were the first to preach the gospel, and they led the church in Jerusalem, from which they established churches in other places. They performed signs and wonders, which confirmed their message; they established authoritative doctrine and practice for the church; and some wrote Scripture. *See also* apostolicity.

APOSTLES' CREED   An early confession of faith that articulated essential doctrines of the early church and that continues to guide contemporary churches. Though bearing the name "Apostles," it was not written by them. The creed emerged in the fourth century, though it contained earlier material and would be set in its present form several centuries later. It has a trinitarian structure expressing beliefs about God the Father (almighty Creator), Jesus Christ (Son, Lord, miraculous conception, death, resurrection, ascension, return in judgment), and the Holy Spirit. It also affirms belief in the church, communion of saints, forgiveness, resurrection, and eternal life.

APOSTLESHIP   *See* apostle.

APOSTOLICITY   With respect to ecclesiology, one of the four traditional attributes of the church (the others being unity, holiness, and catholicity). From the Greek (*apostolos*, "messenger"), *apostolicity* signifies that the church is founded on the apostles. For the Catholic Church, its apostolicity means apostolic succession, the doctrine that Christ authoritatively instituted an unbroken line of successors from his apostles to today's bishops, who continue to wield ultimate authority in the Church. For evangelicals, apostolicity is associated with the apostles' writings. The church preaches, hears, believes, and obeys the teachings of the apostles, written down in the canonical New Testament books. *See also* apostle; catholicity; holiness of the church; unity.

AQUINAS   *See* Thomism / Thomas Aquinas. 阿奎那

ARCHANGEL   A leading or ruling angel. Angels are an order of immaterial/spiritual beings (creatures that have been created without a body) that are very intelligent, moral creatures who worship and serve God. Only one angel, named Michael, is referred to as an archangel, or ruler (Gk. *archē*) of angels (Jude 9). He is portrayed as leading an angelic army against the dragon (Satan) and his demons during a war in heaven (Dan. 10:13). When Christ returns, his descent from heaven will be accompanied by "the voice of an archangel" (1 Thess. 4:16). This could be Michael or some other archangel. *See also* angels; demons; Satan.

阿里乌斯派

ARIANISM   With respect to Christology, the denial of the deity of the Son of God. Major tenets: (1) God created a Son as the first and highest of all created beings. (2) Through him, God created everything, yet the Son is a created being. (3) The Son is not eternal, meaning that he is *heteroousios*, of a different nature from, not *homoousios*, of the same nature as, the Father. The Council of Nicea I (325), in its Creed of Nicea, condemned Arianism, which flourished for a half century until the Council of Constantinople I (381), in its Nicene-Constantinopolitan Creed, defeated it. *See also* Council of Nicea (I, II); Creed of Nicea; *heteroousios*; *homoousios*; Jesus Christ, deity of; Nicene-Constantinopolitan Creed.

亚里士多德哲学

ARISTOTELIANISM   The philosophy of Aristotle (384–322 BC) that influences Western thought and Christian theology. It is both a method and a philosophy that was incorporated by Roman Catholic scholasticism in the medieval period and by Protestant scholasticism in the post-Reformation era. Aquinas adapted Aristotelianism to theology. Key tenets: (1) The divine image consists in rationality, with people able to prove God's existence by reason. (2) Transubstantiation is a change in substance without a change in accidents (characteristics like taste and smell). (3) The causes of salvation are material (Christ's sacrificial death), formal (justification), instrumental (both faith and baptism), efficient (divine grace), and final (God's glory). *See also* Platonism; scholasticism (Catholic); scholasticism (Protestant); Thomism / Thomas Aquinas; transubstantiation.

ARMINIAN THEOLOGY The Protestant tradition that originated with Jacob Arminius (1560–1609) and whose churches include Methodist, (many) Baptist, and Nazarene. In part a reaction to Calvinism, its differences include the following: (1) Predestination is conditional, based on God's foreknowledge of people's response to grace, rather than unconditional. (2) Christ's death was for all; the atonement is unlimited, not limited. (3) Prevenient grace, which is given to all people, restores their ability to embrace Christ; there is no special saving grace for the elect. (4) Grace can be rejected; it is not irresistible. (5) Christians can lose their salvation, so perseverance is not guaranteed. *See also* order of salvation (*ordo salutis*); Reformed theology; Wesleyanism / John Wesley.

ASCENSION Forty days after his resurrection, Christ returned to heaven, from where he came and from where he will come again. In ascending, he returned to his former status of glory in heaven, the way to which he opened. He sat down at the Father's right hand, being given all authority and exalted as head to rule over all creation. He defeated God's enemies and sent the Holy Spirit to inaugurate the church, to which he also gave spiritual gifts. Now ascended, Christ prays and prepares a home for his people, whom he will come to save fully at his return. *See also* exaltation of Christ.

ASCETICISM A theology and spiritual movement that emphasizes maturity in holiness and/or meriting of divine favor through severe discipline. Asceticism (from Gk. *askēsis*, "exercise") has appeared in various forms: personal approaches to sanctification; church movements like monasticism; and the Catholic evangelical counsels of poverty, chastity, and obedience. At its core is the elevation of spiritual habits over fleshly desires; the former must be nurtured in order to dissipate the latter. The denial of otherwise legitimate physical pleasures takes the form of eating and drinking only certain foods and beverages, sleeping on the floor, forgoing marital sexual intercourse, and more. *See also* gnosticism; monasticism.

ASSURANCE OF SALVATION   With respect to the doctrine of salvation, the subjective confidence that is the privilege of all genuine believers that they will remain Christians throughout their life. This doctrine is dependent on the doctrine of perseverance, which is God's mighty act to preserve true Christians by his power through their ongoing faith, until their salvation is complete (1 Pet. 1:5). Such assurance is experienced by means of Christ's sacrificial death (Heb. 10:19–20), through the inner testimony of the Holy Spirit (Rom. 8:16), and by the confidence that comes through faith in the promises of Scripture (1 John 5:11–13). *See also* inner testimony of the Spirit; perseverance.

ATHANASIUS   Fourth-century bishop of Alexandria (Egypt) whose work as secretary at the Council of Nicea I (325) exposed him to Arianism, the heresy against which he fought for many decades. Though he suffered five exiles as an unwelcome defender of the Nicene faith, Athanasius championed the deity of Christ and paved the way for the ultimate defeat of Arianism. Specifically, he contended for the Nicene affirmations that the Son is eternal and not a created being and is of the same essence (*homoousios*) as the Father. A creed named for Athanasius is a classical expression of sound trinitarian theology and Christology. *See also* Arianism; Council of Nicea (I, II); *homoousios*.

ATHEISM   The position that God does not exist. Atheism (from Gk. *a-*, "no"; *theos*, "god") goes beyond agnosticism's view, that one cannot know if God exists, to the denial that God exists. Strong atheism asserts there is no God because (1) there is insufficient evidence for God's existence or (2) the evidence contradicts God's existence. Strong atheism puts the burden of proof on theism. Weak atheism is a practical lifestyle characterized by disregard for God. Atheism dismisses arguments for God's existence, underscores the problem of evil for theism, and regards belief in God as superstition or a psychological crutch. *See also* agnosticism; evil, the problem of; theism.

ATONEMENT The death of Christ on the cross, and what it accomplished. Because of human fallenness, a sacrifice for sin is necessary to avert condemnation and restore people to God. Old covenant sacrifices made provisional atonement, looking forward to the work of Christ: his death brought propitiation, expiation, redemption, and reconciliation. Models of the atonement, or theories of what Christ's death accomplished: (1) Penal substitution: Christ died in the place of sinners to pay the penalty for their sin. (2) Satisfaction: Christ's death restored the honor of which God had been robbed through people's sin. (3) Cosmic victory: Christ defeated Satan and triumphed over all created things. See also *Christus Victor*; governmental theory; moral influence theory; penal substitution theory; ransom to Satan theory.

ATTRIBUTES *See* communicable attributes; incommunicable attributes.

AUGSBURG CONFESSION One of two primary Lutheran confessions of faith (the other being the Formula of Concord). Written by Philip Melanchthon and approved by Martin Luther and the Lutheran churches (1530), it is a defense of Protestant theology that enjoyed broad support in the early years of the Reformation. Its key doctrines include God, original sin, the incarnation and reconciling work of the Son of God, justification by faith, preaching, good works as the fruit of justification, the two marks of the church, the sacraments of baptism and the Lord's Supper, confession and repentance, state-church relationships, Christ's return, and free will. *See also* Formula of Concord; Lutheranism / Martin Luther.

AUGUSTINIAN THEOLOGY The doctrinal tradition that originated with Augustine (354–430) and significantly influenced Catholic and Protestant theologies. Key tenets: (1) Trinitarian doctrine is central to Christian theology. (2) The original creation was good but is now fallen. (3) Adam's sin not only affected him but plunged all humanity into sin. (4) Original sin consists of guilt before God and corrupt human nature. (5) The elect are unconditionally chosen by God, who alone graciously saves people. (6) The whole Christ (*totus Christus*)—divine and human natures, and body—is present in his church, rendering it and its sacraments necessary for salvation. *See also* Protestantism; Roman Catholicism.

AUTHORITY The prerogative possessed by God, people, or institutions to establish laws, give orders, demand obedience, and mete out rewards and punishments. Because God is the sovereign King, he is the source of authority in the creation; indeed, all human authority derives from him (Rom. 13:1–2; 1 Pet. 2:13–17). Ideally, human authority reflects divine authority, being oriented toward human flourishing. Christians are to pray for the increase of this authority (1 Tim. 2:1–2). When authority is abused and oriented toward evil, Christians are to follow Jesus's example and submit to those over them (1 Pet. 2:18–25) while standing against injustice. *See also* government; sovereignty.

AUTHORITY OF SCRIPTURE A property of Scripture whereby it possesses the right to command what believers are to do and prohibit what they are not to do. Such authority is a corollary of inspiration: because God is its author, Scripture possesses divine authority. Evidences of biblical authority include the prophets' messages ("Thus says the LORD"), Jesus's attitude toward the Bible ("Scripture cannot be broken"; John 10:35), and Paul's consciousness of writing from divine imperative (1 Thess. 4:1–2). Reformed theology emphasizes Scripture's self-attesting authority and the role of the Holy Spirit in witnessing to Scripture as the authoritative Word of God.

B

BAPTISM   One of two ordinances or sacraments of the Christian faith. The meanings of baptism include association with the triune God (Matt. 28:19), identification with the death and resurrection of Christ (Rom. 6:3–5), cleansing from sin (Acts 22:16), escape from divine judgment (1 Pet. 3:20–21), and obedience to Christ for incorporation in his church (Acts 2:38–47). Though almost all Christians agree that baptism is the initiatory rite, disagreement exists regarding who should be baptized. Some churches baptize infants and others baptize believers. Disagreement also exists as to its mode. Some churches baptize by immersion and others by sprinkling or pouring water. *See also* baptismal regeneration; believer's baptism; immersion; infant baptism; ordinance; pouring; sacrament; sprinkling.

BAPTISM WITH/IN/BY THE HOLY SPIRIT   The mighty work of Jesus Christ by which he inundates people with the Holy Spirit for incorporation into his body. Jesus is the baptizer (John 1:33), the Christian is the one baptized, the Spirit is the element, and the purpose is incorporation into the church (1 Cor. 12:13). A debate concerns when this baptism occurs. According to Pentecostal theology, it takes place subsequent to conversion, following salvation either logically or temporally (e.g., the Samaritans; Acts 8:12–17). The traditional view is that it occurs at the moment of salvation, along with justification, regeneration, adoption, and more. Its relation to water baptism is also debated. *See also* charismatic movement; filled with the Holy Spirit; Pentecost; Pentecostalism; third wave evangelicalism.

BAPTISMAL REGENERATION   The position that immersion in or sprinkling with water effects the new birth. A key doctrine of

Catholicism, baptismal regeneration appeals to Jesus's charge that a person must be born again, or born of water and of the Spirit, to enter God's kingdom (John 3:1–10). Accordingly, when the Church confers baptism (usually on infants, but also adults), the administration of that sacrament effects cleansing from original sin and regeneration. Lutheran theology also embraces baptismal regeneration but grounds the sacrament's efficacy in the Word of God and faith. Objections focus on its misinterpretation of "born of water" (John 3:5). *See also* baptism; Lutheranism / Martin Luther; Roman Catholicism.

BAPTISTIC THEOLOGY   The key doctrines and practices of Baptist churches that distinguish them from other churches. Originating in the seventeenth century in England, Baptistic theology's characteristics include (1) baptism by immersion for believers; (2) congregational form of church government, with each church being autonomous; (3) involvement in missional endeavors; (4) separation of church and state, with the state playing no role in church government, selection of officers, and so on; (5) biblical authority; (6) soul competency, the responsibility of each person to embrace the gospel; and (7) the priesthood of believers, meaning there are no mediators between God and people other than Christ. *See also* authority of Scripture; baptism; believer's baptism; congregationalism; immersion; mission; priesthood of believers.

BARTH, KARL   Twentieth-century Swiss pastor and theologian who was very influential through his development of neo-orthodoxy and his stand against theological and ecclesiastical compromise under German Socialism during World War II. Although influenced by liberal Protestants like Schleiermacher, von Harnack, and Herrmann, Barth rejected this early training and embraced the existentialism of Kierkegaard. The neo-orthodoxy that resulted was far more conservative in nature yet still not fully orthodox in certain areas like the doctrines of revelation and Scripture. His many contributions include his *Commentary on Romans* (1919; rev.

1921), the Barmen Declaration (1934), and his massive *Church Dogmatics*. *See also* dialectical theology; neo-orthodoxy.

BEATIFIC VISION   The sight of God given to believers after death. This vision is called "beatific" (Lat. *beatifica*, "blessed") because it is given to the blessed in heaven. It is termed a "vision" because it is seeing God, in accordance with biblical promises (Matt. 5:8; 1 Cor. 13:12; 1 John 3:1–3). In contrast to the mediated, partial knowledge of God experienced by believers during their earthly existence, the beatific vision is immediate and full, because the blessed in heaven gaze on God in his majesty. While some Protestant theologies hold to a beatific vision, it is commonly found in Catholic theology.

BEGOTTEN   *See* eternal generation.

BELGIC CONFESSION   *See* Three Forms of Unity.

BELIEVER'S BAPTISM   The practice of administering baptism to those who have heard the gospel, repented of their sins, and believed in Christ for salvation. Also called credobaptism (Lat. *credo*, "I believe"), believer's baptism is supported by Jesus's command to baptize disciples, or those who follow him (Matt. 28:19); biblical illustrations of baptism, all of which portray believers, and not infants, as being baptized (e.g., Acts 8:5–12, 26–40); and discussions that link baptism with explicit faith in Christ (e.g., Gal. 3:26–27). Accordingly, a credible profession of repentance and belief must precede the baptism of a believer. It contrasts with infant baptism. *See also* immersion; infant baptism; profession of faith.

BIBLE   *See* Scripture.

BIBLICAL CRITICISM   Historical-critical approaches to Scripture that depart from traditional methodologies. Biblical criticism began in the seventeenth century with doubts about the authorship of certain books (e.g., the Mosaic authorship of the Pentateuch, from which the documentary hypothesis developed). Its varieties include (1) *form criticism*: identifies the types of biblical literature and their original oral traditions; (2) *source criticism*: detects the precursors of current biblical texts; (3) *redaction criticism*: ascertains the changes introduced in original texts by editors as they collected and arranged those texts; (4) *canonical criticism*: focuses on the final form, rather than earlier stages, of biblical texts. *See also* documentary hypothesis.

BIBLICAL THEOLOGY The discipline that describes the progressive revelation found in Scripture by examining the theology of its various groupings (e.g., the theology of the Pentateuch; the theology of the Synoptic Gospels). Biblical theology also traces the numerous themes in these groupings and notes their development over time (e.g., worship using altars, worship in the tabernacle and temple, worship in spirit and truth). Biblical theology as a Christocentric approach to Scripture is also quite common. Though referred to as "biblical," this theology is not alone in having Scripture as its source; the same is true of exegetical and systematic theology. *See also* exegesis / exegetical theology; progressive revelation; systematic theology; theological method.

BIBLIOLOGY One of the topics of systematic theology, being the doctrine of Scripture (Gk. *biblos*). It treats Scripture's inspiration (its God-breathed nature), authority (its supreme right to command faith and obedience), truthfulness (all its affirmations are wholly true), sufficiency (it provides wisdom leading to salvation and all the instructions that Christians need to fully please God), necessity (it is the ultimate way in which God communicates), clarity (ability to be understood), power (it effects salvation and transformation of life), and canonicity (the list of inspired writings that properly belong in Scripture). Bibliology also defends, and addresses challenges to, these matters. *See also* Scripture.

BISHOP One who ministers in the office of oversight, or bishopric. The Greek term *episkopos* ("bishop") is used interchangeably in Scripture with *presbyteros* ("presbyter, elder") and *poimēn* ("pastor"); thus, *bishop*, *elder*, and *pastor* refer to the same office. However, some denominations distinguish between bishop and elder and elevate the former office above the latter. In this case, the highest authority resides in the bishop, who consecrates other bishops and ordains elders/pastors and deacons. The qualifications for overseers are listed in 1 Timothy 3:1–7 and Titus 1:5–9. Bishops are responsible for teaching, leading, praying, administering the sacraments, and ordaining. *See also* deacon/deaconess/diaconate; elder/eldership; episcopalianism; ordination.

BLASPHEMY   Speech (sometimes a thought or act) that insults, shows contempt for, or fails to give due reverence to God. In the Old Testament, the punishment for blasphemy is death (Lev. 24:10–16). This penalty was assessed against Jesus: he was accused of blasphemy—being a man, yet claiming to be God (John 10:30–33)—and was condemned to death for committing it (Matt. 26:63–65). Blasphemy against the Holy Spirit—slandering his work in Christ and attributing it to Satan—is unpardonable (Matt. 12:31). Secondarily, blasphemy is directed at people through slandering their character or acts (1 Cor. 4:13; Titus 3:2). *See also* unpardonable sin.

BODILY ASSUMPTION OF MARY   A Catholic doctrine proclaimed in the encyclical *Munificentissimus Deus* (November 1, 1950): "The Immaculate Virgin, preserved free from all stain of original sin, when the course of her earthly life was finished, was taken up body and soul into heavenly glory, and exalted by the Lord as Queen over all things." Thus, Mary has uniquely experienced the resurrection, such that she is the only believer in heaven who is embodied. Protestantism rejects this doctrine because it is based on Mary's sinlessness (which contradicts Scripture's affirmation of universal human sinfulness) and because after death, people are disembodied in heaven, awaiting the resurrection. *See also* immaculate conception; Mariology; Mary.

BODY, HUMAN   *See* embodiment.

BODY OF CHRIST   A key metaphor for the church. The Father exalted his Son as the head over all created things and gave him as cosmic head to the church, his body (Eph. 1:20–23). The significance is that the church submits to Christ its head. Additionally, the church is composed of many members who work together and use their gifts to build up the body (Eph. 4:11–16). In a second sense, the *body of Christ* refers to the bread of the Lord's Supper. For Catholics, the bread becomes the actual body of Christ. For evangelicals, the bread symbolizes Christ's body, prompting remembrance of his crucifixion and/or promising his spiritual presence. *See also* church; Lord's Supper.

BORN AGAIN   *See* regeneration.

C

CALL   *See* effective/internal call.

CALVINISM / JOHN CALVIN   Calvinism is the doctrinal tradition that originated with John Calvin (1509–64) and significantly influences Reformed theology. Key contributions of the Reformer: (1) Calvin's *Institutes of the Christian Religion* and commentaries promoted the Reformation. (2) His association of the knowledge of God the Creator and the knowledge of self, together with his insistence on the knowledge of God the Redeemer, initiated Reformed epistemology. (3) His doctrines of sin and salvation, derived from Augustinianism, underscored total depravity and total inability, divine sovereignty, predestination, union with Christ, justification, and perseverance of Christians. (4) He joined the Word of God and the Spirit of God in balance. *See also* Protestantism; Reformed theology.

CANON OF SCRIPTURE The list of which writings belong in the Bible. The Protestant canon is sixty-six books—thirty-nine Old Testament writings and twenty-seven New Testament writings. The Catholic canon is more extensive, including in its Old Testament the apocryphal writings—Tobit, Judith, Ecclesiasticus, Wisdom of Solomon, Baruch, 1 and 2 Maccabees, additions to Esther, and additions to Daniel. The Orthodox canon is more extensive still. The church inherited a closed canon of the Old Testament from the Hebrew Bible and, guided by the Holy Spirit over the course of four centuries, acknowledged the writings belonging to its New Testament. *See also* Apocrypha.

CANONICAL CRITICISM *See* biblical criticism.

CANONS OF DORDT *See* Three Forms of Unity.

CAPPADOCIAN FATHERS Three theologians—Gregory of Nazianzus, Basil (the Great) of Caesarea, and Gregory of Nyssa—from the region of Cappadocia (modern-day Turkey). Their development of trinitarian theology and Christology was extensive. They (1) defended the Creed of Nicea's belief that the Son is of the same essence as the Father, and that he is fully human; (2) championed the deity of the Holy Spirit; (3) articulated the eternal generation of the Son and the eternal procession of the Holy Spirit; (4) expressed the Trinity as one essence in three persons; and (5) combated heresies, including Arianism, Eunomianism (an extreme Arianism), and Apollinarianism. *See also* Creed of Nicea; eternal generation; eternal procession; Trinity.

CATECHISM/CATECHESIS A teaching tool that is used for the process of instructing Christians in the faith and its practice. From the Greek (*katēcheō*, "to instruct"), *catechism* refers to the doctrine and practice that is communicated, and *catechesis* refers to the process of imparting the faith. These terms are often associated with the period of preparation leading up to one's baptism, and specifically with formal classes for this purpose. But passing on the faith involves many aspects: memorizing answers to doctrinal questions (e.g., Westminster Shorter Catechism), learning gospel rhythms through the Sunday liturgy, participating in the sacraments, and reciting the creed.

CATHOLIC CHURCH   *See* Roman Catholicism.

CATHOLIC SCHOLASTICISM   *See* scholasticism (Catholic).

CATHOLICITY   With respect to ecclesiology, one of the four traditional attributes of the church (the others being unity, holiness, and apostolicity). *Catholicity* (from Gk. *katholikos*, "universal") signifies that the church is universal. For the Catholic Church, its catholicity depends on its claim that Christ, in the totality of his divine and human natures, together with his body, is found in the Church. For evangelicals, catholicity is associated with the Great Commission and is the divinely given goal of the church in terms of its extension: complete universality as the gospel of Christ advances into every corner of the inhabited world. *See also* apostolicity; holiness of the church; unity.

CELIBACY   The state of singleness, or abstinence from marriage. According to Catholicism, celibacy is one of the three evangelical counsels or vows (with poverty and obedience) that are taken by priests, monks, and nuns. Support includes Jesus's instructions about eunuchs (Matt. 19:12). According to Protestant theology, celibacy is a choice not to get married, which believers may make as they are sustained by the gift of celibacy from God (1 Cor. 7:7). Protestantism objects to Catholicism's mandatory celibacy for its priests because Scripture certainly allows for—or, better, envisions the common practice of—marriage for church leaders (1 Tim. 3:2). *See also* marriage.

CESSATIONISM   With respect to spiritual gifts, the position that whereas many of the gifts continue to be exercised, the so-called miraculous gifts (prophecy, speaking in tongues, interpretation of tongues, word of knowledge, word of wisdom, miracles, healings) have ceased to operate in the church today. Their cessation is due to these gifts serving to confirm the gospel at the founding of the church and, with the church's foundation having been laid, no longer being needed for its ongoing development. Cessationism does not deny that God heals and performs miracles, but it denies that he operates through people given such gifts. *See also* continuationism; miraculous gifts; spiritual gifts.

CHALCEDONIAN CREED   The statement from the Council of Chalcedon (451) affirming the hypostatic union, the union of two natures—one divine, one human—in the one person of Christ. It also condemned four heresies: Against Arianism, it underscored the full deity of the Son, who is of the same nature as the Father. Against Apollinarianism, it asserted the full humanity—soul and body—of Christ. Against Nestorianism, it confirmed that Christ had two natures that united in one person, not two persons cooperating together. Against Eutychianism, it declared that Jesus's human nature remained human and his divine nature remained divine. *See also* Christology; Council of Chalcedon; hypostatic union; Jesus Christ, deity of; Jesus Christ, humanity of.

CHARISMATIC MOVEMENT   A development within mainline churches and denominations (e.g., Anglican, Catholic), beginning in the 1960s, that embraced certain doctrines and experiences of Pentecostal theology. These commonalities were (1) baptism in the Holy Spirit as a mighty act of God in the lives of Christians sometime after their conversion; (2) speaking in tongues as a sign of such Spirit baptism; and (3) the continuing reception and exercise of all the spiritual gifts described in the New Testament, including the miraculous gifts of prophecy, speaking in tongues, interpretation of tongues, word of knowledge, word of wisdom, miracles, and healings (some include exorcisms). *See also* baptism with/in/by the Holy Spirit; continuationism; Pentecostalism; third wave evangelicalism.

CHERUBIM In regard to angelology, an order of immaterial/spiritual beings (creatures that were created without a body) presented in Scripture. When God exiled Adam and Eve from the Garden of Eden, he placed cherubim and a flaming sword to prevent their return (Gen. 3:24). Two winged cherubim, forged out of gold, were constructed on the ends of the mercy seat in the tabernacle; God's presence dwelled above the seat and between the cherubim (Exod. 25:17–22). Cherubim continued to accompany God and his glory and could take on human characteristics (Ezek. 10; Ps. 18:10). Their relationship to angelic beings is unknown.

CHICAGO STATEMENT ON BIBLICAL INERRANCY The written outcome of a consultation of leading evangelicals (Chicago, 1978) that addressed the truthfulness of Scripture. It affirmed both the infallibility and inerrancy of Scripture, stood against a limited view of Scripture's truthfulness (restricted to matters of faith and salvation), linked inspiration and inerrancy, addressed some current challenges, and affirmed the doctrine of inerrancy as the church's historical view of Scripture. The Chicago Statement also denied that inerrancy is defeated by lack of precise language, grammatical irregularities, the use of figurative language, chronological problems, variant accounts, or citations that are not word for word. *See also* inerrancy; infallibility of Scripture.

CHRIST *See* Jesus Christ, deity of; Jesus Christ, humanity of; Messiah.

CHRISTIAN One who belongs to and follows Jesus Christ. From the Greek *Christos*, meaning "anointed one" and referring to the Messiah, *Christian* means "belonging to the anointed one" and refers to those who acknowledge Jesus to be the Christ. His disciples were first called Christians in Antioch (Acts 11:26), and that is the common term still used today. This contemporary usage can also refer to the cultural adherents of the three major divisions of Christianity—Roman Catholics, Eastern Orthodox, and Protestants—in distinction from the cultural proponents of other religions such as Jews, Muslims, Hindus, Buddhists, Taoists, and the like. *See also* Eastern Orthodoxy; Messiah; Protestantism; Roman Catholicism.

CHRISTOLOGY One of the topics of systematic theology, it treats the person and work of Christ (Gk. *Christos*, "anointed one"). This doctrine affirms the preexistence of the Son of God; his eternal generation from the Father; and his work of creation, providence, redemption, and consummation. It treats his state of humiliation: the taking of human nature in the incarnation, his holy life, suffering, crucifixion, burial, and death. It covers his state of exaltation: his resurrection, ascension, session to the right hand of the Father, and future return. It further rehearses Christ's work as prophet, priest, and king, with emphasis on his atoning sacrifice. *See also* atonement; consummation; cross/crucifixtion; eternal generation; exaltation of Christ; humiliation of Christ; incarnation; Jesus Christ, deity of; resurrection of Christ; second coming; session of Christ.

CHRISTUS VICTOR In respect to Christology, a model of the atonement that emphasizes Christ as conqueror of the evil powers of the world in opposition to God and human beings. These powers are sin (that enslaves humanity), death (humanity's "last enemy"; 1 Cor. 15:26), the law (which brings "death"; Rom. 7:10), and Satan and demons ("the god of this world"; 2 Cor. 4:4). Christ fought against and triumphed over these enemies through his death on the cross (Col. 2:15; Heb. 2:14–15; 1 John 5:19). Gustaf Aulén developed the twentieth-century *Christus Victor* model, but it bears some resemblance to the early church's ransom to Satan theory of the atonement. *See also* atonement; governmental theory; moral influence theory; penal substitution theory; ransom to Satan theory; satisfaction theory.

CHURCH   The people of God who have been saved through repentance and faith in Christ and incorporated into his body through baptism with the Spirit. It consists of two interrelated elements: (1) the universal church, composed of all Christians both in heaven and on earth; and (2) local churches, which are oriented to God's glory, Word centered (on both Christ and Scripture), Spirit activated, covenantal (the new covenant and church covenant), confessional (personal confession of faith and corporate confession of the faith), missional (sent on the mission of God), and assembled as pilgrims on the way to a future hope. *See also* body of Christ.

CHURCH DISCIPLINE   The process of rebuking and correcting sinful members of the church. It consists of four steps (Matt. 18:15–20): a personal confrontation; rebuke by two or three people; admonition by the whole church; and excommunication, or removal from membership. Whenever repentance occurs, the process is terminated and the member is restored. Church discipline is an anticipation of the future judgment that awaits sinful members if they persist in their sin. Its goal is always restoration, but it serves also to rid the church of sinful examples that tend to prompt more sin, and it protects the honor of Christ. *See also* excommunication.

CIRCUMCISION   The removal of the foreskin of the penis, serving as the sign of the Abrahamic covenant. After reiterating his covenant with Abraham, God commanded him to circumcise himself and every eight-day-old male as a sign of the covenant (Gen. 17:1–14). Circumcision thus signified physical descent from Abraham. Tragically, many Jews relied on this mark for their standing before God, a miscalculation denounced by the prophets, Jesus, and the church. Circumcision of the heart (regeneration), not physical circumcision, counts before God (Gal. 6:15). A lingering question is whether the regulations for circumcision apply to Christian baptism (e.g., administrated to infants). *See also* Abrahamic covenant; infant baptism.

CLARITY OF SCRIPTURE   *See* perspicuity of Scripture.

41

CLERGY One of two categories of church members or religious organizations, the other being laity. Clergy (from Gk. *klēros*, "lot" [i.e., chosen by drawing lots]) are ordained, while laity are not ordained. Clergy go by several titles: bishop, pastor, elder, priest, deacon, and minister. Their primary responsibilities are preaching the Word of God and praying, administering the sacraments or ordinances, and leading the church. According to Catholicism, clergy, who have received the sacrament of holy orders, differ in essence from laity. According to Protestantism, the difference is only one of office: clergy are responsible to minister; laity are not. *See also* holy orders; laity; ordination.

COMMON GRACE The universal favor that God grants to all people, both believers and unbelievers. This grace is termed "common" to distinguish it from "saving" grace. Thus, common grace is not designed to save sinful people. Rather, it consists of the blessings of God given to all his image bearers in many realms: intellectual (e.g., scientific discoveries), artistic (e.g., musical talents), social (e.g., governments; Rom. 13:1–7), relational (e.g., families), athletic (e.g., sprinters), physical (e.g., rain for crops; Acts 14:16–17), and moral (e.g., the conscience; Rom. 2:12–15). Common grace prompts unbelievers to embrace the gospel, and it evokes thanksgiving from believers. *See also* saving grace.

COMMUNICABLE ATTRIBUTES With respect to the doctrine of God, God's characteristics or perfections, as revealed in Scripture, that he communicates, or shares, with human creatures made in his image. These attributes include knowledge, wisdom, truthfulness, faithfulness, goodness, love, grace, mercy, patience, holiness, jealousy, wrath, righteousness/justice, and power. Communicable attributes are distinguishable from incommunicable attributes, those characteristics (independence, immutability/unchangeableness, eternity, omnipresence, simplicity, and spirituality/invisibility) that God does not communicate, or share, with human beings. God calls his image bearers to mirror him by reflecting his communicable attributes (e.g., his holiness, 1 Pet. 1:14–16; his mercy, Luke 6:35–36) in the world. *See also* incommunicable attributes.

COMMUNICATION OF ATTRIBUTES   The view that whatever may be said of Christ's divine nature, and whatever may be said of his human nature, may be said of his person. For example, "crucified the Lord of glory" (1 Cor. 2:8) ascribes what is true of the human nature—it dies—to the exalted person of Christ. It does not mean that the divine or human natures changed, nor that the natures mixed together. This view should not be confused with the communication of properties, which holds that divine characteristics like omnipresence were communicated to Christ's human nature, making it everywhere present.

COMMUNION   *See* Lord's Supper.

COMPATIBILISM   The position that divine sovereignty and human responsibility hold together. Compatibilism maintains that the following two affirmations are compatible: (1) God is absolutely sovereign, but his sovereignty never functions in such a way that human responsibility is minimized or destroyed; (2) human beings are morally responsible creatures—they obey, trust, disobey, rebel—but this characteristic never functions so as to make God dependent on them. Compatibilism is a framework for understanding the divine plan and human treachery in the crucifixion of Christ (Acts 2:23) and divine election and the human response to the gospel in salvation (2 Thess. 2:13). *See also* determinism; incompatibilism.

COMPLEMENTARIANISM   The position that men and women are complementary to one another, equal in nature yet distinct in relationships and roles. These distinctions are found in (1) the home, with the husband leading and the wife submitting to him; and (2) the church, with men and women serving in all its ministries except for elder responsibilities, which are reserved for qualified men. Some complementarians apply this position to distinctions in (3) society, with men leading governments and companies and women serving in positions of lower authority. Complementarianism stands in contrast to egalitarianism, which objects to some or all of the distinctions. *See also* egalitarianism.

CONCOMITANCE   With respect to Catholic theology of the Eucharist, the doctrine that Christ is present in the totality of both his divine and human natures. He is present whole and entire in the consecrated wafer, and in each of its grains, and he is present whole and entire in the consecrated wine, and in each of its drops. Accordingly, the faithful participating in the Eucharist do not receive more or less of Christ if they take communion in one kind, receiving the consecrated wafer only, or if they take communion in two kinds, receiving both the wafer and the wine. *See also* Eucharist; real presence of Christ; transubstantiation.

CONCUPISCENCE   The inclination to sin. According to Catholic theology, concupiscence is associated with the pleasures of the senses, coveting earthly things, and self-assertion. Fallen human beings have a tendency that lures them toward and ends in actual sin. However, this inclination is not sin itself. Evangelical theology dissents from this position, insisting that fallen human nature, which produces the tendency to sin (concupiscence), is an aspect of original sin and thus incurs the wrath of God (Eph. 2:1–3). Indeed, this concupiscence is insurmountable; only God's grace—and not human beings cooperating with the divine grace—is capable of overcoming it.

CONCURRENCE   An aspect of divine providence by which God collaborates with everything that he has created in every action and development. Concurrence is God's all-encompassing cooperation with this creation: plants and animals, to prompt their flourishing or to terminate their existence; angelic beings, to employ holy angels in his service and permit evil ones to wreak limited havoc; and human beings, to responsibly will and work for his good pleasure, or to culpably reject his kindness out of hardness of heart. Concurrence raises many questions about God's relationship with evil. Indeed, some theologies deny this all-encompassing nature of divine concurrence. *See also* providence.

CONDEMNATION The divine verdict of guiltiness and eternal rejection that is the result of unforgiven sin. Condemnation is both the liability to suffer punishment for those still awaiting the judgment, and the imposition of that punishment for those judged to be guilty. It is the opposite of justification, the divine verdict that those who embrace the gospel are not guilty but righteous instead, because of the forgiveness of sins and the imputation of Christ's righteousness. All people are condemned before God through their association with Adam, their dismissal of general revelation, their actual sins, and/or their rejection of the gospel. *See also* eternal conscious punishment; hell; justification.

CONDITIONAL ELECTION The position that God's choice of people for salvation is dependent on their faith in the gospel and continuation in Christ, which God foreknows. Key tenets: (1) God desires all people to be saved; (2) although all people are hopelessly sinful, prevenient grace restores the ability to believe the gospel; (3) in his perfect foreknowledge, God foresees those who will embrace salvation and elects them accordingly. This view contrasts with unconditional election: God's choice of people is based not on his foreknowledge of people's faith and perseverance but on his sovereign will and good pleasure to save them. *See also* decree; election; foreknowledge; prevenient grace; unconditional election.

CONDITIONAL IMMORTALITY With respect to eschatology, the position that God alone possesses immortality; believers by God's grace receive eternal life—immortality—by becoming partakers of his nature. Unbelievers, who do not possess or receive immortality, naturally die. Conditional immortality differs from universalism because it denies that everyone will be saved. It differs from the church's historic position—that the wicked will experience eternal conscious punishment in hell—because it considers that view to be based on the immortality of the soul, a belief it deems not a biblical teaching. Rather, believers receive immortality, and unbelievers cease to exist. *See also* annihilationism; condemnation; eternal conscious punishment; hell; immortality.

CONFESSION   The admission of sin and guiltiness, and the expression of belief. In the first sense, confession follows an act of sin and is the sincere acknowledgment of the wrongness of that act and the guilt that it brings before God. Confession also recognizes and embraces the forgiveness of that sin by Christ. In the second sense, confession is both (1) the profession of faith in Christ following the announcement of the gospel, and (2) the verbalization of the faith, or what the church believes about God, Christ, salvation, the Holy Spirit, and more (e.g., recitation of the Apostles' Creed). *See also* faith; *fides qua creditur / fides quae creditur*; saving faith.

CONFIRMATION   A period of preparation for conversion to, or growth in, the Christian faith, and the corresponding sacrament. While most Protestant churches do not consider confirmation to be a sacrament, they incorporate some type of confirmation to prepare people to become Christians (commonly at the age of accountability) or to take a major step of growth (e.g., to become church members). This preparation often consists of communicating the gospel, imparting Scripture, teaching doctrine, and explaining a catechism. For Catholicism, confirmation is a sacrament because it ratifies and reinforces baptismal grace and confers the special strength of the Holy Spirit. *See also* catechism/catechesis; indelible mark.

CONGREGATIONALISM   In terms of church government, congregationalism is government by the local congregation, in whose members ultimate authority resides. Each church is an autonomous entity, with no person (a bishop, as in episcopalianism) or structure (a presbytery or synod, as in presbyterianism), except for Christ himself, above it. Congregationalism is based on two principles:

(1) autonomy, that is, each church is independent and self-govern-ing, being responsible for its own leadership, finances, buildings, and ministries; and (2) democracy, that is, authority in each church resides in its members, who together participate in congregational decisions through some process of affirmation or denial. *See also* Baptistic theology; episcopalianism; presbyterianism.

CONSCIENCE An internal sense of right and wrong, and the perception of moral accountability that accompanies it. God has created everyone with a conscience and expects them to follow it by doing what is right and avoiding what is wrong (Rom. 2:12–16). In the case of failure, a guilty conscience convicts of wrongdoing; repeated violations of conscience may render it seared (1 Tim. 4:2). Believers are to live with a clear conscience (1 Pet. 3:16), fol-low and not violate their own conscience when making decisions, encourage freedom of conscience, and not bind the conscience (theirs or others) beyond Scriptural commands and prohibitions.

CONSUBSTANTIATION With respect to Lutheran theology of the Lord's Supper, the doctrine (also called the sacramental union) that Christ is truly and completely present in the sacrament. Specifically, the body of Christ is present "in, with [Lat. *com-*], and under" the *substance* of the bread; the same is true of the blood of Christ and the wine. Jesus's words "This is my body" are understood literally, and Christ's sitting at the right hand of God means that he is present everywhere. Thus, Christ is in heaven, and his body and blood are in the Lord's Supper at the same time. *See also* "in, with, and under."

CONSUMMATION The climax of this world's existence and his-tory. As the final chapter in the biblical metanarrative of creation, fall, redemption, and consummation, it is the future that the people of God anticipate in hope. Several climactic, epoch-changing events constitute the consummation: Christ's return, the resurrections, the last judgment, the eternal blessing of the righteous and the eternal judgment of the wicked, and the eternal state of the new heaven and new earth. Some (postmillennialists, premillennialists) would add a future millennium as well. Christ will be preeminent, believers will become eminent (Rom. 8:29), and God will be all in all (1 Cor. 15:28). *See also* great white throne judgment; new heaven and new earth; resurrection of people; second coming.

CONTEXTUALIZATION The adaptation of the gospel and the church it brings forth in different contexts. Because the church engages with cultures of all types, it must adjust its message, and the expression of its worship and discipleship, in the different settings into which it expands. Contextualization is seen in Peter's Old Testament–rich proclamation to his Jewish audience on Pentecost (Acts 2:14–41), Paul's simple words to the peasants of Lystra (14:8–18), and his address to the philosophically sophisticated Athenians (17:16–34). The path to proper contextualization is fraught with pitfalls, with both undercontextualization and over-contextualization, or syncretism, being two extremes to avoid.

CONTINGENCY That which is dependent on someone or something else. Contingency is one of three modes of existence: something necessary must exist, something impossible cannot exist, and something contingent may or may not exist. The doctrine of God emphasizes that necessary existence is true of God alone. Contingent existence is true of everything created: apart from God's will, nothing would exist. Theological anthropology emphasizes the importance of human beings recognizing their contingency: they live because God purposed for them to be his image bearers and their parents provided the biological life for their existence. This acknowledgment fosters humility and dependence.

CONTINUATIONISM With respect to spiritual gifts, the position that all the gifts, including the miraculous gifts (prophecy, speaking in tongues, interpretation of tongues, word of knowledge, word of wisdom, miracles, and healings), continue to operate in the church today. Because spiritual gifts are given to foster the church's growth by equipping its members for ministry, all of them are needed and should be exercised. Continuationism stands in contrast with cessationism, the position that the miraculous gifts served to confirm the gospel at the founding of the church and, with its foundation having been laid, are no longer needed today. *See also* cessationism; miraculous gifts.

CONVERSION   In regard to the doctrine of salvation, the human response to the gospel. It consists of two aspects: (1) repentance, or sorrow for sin, hatred of it, and resolve to turn from it, and (2) faith, or belief in God's provision of forgiveness and trust in Christ for salvation. Though it is a thoroughly human response, it is not merely human, because it is gospel prompted (Rom. 10:17) and grace stirred (Acts 18:27). Reformed theology holds that regeneration, being born again and thus able to respond to God, precedes conversion. Arminian theology maintains that conversion, enabled by prevenient grace, precedes regeneration. *See also* faith; prevenient grace; regeneration; repentance; saving faith; saving grace.

CORRUPTION   With regard to the doctrine of sin, one aspect of original sin. Original sin is the state of all human beings at birth, a condition that consists of (1) original guilt, or the liability to suffer eternal condemnation (some theologies deny this element); and (2) original corruption, or sinful nature, the tendency toward evil. Some theologies further detail this corruption as consisting of (a) total depravity, meaning that every aspect of human nature is infected with sin, and (b) total inability, referring to the absence of all spiritual goodness and the incapacity to reorient oneself from self-centeredness to God. *See also* guilt; original sin; total depravity; total inability.

COSMOLOGICAL ARGUMENTS   A category of rational arguments for God's existence. Cosmological (from Gk. *kosmos,* "world") arguments have to do with this world. As *a posteriori* arguments, they are based on experience, specifically causation. An example is Aquinas's argument from efficient cause: (1) there are efficient causes in the world (e.g., an author is the cause of a book); (2) nothing can be the cause of itself; (3) an actual infinity of efficient causes is impossible; (4) if there is no first cause, there is no effect, which is false, because the world is an effect; (5) therefore, there is a first cause, who is God. See also *a posteriori / a priori*; Five Ways, the; God; knowability; moral arguments; ontological arguments; teleological arguments.

COUNCIL, GENERAL   A historically important and highly influential assembly of leaders from a wide representation of churches. Convened to articulate the church's orthodox theological stance in light of biblical teaching and to refute heresies, these councils often bear the title "general" or "ecumenical" (in contrast to "local" or "regional") because of the participation of church leaders from various Christian traditions and geographical locations. Key political figures were often involved as well. These councils, and the creeds and decisions that flowed from them, are accorded different levels of authority by Catholicism, Orthodoxy, and Protestantism. The following chart presents the first seven general councils:

Council (date)	Key doctrines formulated	Key heresies condemned
Nicea I (325)	Deity of the Son	Arianism
Constantinople I (381)	Affirmed Nicea I; deity of the Spirit	Apollinarianism
Ephesus (431)	Unity of two natures in Christ	Nestorianism
Chalcedon (451)	Hypostatic union	Eutychianism; earlier three
Constantinople II (553)	Clarified Chalcedon	Nestorianism; Origenism
Constantinople III (680/81)	Dyothelitism (two wills in Christ)	Monothelitism
Nicea II (787)	Affirmed veneration of icons	

COUNCIL OF CHALCEDON   The fourth general council of the early church (451), Chalcedon condemned the heresies of Arianism (denying Christ's deity), Apollinarianism (denying Christ's full humanity), Nestorianism (separating the two natures into two persons), and Eutychianism (fusing the two natures). It also articulated the orthodox doctrine of the hypostatic union, that is, the union of the two natures—one divine nature, one human nature—in the one person of Jesus Christ. The Creed of Chalcedon, one of the fruits of the council, stands as the classical expression of Christology and has been the standard of orthodoxy ever since its promotion. *See also* Chalcedonian Creed; council, general; hypostatic union.

COUNCIL OF CONSTANCE The sixteenth general council (1414–18) as acknowledged by the Catholic Church but rejected by Orthodoxy and Protestantism. Constance condemned the teachings of John Wycliffe (45 heresies) and John Hus (30 heresies). Because of the existence of two popes at the time, the council sought to heal the schism by deposing both and installing its own, resulting in three popes. Finally, Martin V was elected pope. This council issued two significant decrees, asserting that a general council is superior to the pope and that such councils should meet frequently to govern the Church. Eventually, these decrees were dismissed. *See also* council, general.

COUNCIL OF CONSTANTINOPLE (I, II, III) The second, fifth, and sixth general councils of the early church. Constantinople I (381) confirmed the doctrinal decisions of the Council of Nicea I (325), condemned Apollinarianism, and supported the deity of the Holy Spirit. Constantinople II (553) further condemned the heresies of Origen and Nestorius while upholding Chalcedon's doctrine of two natures (divine and human) united in the one person of Jesus Christ. Constantinople III (680–81) stood against the view that Christ has only one (divine) will, insisting instead that because Christ has two natures, he must necessarily have two wills (divine and human). *See also* Chalcedonian Creed; council, general; hypostatic union; Nicene-Constantinopolitan Creed.

COUNCIL OF EPHESUS The third general council of the early church (431), Ephesus condemned the heresy of Nestorianism, that two persons—one divine person, one human person—cooperated together in Christ. Nestorius was reluctant to affirm that Mary is *theotokos* ("one who bore God") without also affirming she is *anthrōpotokos* ("one who bore a man"), seemingly affirming two distinct persons. This council proclaimed that Mary is *theotokos*, signifying that her son is the Son of God and fully divine. It also upheld the unity of the two natures—one divine nature, one human nature—in the one person of Christ. *See also* council, general; hypostatic union; *theotokos*.

COUNCIL OF NICEA (I, II)* The first and seventh general councils of the early church. Nicea I (325) condemned the heresy of Arianism and defended the deity of the Son of God. It coined the term *homoousios* to affirm that the Son is of the same nature as the Father. It also denied that the Son is a created being who is not eternal. Nicea II (787) reversed the ban against the use of icons (physical representations of Christ, Mary, angels, and the saints), affirming instead that such holy images may be venerated (adored, but not worshiped) by the church. *See also* council, general; Creed of Nicea; *homoousios*.

COUNCIL OF TRENT The nineteenth general council as acknowledged by the Catholic Church but rejected by Orthodoxy and Protestantism. Meeting in three phases between 1545 and 1563, it affirmed the Church's views on the doctrines of Scripture, original sin, justification, the seven sacraments, the administration of the Eucharist, the mass, purgatory, indulgences, and other matters. It also condemned Protestant doctrines as part of the Counter-Reformation against the heresy of Protestantism. Finally, the council sought to reform the Church by correcting its many abuses and promoting a new creed (the Profession of the Tridentine Faith) and a new liturgy (the Tridentine Mass). *See also* council, general.

COVENANT A structured relationship between God and his people, consisting of typical features. A covenant (1) is unilateral, initiated by God alone; (2) creates a structured relationship, or

---

* "Nicea" is often spelled "Nicaea."

formalizes an already existing relationship, between God and his partners; (3) features binding obligations on the part of God, who commits himself to be God and do certain things, and on the part of the partners, who commit themselves to be faithful and obedient to the covenant terms; and (4) involves covenantal signs or the swearing of oaths. Biblical covenants are the Adamic, Noahic, Abrahamic, old (or Mosaic), Davidic, and new covenants.

COVENANT OF GRACE   An aspect of the Reformed framework for constructing theology, treating how God mercifully saves people. Following their fall into sin, God established a pact to save his people by grace. This one covenant encompasses the Noahic, Abrahamic, old (or Mosaic), Davidic, and new covenants. Though each covenant features different partners, each promises salvation for them through God's grace appropriated by faith that results in obedience. Because all these covenants feature grace, there is significant continuity between them. For example, regulations concerning circumcision, the initiating rite of the old covenant, impact (infant) baptism, the initiating rite of the new covenant. *See also* covenant of redemption; covenant of works; Reformed theology.

COVENANT OF REDEMPTION   An aspect of the Reformed framework for constructing theology, the eternal agreement established among the Trinity about accomplishing salvation through the Son. This eternal covenant involves the Son becoming incarnate, living his life under the covenant of works as the representative of God's people, and offering himself as a payment for sins to redeem his people. The Father agreed to send the Son; the Son agreed to become incarnate, redeem his people, and preserve them forever; and the Spirit agreed to effect the incarnation, empower Christ during his ministry, and apply Christ's saving work to his people. *See also* covenant of grace; covenant of works; Reformed theology.

COVENANT OF WORKS   An aspect of the Reformed framework for constructing theology, the divine pact established with Adam and Eve that would reward their obedience with eternal life and punish their disobedience with eternal death. The specific requirement that God gave them to obey in the Garden of Eden was the prohibition not to eat of the tree of the knowledge of good and evil. The explicit promise for disobedience was death; the implicit reward for obedience was eternal life through the tree of life. Adam and Eve's failure to keep this covenant necessitated the covenant of grace for salvation. *See also* Adamic covenant; covenant of grace; covenant of redemption; Reformed theology.

COVENANT THEOLOGY   A Reformed framework for constructing theology that employs the concept of covenant as its organizing principle. Three covenants compose the structure of God's activity. (1) The *covenant of redemption* is the eternal agreement of the triune God about accomplishing salvation through the Son. (2) The *covenant of works* is the divine pact established with Adam that would reward obedience with life and punish disobedience with death. Adam's failure to keep the covenant necessitated the next covenant. (3) The *covenant of grace* is the overarching covenant that promises salvation to people by faith and obedience. It encompasses the Noahic, Abrahamic, old (or Mosaic), Davidic, and new covenants. *See also* covenant of grace; covenant of redemption; covenant of works; Reformed theology.

CREATION *EX NIHILO*   The divine work to bring this universe into existence out of nothing (Lat. *ex*, "out of"; *nihilo*, "nothing"). Support includes the Hebrew word for "create" (Gen. 1:1) and the affirmation that God "calls into existence the things that do not exist" (Rom. 4:17); still, creation *ex nihilo* is embraced by faith (Heb. 11:3). God spoke everything into existence through his Word ("God said," ten times in Gen. 1), who is the agent through whom everything was created (John 1:3; Col. 1:15–16), with the Spirit (Gen. 1:2). The original world was very good, created to reveal and glorify God. *See also* evolution.

CREATIONISM   With regard to theological anthropology, the view that the soul of a person is created by God and then united to a sinful body that is generated through procreation by parents. Support includes the creation of Adam, to whom God imparted a soul (Gen. 2:7); the soul's immortality, which means that it cannot be created physically; and the dichotomy between the body, which is inherently evil, and thus from parents, and the soul, which is inherently good, and thus from God. Creationism is opposed by traducianism, the view that both the body and the soul are generated by parents. *See also* preexistence of the soul; soul; traducianism.

CREATIONISM, OLD EARTH   The position that God created the universe long ago, as supported by science, but without using evolution. Several varieties: (1) The day-age theory holds that the "days" of Genesis 1 were actually lengthy periods of time. (2) The intermittent-day theory maintains that the actual days were separated by long periods of time. (3) The gap theory proposes a lengthy period of time between the original creation (Gen. 1:1), which became ruined ("without form and void"; 1:2), and God's re-creation of it recently in six actual days (1:3–31). These long periods of time account for the earth's old age. *See also* creationism, young earth.

CREATIONISM, YOUNG EARTH   The position that God created the universe fairly recently, perhaps just six thousand years ago. This has been the church's historical view. Its contemporary expression is advanced against evolution and old earth creationism, and in light of scientific creationism. It critiques evolution's contradiction of the laws of thermodynamics, its reliance on natural selection and mutations, and its failure to account for gaps in the fossil record. It criticizes old earth proposals for their misinterpretations of Genesis 1, especially its straightforward narration of the days of creation, and the Fourth Commandment's grounding of Sabbath rest on those being actual days (Exod. 20:8–11). *See also* creationism, old earth.

CREDIBLE PROFESSION OF FAITH   *See* profession of faith.

CREED A profession of faith that summarizes the affirmations of Scripture, exposes and condemns heresy, and constitutes presumptive, not ultimate, authority for the church's beliefs. Early church councils account for most of these creeds, which include the Creed of Nicea (Council of Nicea I, 325), the Nicene-Constantinopolitan Creed (Council of Constantinople I, 381), the Chalcedonian Creed (Council of Chalcedon, 451), and the Apostles' Creed (third–fourth century). These creeds address the doctrines of the Trinity, Christ, the Holy Spirit, the church, forgiveness of sins, the resurrection, final judgment, and the age to come. Heresies condemned include Arianism, Apollinarianism, Nestorianism, and Eutychianism.

CREED OF NICEA* A confession of faith composed at the Council of Nicea I (325), condemning Arianism and defending the deity of the Son of God. It affirms that the Son is "begotten of the Father," "only begotten," and "begotten, not made," distinguishing his existence from that of all creatures: they all were made, but the Son was not created. The creed affirms that the Son is *homoousios*, of the same substance as the Father, and thus fully God. The creed also condemns specific errors of Arianism: the Son is created, not eternal, and of a different nature from the Father. *See also* Council of Nicea (I, II); *homoousios*; Nicene-Constantinopolitan Creed.

CROSS/CRUCIFIXION A cross is the two-piece wooden instrument on which Jesus was crucified. It consisted of a vertical piece stuck into the ground and to which his legs were nailed, and a horizontal piece to which his hands were nailed. As a form of execution, crucifixion was reserved for the most heinous criminals; still, the innocent Jesus died on a cross. Derivatively, the cross symbolizes (1) reconciliation between holy God and sinful people (Eph. 2:16); (2) the gospel message (1 Cor. 1:18); (3) Christians' death to this world (Gal. 6:14); and (4) the daily death to self to which Christians are called (Matt. 16:24).

---

* "Nicea" is often spelled "Nicaea."

D

DAMNATION   *See* condemnation; hell.

DAVIDIC COVENANT   The structured relationship that God established with David (2 Sam. 7), consisting of typical covenantal features. This covenant (1) was unilateral, initiated by God, who had raised up David the shepherd; (2) formalized a structured relationship between God and his partners: David, as referring to King David himself; David's immediate offspring, Solomon; David's descendants, the Davidic kings; and an eternal Davidic king, Jesus Christ; (3) featured binding obligations, including (a) on God's part, to be a loving father; and (b) on David's part, to be a faithful son; (4) involved God swearing an oath to uphold the covenant.

DAY OF THE LORD   The future climactic event encompassing Christ's return; universal judgment, including condemnation and salvation; and ultimately the new heaven and new earth. The Old Testament associates the day with Israel's expectation of God's decisive intervention to rescue his people. At the same time, the prophets dash that hope, portraying the day as one of wrath and the destruction of God's sinful people. The New Testament transforms it into the day of Christ, associated with his second coming. It also presents that future finale as having already invaded this world through Christ's inauguration of the kingdom of God. *See also* second coming.

DEACON/DEACONESS/DIACONATE   Deacons are those who serve in the office of service. From the Greek (*diakonia*, "service"; *diakonos*, "servant"), these terms are used generically to refer to anyone who engages in service and used technically for a person who is a publicly recognized officer serving in a church. This office (diaconate) is to be distinguished from the office of bishop (bishopric) and the office of elder (eldership), which in the New Testament and in many churches are one office. The qualifications for men and women to serve are listed in 1 Timothy 3:8–13. Deacon responsibilities do not include leading and teaching but consist of serving in ministries. *See also* bishop; elder/eldership.

DEATH The cessation of the functioning of a person's material element (body), and its temporary separation from the immaterial element (soul). Created by God as a complex reality, consisting of a material aspect and immaterial aspect intimately joined together, a person is given life and exists as a body-soul unity. Death, which is the penalty imposed by God because of human sin, is the demise of the body and the undoing of this unity. The lifeless body is sloughed off at death, and there is a separation of the two elements until their reuniting at the resurrection of the body. *See also* embodiment; human nature; intermediate state; soul.

DECREE The eternal purpose of God for everything that happens. The divine decree was determined before the creation of the world and regards everything that occurs in it: the formation of Adam and Eve and their fall into sin, the crucifixion of Christ and the eternal destinies of all people, the moral evil of terrorist attacks and the natural evil of hurricanes, the fulfillment of the Great Commission and the return of Christ. Some theologies deny this all-encompassing nature of the divine decree, seeing it more like a dynamic program whose outworking depends in part on human decisions and actions. *See also* God; independence; necessity; open theism; predestination.

DEIFICATION A view of salvation as becoming more like God. Also called theosis and divinization, deification is the prevalent model and aim of Christian maturity in Eastern Orthodoxy. The affirmation that believers "become partakers of the divine nature" (2 Pet. 1:4) is biblical support. The incarnation—"God became man that men might become gods" (Athanasius)—is the ground for the faithful's divinization: not becoming God, taking on his essence, but like him, permeated by his energies. The vision of God, mortification of sin, mystical union, the Spirit, spiritual disciplines, and more enable people to cooperate with grace to foster deification. *See also* Eastern Orthodoxy; energies.

DEISM   An eighteenth-century movement that undermined historic Christianity. Deism exchanged God's personal care for the world for a mechanistic model: God is like a watchmaker who created the world, including the natural laws it needs for continuous operation, wound it up, and let go, never to intervene. Its five tenets: (1) God exists; (2) people are to worship this God; (3) such worship is achieved through moral living; (4) people must repent of sins; and (5) there is a future judgment of good and bad works. The supernatural nature of Christianity was replaced with a code of ethical conduct. *See also* providence.

DEMON POSSESSION   The sinister mastery of people by demons. Jesus's ministry was characterized by liberating demon-oppressed people (Matt. 4:24) through a word of rebuke (8:16); examples include two demoniacs (8:28–34) and an epileptic boy (17:14–21). Jesus's enemies attributed his exorcisms to Satan (9:32–34), but Jesus exposed that irrational explanation and clarified that he cast out demons by the Spirit (12:22–32). Jesus gave his disciples authority to cast out demons (10:1); an example is Paul's exorcism of a fortune teller (Acts 16:16–18). Demon possession manifests itself in sickness, mental instability, physical torment, and unusual strength. Demons are exorcised in Jesus's name. *See also* demons; exorcism; Satan.

DEMONS   A subcategory of angels, creatures that were created as immaterial (without a body) beings. Though all angels were originally created good, those now known as demons followed their head, Satan, in rebelling against God, lost their original goodness, and seek to oppose God and his work. Their evil activities with reference to human beings include temptation, deception, lying, false belief, torment, sickness, and even possession leading to self-destructive activity, mental instability, pronounced strength to harm others, and anguish. Called "rulers," "authorities," "cosmic powers," and "spiritual forces of evil," demons are to be resisted by spiritual warfare (Eph. 6:10–18). *See also* angels; demon possession; Satan.

DEMYTHOLOGIZATION   Rudolph Bultmann's method of interpreting the New Testament, demythologization is the attempt to recover the deeper meaning behind Scripture's many mythological elements. Bultmann made a radical dichotomy between the historical Jesus of Nazareth, about whom almost nothing can be known, and the "kerygmatic" Christ of faith, who was preached by the first disciples and, as the product of the early church, was covered with mythology (e.g., Jesus's resurrection and ascension). Accordingly, biblical interpretation demands acknowledging that its preaching and its mythological elements conceal a deeper meaning under the cover of mythology. By stripping away these legendary coverings, this deeper meaning can be uncovered. *See also* hermeneutics.

DENOMINATION/DENOMINATIONALISM   A denomination is an authoritative association of churches and institutions that distinguishes itself from other alliances by common heritage, self-governance, liturgy, organizational structure, theological distinctives, and missions agencies. Many denominations, while considering themselves to be the most pure expression of Christianity, encourage cooperation with other legitimate denominations, thus fostering catholicity and avoiding sectarianism. Denominationalism, then, is the spirit of participating in a denomination; it stands in contrast with nondenominationalism, which encourages the commonalities shared by a broad sweep of Christianity as seen in shared educational institutions, missions networks, broadcast media, evangelistic ministries, and more. Ecumenism reverses denominationalism by encouraging mergers of denominations. *See also* catholicity; ecumenism.

DEPOSIT OF FAITH   *See* creed.

DEPRAVITY, TOTAL   *See* total depravity.

DESCENT INTO HELL   According to the Apostles' Creed, the state of Christ between his crucifixion and resurrection. The creed, relying on 1 Peter 3:18–19, affirms Christ "descended into hell." His purpose may have been to proclaim the gospel (1 Pet. 4:6) and thereby rescue the righteous who had gone before him. The affirmation has difficulties: (1) the earliest versions of the creed did not include it; (2) its two clearest attestations come in the fourth and seventh centuries; (3) 1 Peter 3:18–19 may refer to the preexistent Christ's proclamation of salvation through Noah to the people living before the flood.

DETERMINISM   The position that for every decision and action that happens, causal conditions exist such that, given those conditions, no other decision or action could happen. These conditions decisively incline the person's will in one direction or another; consequently, the person could not have done otherwise. Causal conditions include God's choice and call of the elect, the conviction of the Spirit, dissatisfaction with sin, and the powerful gospel. Hard determinism embraces coercion: people are constrained in their decisions and actions. Soft determinism accounts for significant human freedom: causal conditions decisively prompt people to decide and act in accordance with their will. *See also* compatibilism; incompatibilism.

DEUS ABSCONDITUS / DEUS REVELATUS   Martin Luther's paradoxical theology that God is both "hidden" (*absconditus*) and "revealed" (*revelatus*). The hidden God reveals himself, specifically in the cross of Christ, and the revealed God hides himself, as the cross of humiliation and shame shrouds his glory from human wisdom. God is incomprehensible, because he "dwells in unapproachable light" (1 Tim. 6:16); seeking to know the unknowable God is destructive, prideful speculation. Still, the glorious God conceals his majesty through the human nature of the incarnate Son, and Christ reveals the hidden God. Ultimately, the divine glory is hidden in the sufferings of the cross. *See also* incomprehensible; Lutheranism / Martin Luther.

DIALECTICAL THEOLOGY The theological method of neo-orthodoxy in general and of Karl Barth in particular. *Dialectical* emphasizes the paradoxical nature of theology due to the infinite distinction between the Creator and his creatures. Revelation and hiddenness, transcendence and immanence, grace and judgment are paradoxes that cannot be synthesized into a higher unity nor reduced to the problem of human speech about God; the paradoxes are real. Dialectical theology stands opposed to Protestant liberalism, which explains God in terms of human aspirations. Liberalism is not theology—that is, speaking about God—but anthropology—that is, speaking about human beings "in elevated tone" (Barth). *See also* Barth, Karl; neo-orthodoxy.

DICHOTOMY In regard to the doctrine of humanity, the view that complex human nature consists of two elements: one material aspect, or body, and one immaterial aspect, soul or spirit (which are interchangeable terms). Support includes descriptions of human nature as body and soul (Matt. 10:28) or body and spirit (1 Cor. 5:3, 5). Dichotomy contrasts with trichotomy, the view that human nature consists of three elements: one material aspect, or body, and two immaterial aspects, soul (intellect, emotions, will) and spirit (which relates to God). Both views reject monism's idea that human nature is simple (only body or spirit). *See also* dualism; embodiment; human nature; monism; soul; trichotomy.

DICTATION THEORY With respect to the doctrine of Scripture, the view of its inspiration that the biblical authors had no significant and willful participation in the writing of Scripture. Rather, God dictated the words and caused the authors, as secretaries, to write them. Actually held by few people, the theory is more an accusation by theologians against those who disagree with their view of inspiration. The theory is contradicted by the differences in perspective, vocabulary, writing style, grammatical ability, genre, and so forth that Scripture clearly evidences. These differences are most reasonably attributed to full human participation rather than dictation. *See also* inspiration of Scripture.

DISCIPLE/DISCIPLESHIP   A disciple is a follower of Jesus, and discipleship is the process by which one develops as his follower. Jesus appointed twelve men to be his initial disciples, and having equipped them through his discipling ministry and empowered them with the Spirit, he commissioned them to make disciples everywhere. The church builds and multiplies Jesus's disciples by announcing the gospel, baptizing those who repent and believe in the name of the triune God, communicating Jesus's teachings so they obey him, and training them to multiply themselves through the making of other disciples (Matt. 28:18–20). This process of discipleship is multifaceted and never ending.

DISPENSATIONAL PREMILLENNIALISM   With respect to eschatology, the position that Christ's second coming will occur before (*pre-*) his one-thousand-year (*millennium*) reign on earth. As a view developed by dispensationalism, it differs from historic premillennialism by its belief that prior to the tribulation, Christ will remove the church from the earth (the rapture); thus, it is also called pretribulational premillennialism. Revelation 20:1–6 pictures Christ's rule over the earth (while Satan is bound) for a thousand-year period, which is followed by Christ's ultimate defeat of a released Satan, the last judgment, the resurrection of the wicked, and the new heaven and new earth. *See also* dispensationalism; Great Tribulation; historic premillennialism; rapture.

DISPENSATIONALISM   An evangelical framework for constructing theology that employs the concept of dispensation as its organizing principle. Related to the Greek term *oikonomia* ("administration, arrangement"), dispensationalism in its classical form (nineteenth to mid-twentieth century) featured seven dispensations: innocence, conscience, government, promise, law, grace, and kingdom/millennium. Three other varieties are ultra-, revised, and progressive dispensationalism. Key tenets: (1) a literal interpretation of Scripture (while accounting for figurative language); (2) different divine purposes for Israel and the church, with the latter not replacing the former; (3) blessings for ethnic Israel that are both political/national and spiritual; and (4) premillennial eschatology with a pretribulational rapture of the church. *See also* dispensational premillennialism; hermeneutics; covenant theology; theological method.

DIVORCE The termination of a marriage. Because marriage is a permanent covenant between husband and wife, and divorce severs the bond, God hates it (Mal. 2:16) and prohibits it (Matt. 19:6). In cases of adultery (Matt. 5:31–32; 19:9) and abandonment by an unbelieving spouse (1 Cor. 7:15), however, the covenant is permissibly broken and divorce allowed. Divorce differs from separation, the distancing of two people who remain married, and annulment, a legal declaration invalidating the marriage. Regarding remarriage, several views exist: (1) no remarriage is permitted; (2) with biblically permitted divorce, remarriage is permitted; (3) with all divorces, following repentance, remarriage is permitted. *See also* marriage.

DOCETISM With respect to Christology, the denial of the humanity of Christ. Docetism (from Gk. *dokeō*, "to appear, seem") holds that Christ only seemed to be a man. He was, instead, a spirit being who only appeared as a human being. Scripture warns against this heresy: the refusal to acknowledge "that Jesus Christ has come in the flesh" (1 John 4:1–3). Early church leaders demonstrated that Christ was truly human because he experienced the true activities of human beings: he was born, ate and drank, suffered, and died. Moreover, Christ's followers suffer in reality because Christ was human in reality. *See also* hypostatic union; Jesus Christ, humanity of.

DOCTRINE Christian belief based on Scripture. Examples include God is triune, Jesus is both God and man, and salvation is by divine grace. Doctrine is believed (orthodoxy), confessed (publicly recited), lived (orthopraxy), and taught (Lat. *docere*, from which *doctrine* comes). Sound doctrine is associated with Christian maturity (Eph. 4:14) and the responsibility of church leadership (1 Tim. 4:6). Negatively, an outsider "teaches a different doctrine and does not agree with the sound words of our Lord Jesus Christ" (1 Tim. 6:3). Sound doctrine, or orthodoxy, which reflects in summary what Scripture teaches and what the church is bound to believe, contrasts with heresy, which contradicts it. *See also* heresy; orthodoxy.

DOCUMENTARY HYPOTHESIS   A critical proposal that the Pentateuch is a collection of selections from several written documents (abbreviated *JEDP*) that were composed by different authors over a period of five centuries. A key tenet is that different divine names indicate different sources. Genesis 1 employs *E*lohim to refer to God, while Genesis 2 uses Yahweh (or Jehovah). This accounts for two sources, *J* and *E*. Deuteronomy was written in 621 BC and was the third source, *D*. A Priestly Code about holiness was composed later and became the fourth source, *P*. This *JEDP* hypothesis denies that Moses wrote the Pentateuch. *See also* biblical criticism.

DOGMA/DOGMATICS   *See* doctrine.

DOMINICAL SAYING   A dominical saying is anything that Jesus spoke. From the Latin (*dominus*, "Lord"), *dominical* refers to anything relating to the Lord. Scripture presents few of Jesus's exact (Aramaic) words: *Talitha cumi* ("Little girl, I say to you, arise"; Mark 5:41), *Ephphatha* ("Be opened"; Mark 7:34), and *Eloi, Eloi, lema sabachthani* ("My God, my God, why have you forsaken me?"; Mark 15:34). Because the Gospels were written in Greek, the dominical sayings reflect Jesus's exact voice: their Greek versions are faithful renditions of Jesus's Aramaic sayings, which he indeed spoke (the disciples did not invent them and attribute them to Jesus).

DONATISM   A movement of separatist churches in the fourth and fifth centuries. At issue was the consecration of bishops by others who had denied the faith by betraying Christians and handing over Bibles during persecution. Donatus, a church leader in Carthage, adopted a hard-line stance: any bishop consecrated by a compromised bishop was himself compromised and could not validly administer the sacraments. The church in Rome and, later, Augustine, took the opposite view: these fallen leaders could be forgiven, and the sacraments that they administered were effective merely by being administered. Donatism and its rigorist churches were eventually condemned. *See also* Novatianism.

DUALISM The philosophical position that reality is complex, consisting of two categories, and the one cannot be reduced to the other. Several forms of dualism exist: Moral dualism holds that two different yet equal forces—good and evil—eternally conflict. Substance dualism, proposed by Descartes, affirms that the mind and body are completely different substances. Emergent dualism proposes a closer connection between mind and matter, with the mind emerging from the brain yet not reducible to it. Dualism contrasts with monism, the view that reality is simple, most commonly material. Unlike monism, dualism accounts well for the disembodied intermediate state. *See also* monism.

E

EASTERN ORTHODOXY A family of self-governing national churches (e.g., Russian Orthodox, Greek Orthodox) and one of three branches of Christendom, along with Catholicism and Protestantism. The initial division between Orthodoxy (the Eastern church) and Catholicism (the Western church) occurred in 1054 when the pope's representative and the patriarch of Constantinople exchanged excommunications. Key distinctives: (1) The Eastern Church believes the Spirit proceeds from the Father, while the Western churches (Catholic and Protestant) believe he proceeds from the Father *and the Son*. (2) Eastern Orthodoxy believes the pope has primacy of honor, while the Catholic Church believes he exercises ultimate authority. (3) Eastern Orthodoxy embraces the first seven ecumenical councils, while Catholicism endorses twenty-one. *See also* Christian; eternal procession; *filioque*; Protestantism; Roman Catholicism.

EBIONISM   With respect to Christology, the denial of the deity of Christ. Ebionism bears some similarities to adoptionism. Major tenets: (1) Jesus was an ordinary, though unusually holy, man who was born to Mary and Joseph in a normal way. (2) At Jesus's baptism, the "Christ" (the power and presence of God) came upon him. At that point, God "adopted" Jesus as his son, conferring on him supernatural powers and rendering him the Messiah. (3) On the cross, as Jesus cried out, "Why have you forsaken me?" the Christ withdrew from him. Early church leaders condemned Ebionism as a heresy. *See also* adoptionism/adoptianism; Jesus Christ, deity of; virgin birth / virginal conception.

ECCLESIOLOGY   One of the topics of systematic theology, it treats the biblical material regarding the church. Ecclesiology (from Gk. *ekklēsia*, "assembly") presents the definition of the church and discusses its covenantal relationship with God, as well as its relationship to Israel and the kingdom of God. Ecclesiology further develops the church's nature (e.g., gospel centered, Spirit empowered, confessional, missional), its attributes (e.g., unity, purity, apostolicity, catholicity), and its marks (e.g., preaching, administering the sacraments, church discipline). Ecclesiology also considers the church's offices (e.g., eldership, diaconate) and government (e.g., episcopalianism, presbyterianism, congregationalism), as well as its ministries (e.g., worship, preaching, mission, discipleship). *See also* church.

ECONOMIC SUBORDINATION   *See* subordinationism.

ECONOMIC TRINITY   Perspective on the three persons of the Godhead in terms of the distinction in their roles. *Economic* (from Gk. *oikonomia*, "an ordering of activities") *Trinity* refers to the different roles the three persons exercise in creation, salvation, and sanctification. The Father exercises the primary role in creation, the Son exercises the primary role in salvation, and the Spirit exercises the primary role in sanctification. Still, the inseparable operation of the three means that the Father, Son, and Spirit are united in their work. Thus, the distinction in roles is a distinction within the one work of the one God. *See also* ontological Trinity; social Trinity; Trinity.

ECUMENISM   The position or movement that promotes unity among churches. Ecumenism (from Gk. *oikoumenē*, "the inhabited world") appeals to Jesus's prayer for his disciples' unity (John 17:21) and insists that such unity must be visible. The early Christians confronted heretical opponents who split from the catholic (universal) church. When Christendom divided into Eastern (Orthodox) and Western (Catholic) churches (and Western Christendom later separated into Catholicism and Protestantism), ecumenical efforts failed to heal the ruptures. Evangelicals are often suspicious of contemporary ecumenism (World Council of Churches, Catholic-Orthodox-Protestant dialogues) because of its perceived doctrinal and evangelistic weaknesses and its liberal political ideology.

EDWARDS, JONATHAN   One of America's leading theologian-philosophers (1703–58), whose influence contributed significantly to the First Great Awakening. Through his preaching on divine sovereignty, justification, and conversion, Edwards's church experienced revival, which in turn spread to other churches. Through *A Faithful Narrative of the Surprising Work of God, Distinguishing Marks of a Work of the Spirit of God*, and *Some Thoughts Concerning the Present Revival*, Edwards explained and defended this revival. He also addressed topics like sin and the human will and analyzed religious experience, drawing conclusions about true and false signs of conversion in *Treatise Concerning Religious Affections*.

EFFECTIVE/INTERNAL CALL The summons to embrace salvation that is extended to the elect through the proclamation of the gospel and that guarantees a response of repentance and faith. It is associated with the external call yet distinguished from it. Whereas both kinds of call come through the gospel, the effective call is an additional mighty work of God directed at the elect only, drawing them with certainty to turn from sin and trust Christ for salvation. God the Father calls his chosen people into his kingdom and glory and into fellowship with his Son (1 Cor. 1:9; 1 Thess. 2:12). *See also* election; external call.

EGALITARIANISM The position that men and women are equal to one another in nature, relationships, and roles. These equalities may be found in (1) the home, with the husband and the wife sharing equal authority and submitting to each other; (2) the church, with men and women serving in all its ministries, including elder responsibilities (traditionally reserved for qualified men); (3) the society, with men and woman leading governments and companies; or (4) some combination of these three. Egalitarianism stands in contrast to complementarianism, which believes men and women to be equal in nature yet distinct in relationships and roles. *See also* complementarianism.

ELDER/ELDERSHIP One who ministers in the office of oversight, or eldership. The Greek term *presbyteros* ("presbyter, elder") is used interchangeably in Scripture with *episkopos* ("bishop") and *poimēn* ("pastor"); thus, *elder*, *bishop*, and *pastor* refer to the same office. However, some denominations distinguish between elder and bishop and elevate the latter office above the former. The qualifications for elders are listed in 1 Timothy 3:1–7 and Titus 1:5–9. Elders are entrusted with four responsibilities: teaching, or communicating sound doctrine; leading, or providing overall direction; praying, especially for the sick; and shepherding, or guiding, nourishing, and protecting the church. *See also* bishop; deacon/deaconess/diaconate.

ELECTION   In terms of the doctrine of salvation, God's purpose regarding the redemption of people. According to Reformed theology, election is the sovereign, eternal purpose of God to save certain people through his gracious work in Christ. Election is unconditional: it is not based on foreknowledge of people's faith and good works; rather, it is grounded in God's good pleasure. According to Arminian theology, election is God's purpose to save people who, through prevenient grace, repent and believe in Christ and continue in salvation. Election is conditional: it is based on foreknowledge of people's faith and perseverance throughout their life. *See also* conditional election; decree; foreknowledge; reprobation; unconditional election.

ELEMENTS   *See* Lord's Supper.

EMBODIMENT   The divinely designed state of human existence. In contrast with angels, who are created to be nonembodied beings, humans are created beings that consist of both an immaterial aspect and a material aspect. Thus, the proper state of human beings is embodiment. This affirmation does not overlook the intermediate state in which people continue to exist after death as disembodied beings. Importantly, this state of disembodiment is abnormal, not the way human beings are designed to be, as evidenced by Paul's expression of horror when considering disembodiment ("naked," "unclothed"; 2 Cor. 5:1–9) and the reembodiment of people at the resurrection. *See also* death; intermediate state; neurophysiology; soul.

ENERGIES   In Eastern Orthodox theology, the activities of God in this world, as distinct from his essence. The divine essence exists by itself. It is uncreated and unknowable; consequently, no one can participate in God's essence. The divine energies are also uncreated, but through them God creates and sustains the world.

Because of his energies, God is present and can be experienced: through the process of deification (*theosis*), the faithful participate in God's energies. The essence-energies distinction preserves the reality of God's transcendence and immanence without falling into panentheism. Catholic and Protestant theologies minimize or reject the doctrine of energies.

ENHYPOSTASIS   *See* hypostatic union.

ENLIGHTENMENT, THE   Various philosophical, scientific, and political movements in Europe during the seventeenth and eighteenth centuries that contributed to the rise of modernity. According to Immanuel Kant, the Enlightenment was humanity's awakening from its self-imposed immaturity, "the inability to use one's own understanding without the guidance of another" (1784). Its nickname "the age of reason" underscores its emphasis on the role of reason above the traditional sources of knowledge and authority, such as revelation (e.g., Scripture) and religion (e.g., church). The Enlightenment's political systems, naturalistic approaches to science, social upheavals, and antisupernaturalistic philosophies sparked a challenge to and refutation of Christianity. *See also* Kant, Immanuel; rationalism.

EPISCOPALIANISM   With regard to ecclesiology, the type of church government with ultimate authority residing in the bishop (Gk. *episkopos*). Bishops are distinguished from presbyters (elders) and deacons: bishops exercise ultimate authority; presbyters are ordained by, and serve under, bishops; and deacons serve both. Support includes Scripture and tradition. In Scripture, the leadership of James in the Jerusalem church and the proceedings of the Jerusalem Council are prototypes of episcopalianism. Tradition points to the early (second-century) development of a single bishop leading each church and the later development of one regional bishop over numerous churches. Catholicism and Anglicanism adopt episcopalianism. *See also* bishop; congregationalism; presbyterianism.

EPISTEMOLOGY   The branch of philosophy that studies knowledge. Epistemology (from Gk. *epistēmē*, "knowledge") is also known as the theory of knowledge and treats the definition, structure, justification, sources, and limits of knowledge. Epistemology raises and seeks to answer questions such as: What is knowledge? What is the difference between knowledge, belief, and opinion? What can be known? What cannot be known? How is knowledge acquired? What constitutes justification for knowledge? Religious epistemology treats such issues as the existence of God (the ontological, cosmological, teleological, and moral arguments) and how he may be known (through revelation, reason, mystical experience, or more). *See also* ethics; metaphysics.

ESCHATOLOGY   One of the topics of systematic theology, it treats the biblical material regarding the last things (Gk. *eschatos*, "last"). This doctrine is commonly subdivided into personal and cosmic eschatology. Personal eschatology treats the topics of death and the intermediate state, or human existence between death and the resurrection of the body. Cosmic eschatology covers the return of Christ and its relationship to the millennium (amillennialism, postmillennialism, premillennialism) and the tribulation, the resurrection, the last judgment, the eternal blessing of the righteous and the eternal judgment of the wicked, and the eternal state of the new heaven and new earth. *See also* intermediate state; millennium.

ESSENCE   *See* human nature; substance; *substantia*.

ETERNAL CONSCIOUS PUNISHMENT   Regarding eschatology, one of two results of Christ's final judgment of people (the other being eternal life). Following Christ's evaluation of their unbelief and evil deeds, and his proclamation of condemnation, the wicked will consciously experience retribution in hell forever. Biblically supported (e.g., Matt. 25:46) and the historical position of the church, this position contrasts with (1) universalism: all people will be saved; (2) conditional immortality: believers will exist forever, but unbelievers will cease to exist at death; and

(3) annihilationsim: after a period of punishment, the wicked will be destroyed and thus not experience *eternal* punishment. *See also* annihilationism; condemnation; conditional immortality; hell; universalism.

ETERNAL GENERATION   With reference to the Son's relationship with the first person of the Trinity, the Son is eternally generated, or begotten, by the Father. Eternal generation does not mean that the Son was created by the Father, or that the Son's divine nature is derived from his, or that the Son is inferior, but it means that the Son is eternally dependent on the Father for his person-of-the-Son. Affirmations that the Father grants the Son to have life in himself (John 5:26) and that the Son has been born of God (1 John 5:18) point to his eternal generation by the Father. *See also* Jesus Christ, deity of; Trinity.

ETERNAL LIFE   In one sense, the personal knowledge of God and his Son, Jesus Christ (John 17:3), which is granted to his followers through their belief in the gospel (3:16; 5:24). Secondly, eternal life is the continuation of existence after death. Absent their body, Christians continue to exist in heaven with Christ (2 Cor. 5:1–9), awaiting his second coming and the resurrection of their body. Ultimately, they will live eternally in the new heaven and new earth. Thirdly, eternal life is one of two results of Christ's final judgment of people, the other being eternal conscious punishment (Matt. 25:46). *See also* death; eternal conscious punishment; great white throne judgment; new heaven and new earth.

ETERNAL PROCESSION   With reference to the Holy Spirit's relationship with the other persons of the Trinity, he eternally proceeds from both the Father and the Son. This does not mean that he was created by them, or that his divine nature is derived from theirs, or that he is inferior, but it means that he is eternally dependent on them for his person-of-the-Spirit. Jesus's affirmations that the Father and he would send the Spirit (on Pentecost; John 14:26; 15:26; 16:7) point to the eternal procession of the Spirit, who is the Spirit of God and the Spirit of Christ (Rom. 8:9), from them both. See also *filioque*; Holy Spirit, person of; Trinity.

ETERNAL SECURITY   *See* assurance of salvation.

ETERNITY   With regard to the doctrine of God, the divine attribute by which God is not bound by time but always exists. Eternity is God's infinity in relation to time; he exists "before all time and now and forever" (Jude 25). He has no beginning, end, or time-sequenced development in his being. God is not bound by time; indeed, he existed before he created the spatial-temporal universe. Still, he does act in time: prior to time beginning, he chose believers before creating the world (Eph. 1:4); the Son came at the appropriate time (Gal. 4:4); and the resurrection of Christ precedes that of believers (1 Cor. 15:23–28). *See also* infinite.

ETHICS   The discipline that studies moral matters. Ethics (from Gk. *ēthikos*, "habit") focuses on the nature, knowledge, and determination of moral principles; what is right and wrong; and moral obligation. Deontological ethics is the ethics of duty: one does the right and avoids doing the wrong because it is one's duty to do so. Teleological or consequentialist ethics is the ethics of consequences: one does the right and avoids doing the wrong because the former actions produce good consequences and the latter produce harmful consequences. Virtue ethics focuses on promoting right habits (e.g., justice) and avoiding vices (e.g., pride). *See also* epistemology; metaphysics.

EUCHARIST   One of seven sacraments of the Catholic Church. The Eucharist (from Gk. *eucharisteō*, "to thank"; reflective of Jesus's giving of thanks at the last supper) is "the source and summit of the Christian life,"* toward which the other sacraments are oriented. It is a memorial of Christ's sacrifice, with its participants offering to God bread and wine that, through transubstantiation, become

---

* *Lumen gentium*, no. 11 (cf. *Catechism of the Catholic Church*, 1324).

the body and blood of Christ, who is wholly present. Indeed, it is a re-presentation of Christ's one sacrifice for sins and conveys grace to the faithful. Some Protestants, while denying transubstantiation, use the term *Eucharist*. *See also* consubstantiation; Lord's Supper; real presence of Christ; transubstantiation.

EUTYCHIANISM   With respect to Christology, the denial of the hypostatic union, the orthodox doctrine that the incarnate Christ has two distinct natures—one divine, one human—united in one person. Its major tenet is that the incarnate Christ has only one nature, understood in two different ways: (1) the divine nature nearly absorbed the human nature of Christ, meaning that his one nature is DIVINEhuman; (2) the divine and human natures fused, meaning that Christ's one nature is divinehuman. The Council of Chalcedon (451), in its Chalcedonian Creed, condemned Eutychianism as heresy, insisting that Christ has two natures that retain their distinctive properties. *See also* hypostatic union.

EVANGELICALISM   A broad movement of churches, denominations, and institutions for which the evangel (Gk. *euangelion*), or gospel, is central. Derived from the Protestant Reformation, evangelicalism has roots in pietism, Puritanism, Methodism, and North American–British revivalism. In the twentieth century, it separated itself from fundamentalism, maintaining conservative theology while embracing cultural engagement. This theology includes conversionism (the need for personal faith in the gospel and regeneration), activism (living the gospel through missional endeavors and social involvement), biblicism (trust in Scripture as true and the ultimate authority), and crucicentrism (focus on the cross of Christ as the only means of accomplishing salvation). *See also* fundamentalism / fundamentalist-modernist debate; gospel; liberalism.

EVANGELISM   The activity of engaging non-Christians with the gospel. Jesus himself evangelized, announcing salvation especially to his people, the Jews (John 1:11), with some exceptions (e.g., Matt. 15:21–28; John 4:1–42). During his ministry, Jesus sent his disciples to evangelize the Jews rather than the Samaritans and Gentiles (Matt. 10:5–6). At the climax of this ministry, he gave the Great Commission to be the global task of making disciples (Matt. 28:18–20) empowered by the Holy Spirit (Acts 1:8). Accordingly, the church proclaims the good news everywhere, knowing that "faith comes from hearing, and hearing through the word of Christ" (Rom. 10:17). *See also* gospel; Great Commission; mission.

EVIL The absence or opposite of good, or anything that is bad or damaging. Evil is not a thing. Indeed, as originally created, the world was good, without any evil. Through Adam and Eve's *dis*obedience—the converse of obedience—sin entered the world, prompting all that is bad, or moral evil (murder, lying), and all that is damaging, or natural evil (drought, hurricanes). Thus, evil is any thought, motivation, act, word, or inclination, as well as any natural occurrence, that is contrary to God's good plan. Whereas evil pertains to his fallen creation, God is not the author of evil. *See also* sin.

EVIL, THE PROBLEM OF The issue of how believers in God understand and respond to the reality of evil. Two types: (1) The theological problem: "If God is all-good and if God is all-powerful, why is there evil?" The fact that evil exists calls into question God's goodness (though able to prevent evil, God is not willing) or God's power (though willing to prevent evil, God is not able), or both. (2) The personal/religious problem, expressed as "Why am I suffering?" or "Why did God permit this disaster to happen?" Theodicies or defenses are responses to these problems of evil. *See also* suffering; theodicy.

EVOLUTION Since the mid-nineteenth century, the reigning scientific theory that all of life originated from nonliving material and has developed according to natural selection and speciation as random mutations effect changes without purpose or design over billions of years. The modern theory of evolution arose with Charles Darwin's *Origin of Species* (1859) and has produced various responses from Christianity. Some have denounced it as atheistic and incompatible with Scripture. Others have rejected evolution while seeking to reconcile some elements of scientific discoveries with Scripture. Still others have found common ground between evolution and divine action in guiding the process. *See also* creation *ex nihilo*; creationism, old earth; creationism, young earth; evolution, theistic.

EVOLUTION, THEISTIC The theory that all life has developed according to evolutionary processes into which God has at times intervened to accomplish his purpose. It affirms both divine action ("theistic") and evolution. The specific stages of divine intervention are (1) the creation of the material universe, probably fourteen billion years ago; (2) the creation of living organisms from that nonliving matter, about four billion years ago; and (3) the creation of human beings from prehuman life-forms. Evolutionists reject this theory because of its appeal to divine intervention, and creationists find fault because of its nearly full acceptance of evolution. *See also* creation *ex nihilo*; creationism, old earth; creationism, young earth; evolution.

EX NIHILO *See* creation *ex nihilo*.

EX OPERE OPERATO The Catholic view of the validity of the sacraments. A Latin expression, *ex opere operato* ("by the work worked") means the sacraments are effective simply by their administration. For example, when a priest baptizes infants, his action of administering water in a Christian manner cancels the infants' original sin, effects their regeneration, and incorporates them into the Church. The sacrament's effectiveness does not depend on the priest's condition (i.e., he may be a saintly man or entrenched in sin), and it bears no relationship to the infants' faith or disposition to be baptized. Protestantism denies the effectiveness of the sacraments *ex opere operato*, instead grounding it in the Word of God and faith. *See also* Roman Catholicism.

EXALTATION OF CHRIST One of three states of Christ, the others being his preexistent state and the state of humiliation. While preexisting eternally, he entered a state of humiliation through incarnation, suffering, death, and burial. With his humiliation finished, Christ's exaltation began with his resurrection, reuniting him with his (now-glorified) body. After forty days of postresurrection appearances, he ascended into heaven, returning to the realm of glory. Exalted to the right hand of the Father, he sat down as authoritative Lord and intercessor for Christians. The last stage of his exaltation will be his glorious, victorious return to the earth. *See also* ascension; humiliation of Christ; second coming.

EXCLUSIVISM   With regard to Christianity and other religions, the position that salvation comes only through Christ, not through religions like Islam, Buddhism, and Hinduism. Exclusivism makes two affirmations: (1) The person and work of Christ is the ground of salvation; through his life, death, and resurrection, Christ accomplished redemption. (2) Faith in the person and work of Christ is necessary to appropriate salvation; through trust in Christ, sinful people experience redemption. Accordingly, the church is missionally engaged in proclaiming the gospel to make known the salvation accomplished by Christ so it may be believed. Exclusivism contrasts with inclusivism and pluralism. *See also* inclusivism; pluralism.

EXCOMMUNICATION   The last stage of the process of church discipline. Following the failure of the first stage of personal confrontation, of the second stage of two/three-on-one confrontation, and of the third stage of whole church rebuke and admonition, the church is to excommunicate the unrepentant member and treat that person as a non-Christian (Matt. 18:15–20). This action entails removal from church membership and ministry, exclusion from the Lord's Supper, and rupture of relationship with the church and with God. The purpose of excommunication is restoration; the church hopes and prays for repentance, which then leads to reinstatement of the excommunicated person. *See also* church discipline.

EXEGESIS / EXEGETICAL THEOLOGY   Exegesis is the activity of interpreting the Bible by studying (1) the *grammar* of the text:

the meaning of its words, phrases, and sentences; (2) the *historical* context of the text: its author, readership, socioeconomic-cultural background, and purpose; (3) the *genre*, or literary type, of the text: narrative, poetry, prophecy, letter, gospel, and so on; and (4) the *redemptive-historical* context of the text: its place in the canon and the progress of revelation, its connection to earlier texts and anticipation of later texts, its connection to biblical covenants, and the point about Christ that it emphasizes; and by relying on (5) the illumination of the Holy Spirit. *See also* biblical theology; hermeneutics; systematic theology; theological method.

EXISTENTIALISM   Philosophies that emphasize existence rather than essence, as seen in Sartre's expression "existence precedes essence." Originating in the nineteenth century and influential in the twentieth century, existentialism denied the reality of a common human essence and any "givens" in life. Rather, each person is an individual, uniquely and responsibly free, undetermined by anything or anyone else. Indeed, individuals exist in a frighteningly absurd, meaningless world. Key to human existence, therefore, is concrete personal decision, determining for oneself one's values, morals, goals, and actions. Existentialism's impact on theology is seen in Søren Kierkegaard, Rudolph Bultmann, Paul Tillich, and Karl Barth.

EXORCISM   The supernatural activity of casting out demons from demonically oppressed people. Jesus cast out demons by the Holy Spirit (Matt. 12:22–32) through a word of rebuke (Matt. 8:16); examples include the Gerasene demoniac (Mark 5:1–20) and a boy with an unclean spirit (Mark 9:14–29). Jesus gave his followers authority for exorcisms (Luke 9:1); for example, Philip cast out demons tyrannizing the Samaritans (Acts 8:4–8). Exorcism may involve "the [Spirit-given] ability to distinguish between spirits" (1 Cor. 12:10), but it features saying to a demon, "I command you in the name of Jesus Christ to come out of her" (Acts 16:18). *See also* demon possession; demons.

EXPIATION   One aspect of the atonement, that Christ's death removed the liability to suffer eternal punishment because of sin and guilt. The Old Testament background is the blood of sacrifices that was sprinkled on the mercy seat, thereby covering the sins of God's people and cleansing from sin to avoid judgment (Lev. 16). Some theologians object to the idea that Christ's death was a propitiation (assuaging the divine wrath) and maintain instead that his death was an expiatory sacrifice. Scripture affirms both. Christ's sacrifice was an expiation, cleansing and purifying through the removal and forgiveness of sins (Heb. 9:6–15; 10:5–18; 13:10–13). *See also* atonement; penal substitution theory; propitiation.

EXTERNAL CALL   The invitation to embrace salvation through the gospel. The external call comes to every person to whom the good news is announced. It is associated with the effective/internal call yet distinguished from it. The internal call is the summons extended to the elect only that comes through the gospel and that guarantees a response of repentance and faith. Whereas both types of call come through the gospel, the external call results in salvation only when the internal call operates as well. For the nonelect, the external call communicates God's command to trust the gospel, even though they refuse. *See also* effective/internal call.

EXTRA CALVINISTICUM   The position that the Son of God, while fully united to human nature in the incarnation, was not confined to it; thus, the Son existed outside of (*extra*) Christ's human nature. Reflective of traditional Christology, the position, dubbed *extra calvinisticum* by Lutheran opponents, is associated with John Calvin. He maintained that the Son "descended from heaven in such a way that, without leaving heaven, he willed to be borne in the virgin's womb, to go about the earth, and to hang upon the cross; yet he continuously filled the world even as he had done from the beginning!" (*Institutes of the Christian Religion*, 2.13.4). *See also* hypostatic union.

EXTRA NOS   The view that salvation comes from the outside. A Latin expression, *extra nos* ("outside of us") is associated with the theology of Martin Luther. Dissenting from the doctrine of salvation as held by the Catholic Church, which connected salvation with doing what is within one's ability to do, Luther linked salvation with the alien righteousness of Christ. Justification is God's declaration that people are not guilty but righteous instead, not because of any grace infused into them through the sacraments, or some righteousness inherent in them, but because God imputes the righteousness of Christ from outside of them. *See also* imputation; justification.

EXTREME UNCTION   *See* anointing of the sick.

F

FAITH   One aspect of conversion (the other being repentance), which is the human response to the gospel. Faith is belief and personal trust. It involves an understanding of the person and work of Christ to provide salvation; an assent to one's need for forgiveness; and a decision to trust Christ to personally save. Though a fully human response, faith is not merely human, because it is prompted by grace (Acts 18:27). For some, prevenient grace is given to all people, enabling them to believe. For others, saving grace is given only to the elect, enabling them to believe the gospel. *See also* conversion; *fides qua creditur / fides quae creditur*; prevenient grace; repentance; saving faith; saving grace.

FAITHFULNESS   A divine attribute signifying that God never goes back on his word but always fulfills his promises (Num. 23:19).

God's faithfulness does not depend on his people being faithful to him. Indeed, "if we are faithless, he remains faithful—for he cannot deny himself" (2 Tim. 2:13). This means that Christians will never be ultimately overcome by temptation but will certainly persevere in salvation through God's faithfulness to forgive them (1 Cor. 10:13; 1 John 1:9). In a secondary sense, it is a human attribute reflective of divine faithfulness, in which people honor their commitments and fulfill their promises.

FALL The cataclysmic event of Adam and Eve's sin, with devastating consequences for all humanity. Created in the divine image as people of integrity, they were characterized by an upright nature, personal relationship with God, love between them, and harmony with the creation. Tempted by Satan, Eve disobeyed God's prohibition to eat of the tree of the knowledge of good and evil; Adam transgressed that prohibition with full awareness. The results of the fall were universal: a corrupt nature, guilt before God, interpersonal conflict, and disharmony with the creation. These results were transmitted to all humanity after Adam and Eve. *See also* federal headship; natural headship of Adam; original sin; representative headship of Adam; Satan; sin.

FEAR OF GOD The reverence that is owed to God and is the beginning of wisdom. Because God is transcendent and holy, he commands his creatures to honor him alone, forsake sin, and avoid displeasing him. Such fear is seen at the burning bush, when God revealed himself to Moses on holy ground, and "Moses hid his face, for he was afraid to look at God" (Exod. 3:1–6). Proper fear of God is not terror that paralyzes; rather, it is the beginning of wisdom leading to human flourishing, wholehearted love, the obedience of faith, not fearing people, and fruitful service.

FEDERAL HEADSHIP The position that God established a covenant with Adam that constituted him the representative of all human beings, such that as Adam would go, the entirety of the human race would go. The conditions of the covenant were blessings for Adam and humanity should Adam obey the covenant stipulations (i.e., avoid eating the fruit of the tree of the knowledge of good and evil) but curses for all should he disobey. Accordingly, when Adam fell, he plunged not only himself but all human beings who would come from him into a hellish nightmare of sin, death, and condemnation. *See also* Adamic covenant; natural headship of Adam; original sin; Reformed theology; representative headship of Adam; Satan; sin.

FEDERAL THEOLOGY   *See* covenant theology.

FEMINISM / FEMINIST THEOLOGY   A movement or a theology that focuses on women and female perspectives. Feminism developed in the twentieth century in reaction to patriarchalism (systems of male hierarchical authority), male biases, and mistreatment of women (e.g., abuse, barriers to career advancement). Sometimes it criticizes men and male perspectives. Feminist theological proposals include emphasizing the feminine attributes of God, interpreting Scripture from a woman's perspective, and referring to God in feminine terms (e.g., as Mother). Evangelical feminism calls into question traditional complementarian theology and advances egalitarianism, the position that men and women are equal in nature, relationships, and roles in the church and home. *See also* complementarianism; egalitarianism; theological method.

FIDEISM   The position that Christian truth must be acknowledged by faith alone, apart from reason, evidence, and argument. Fideism (from Lat. *fides*, "faith") may adopt a negative stance toward reason due to the conviction that reason is incompatible with or even hostile to faith, or because reason cannot provide the certainty faith can. An example is Søren Kierkegaard, who dismissed arguments for Christianity as irrelevant and presented faith as wholehearted abandonment to God, even against reason. The opposite approach to Christian truth upholds the importance and necessity of reason, as seen, for example, in the proofs for God's existence. *See also* faith; presuppositionalism; reason.

FIDES QUA CREDITUR / FIDES QUAE CREDITUR   Two Latin expressions that refer to two different notions of faith. *Fides qua creditur* ("faith by which [it] is believed") refers to the act of faith. For example, for a person to embrace salvation, that person must have faith in Jesus Christ. The personal exercise of saving faith in Christ is the act of faith. *Fides quae creditur* ("faith that is believed") refers to the substance of faith. For example, the cardinal beliefs regarding the Trinity, the person and work of Christ, human sinfulness, the application of salvation by grace through faith, and more—this sound doctrine constitutes what the church believes and publicly confesses. *See also* confession; faith; saving faith.

FIDES QUAERENS INTELLECTUM   The theological method of "faith seeking understanding" (also, *credo ut intelligam;* "I believe that I may understand"). Associated with Anselm's approach (and Augustine before him), this method prioritizes faith as the starting point and presupposition for theology's task of seeking to reason about God's existence, the Trinity, and more. It is contrasted with a neutral approach, which suspends belief during the theological process, and skepticism, which prioritizes doubt. The priority of faith acknowledges God's creation of human beings in his image, their fall into sin, and grace to restore them to love and know God through understanding. *See also* faith; fideism; presuppositionalism; theological method.

FILIOQUE   In terms of pneumatology, this Latin term translated "and the Son" was inserted into the Nicene-Constantinopolitan Creed at the Synod of Toledo (Spain) in 589. Whereas the original creed affirmed that the Holy Spirit proceeds from "the Father," the addition resulted in the modified creed affirming that the Spirit proceeds from "the Father and the Son." Because the Eastern Church did not participate in this council and dissented from this addition, the double procession of the Spirit from the Father and the Son is a major point of division between Eastern (Orthodox) churches and Western (Catholic and Protestant) churches. *See also* eternal procession; Holy Spirit, person of the; Trinity.

FILLED WITH THE HOLY SPIRIT   To be controlled, permeated, or pervaded by the Spirit. The expression has three uses: (1) as an equivalent of "baptism with the Spirit" (also, the "outpouring," "coming," and "gift" of the Spirit), "being filled" is the initial experience when Jesus baptizes with the Spirit for incorporation into his body (Acts 2:4 with 1:5; 1 Cor. 12:13); (2) subsequent experiences of the Spirit to empower ministry (Acts 4:8); and (3) a characterization of people in relation to the Spirit, acknowledging a praiseworthy Christian lifestyle (Acts 6:3, 5). Christians must be "filled with the Spirit" (Eph. 5:18). *See also* baptism with/in/by the Holy Spirit; Keswick theology.

FINAL JUDGMENT   *See* great white throne judgment.

FIVE POINTS OF CALVINISM   *See* Calvinism / John Calvin.

FIVE WAYS, THE   Proofs for God's existence. From Aquinas's *Summa Theologica*, they consist of four cosmological arguments and a teleological argument. The First Way, an argument from motion, focuses on a necessary first mover, who is God. The Second Way, an argument from causation, focuses on a necessary first cause, who is God. The Third Way, an argument from necessity, focuses on a necessary being, who is God. The Fourth Way, an argument from hierarchy, focuses on the cause of all perfections, who is God. The Fifth Way, a teleological argument, focuses on an intelligent being directing and ordering all things, who is God. *See also* cosmological arguments; teleological arguments.

FLESH   The human body, humanity in general, and sinful nature. (1) *Flesh* refers to (a) the whole body (flesh, bones, blood, and organs), not just the fleshly part (life lived as embodied people; Gal. 2:20); and (b) just bodily tissue (physical circumcision; Rom. 2:28). (2) Flesh is humanity in reference to its origin (Rom. 1:3), including its gifts, abilities, and achievements ("confidence in the flesh"; Phil. 3:4). These generally positive ideas should not be confused with (3) flesh as sinful nature (Rom. 7:18). Flesh in terms of human embodiment is not the same as flesh in terms of human sinfulness. *See also* embodiment; sin nature.

FOREKNOWLEDGE   A divine attribute signifying that God eternally knows all that will transpire in the universe. From eternity, with respect to creation, God has known the end from the beginning (Isa. 46:10). Reformed theology closely joins foreknowledge with foreordination: not only does God know everything, he also purposes and "works all things according to the counsel of his will" (Eph. 1:11). Accordingly, God's foreknowledge of the elect is associated with his choice of them for salvation. Arminian theology affirms foreknowledge without such a close link to foreordination, believing that God foreknows those who will embrace Christ and thus elects them. *See also* conditional election; open theism; unconditional election.

FORENSIC   Having to do with legal matters. From the Latin (*forensis*, "public"), *forensic* emphasizes the judicial nature of some aspects of salvation. For example, justification is a forensic declaration that sinful people are not guilty but righteous instead. They are righteous, not because of any inherent or earned righteousness, but because of God's imputation—again, a legal reckoning—of Christ's righteousness to their account. Indeed, when Abraham believed God's promise, his faith was reckoned as righteousness (Rom. 4:3). Though some aspects of salvation—regeneration, sanctification—are re-creative, other aspects—justification, adoption—are forensic, dealing with one's legal standing before God. *See also* adoption; imputation; justification.

FORGIVENESS   The mighty act of God by which he remits sins, removes his wrath, and extends pardon to sinful people. Forgiveness stems from God's love and justice. While fallen people were still in their sins, God demonstrated his love through the atoning death of Christ, by which he is both just and the justifier of all who receive forgiveness by faith. The divine provision for, and the human experience of, divine forgiveness is a prerequisite for extending and experiencing human-to-human forgiveness. Such forgiveness involves setting aside anger and giving up the right to exact justice or punishment from an offender. *See also* atonement; justice; love; penal substitution theory.

FORMULA OF CONCORD   One of two primary Lutheran confessions of faith (the other being the Augsburg Confession). Written by a group of Lutheran theologians, chief among whom were Jacob Andreä and Martin Chemnitz (1577), it united most Lutherans divided in their loyalty to either Martin Luther or Philip Melanchthon. Affirming Scripture as the norm of faith, the formula's twelve topics are: original sin, free will, the righteousness of faith, good works, law and gospel, the third use of the law (for Christians), the Lord's Supper, the person of Christ, his descent into hell, church ceremonies, election, and sects and heresies. *See also* Augsburg Confession; Lutheranism / Martin Luther.

FOUNDATIONALISM   A philosophy that proposes a ground or starting point for building knowledge. The classical foundationalism of René Descartes—*cogito ergo sum* ("I think, therefore I am")—offered a self-evident, indubitable, and incorrigible foundation for knowledge. Modest foundationalism begins with basic propositions that are regarded as true, though not indubitable, and builds other propositions, derived from those basic ones, on this foundation. Postmodernism rejects foundationalism, denying the existence of basic starting points and holding to theories that knowledge consists of propositions that cohere together (coherentism) or propositions that work (pragmatism). Christian theology is foundationalist by building its doctrines on Scripture. *See also* epistemology; postmodernism.

FOURTH LATERAN COUNCIL   The twelfth general council (1215) as acknowledged by the Catholic Church but rejected by Orthodoxy and Protestantism. Meeting in Rome's Basilica of Saint John Lateran, it affirmed Catholicism's doctrines of the exclusivity of the Catholic Church for salvation and transubstantiation: the body and blood of Christ are truly contained in the sacrament of the Eucharist under the elements of the bread and wine, the bread being transubstantiated (changed) into the body and the wine into the blood by divine power. It also prescribed confession of sins to a priest and participation in the Eucharist at least annually. *See also* Eucharist; real presence of Christ; substance; transubstantiation.

FRAMEWORK HYPOTHESIS   With respect to the doctrine of creation, a literary approach to interpreting the "days" of Genesis 1. Rather than understanding these days as twenty-four literal hours or even lengthy periods of time, this view sees them as an artistic framework paralleling the "days of *forming*" (day 1: light and darkness separated; day 2: waters and sky separated; day 3: dry land and seas separated) with the "days of *filling*" (day 4: sun, moon, and stars as lights in the heavens; day 5: fish and birds fill the waters and sky; day 6: animals and humans fill the land). *See also* creationism, old earth; creationism, young earth.

FREE WILL   The capacity to decide without coercion. Some theologies (Arminian) embrace libertarian freedom: no causal factors (e.g., divine decree, God's grace) can decisively incline a person's will in one direction or another. It is not a random choice, and the person could have chosen something other than they chose. Other theologies (Reformed) embrace significant, but not libertarian, freedom: causal factors can decisively incline a person's will in one direction or another. It is not a forced choice, and the person could not have chosen something other than they chose. One's view of free will impacts one's approach to salvation. *See also* compatibilism; determinism; freedom; incompatibilism.

FREE-CHURCH MOVEMENT   Churches and denominations that embrace the separation of church and state, insisting that civil authorities may not exercise control of churches. Opposed to the centuries-old interdependence between secular governments (e.g., the nation of France) and churches, the movement arose during the Reformation in distinction from both the Roman Catholic

Church and magisterial Protestantism—Lutheran, Reformed, and Anglican churches, in whose affairs the civil authorities exercised control. Anabaptist, Separatist, and Baptist churches decried the interference of the state in church matters and demanded that they be free from governmental control so as to worship God according to Scripture. *See also* Anabaptism; Baptistic theology; magisterial Reformation.

FREEDOM The condition of making decisions and acting without constraint or coercion. The freedom of God means that no external or internal factors (e.g., need to express his power) demand that he purpose and act as he does. God was free to create or not to create, to save or not to save, and more. Christian freedom is twofold. Christians are free through Christ to obey God and not sin. Regarding amoral matters (neither moral nor immoral activities), Christians enjoy liberty to participate or not to participate. Still, they are guided by principles of conscience, deference to others, and more (Rom. 14). See also *adiaphora*; compatibilism; conscience; incompatibilism.

FUNDAMENTALISM / FUNDAMENTALIST-MODERNIST DEBATE
The fundamentalist-modernist debate was an aggressive dispute between conservative and liberal theologies in the early twentieth century. Through the influence of biblical criticism, Darwinism, and naturalism, portions of Protestantism began to accommodate to modern culture. Fundamentalism developed to protect traditional, orthodox theology from this dangerous trend, which was called modernism. Rallying around *The Fundamentals* (1910–15), fundamentalists defended the inerrancy of Scripture; Christ's virgin birth, deity, substitutionary atonement, resurrection, and return; miracles; and more. As fundamentalism identified modernism as non-Christian and called for separation from it, new denominations (e.g., Presbyterian Church of America, Conservative Baptists) and institutions (e.g., World's Christian Fundamentals Association) arose. *See also* evangelicalism; liberalism.

G

GENDER Masculine and feminine. When God created human beings in his image, "male and female he created them" (Gen. 1:27). Thus, gender is a primary characteristic, a fundamental given, rather than a secondary characteristic (blue eyes, curly hair) of people. The dual genderedness of people enables the development of human community reflective of the divine community of the Trinity, and it renders possible the fulfillment of the divine mandate for human beings to engage in procreation and vocation (Gen. 1:28). The expression of gender, flowing from the divinely implanted maleness or femaleness, is nourished by familial, relational, cultural, and ecclesial factors. *See also* embodiment; image of God (*imago Dei*).

GENERAL REVELATION God's communication of himself to all peoples at all times and in all places by which they may know of his existence, some of his attributes, and something of his moral law. General revelation has four modes: the created order (Rom. 1:18–25), the human conscience or internal moral sense (Rom. 2:12–16), God's providential care (Acts 14:8–18), and an innate sense of God (Acts 17:22–31). The intended response to general revelation is worship, thanksgiving, submission, and obedience to God. People respond actually with idolatry, disobedience, and self-reliance. This failed response results in God's righteous judgment falling on rebellious people. *See also* special revelation.

GENERATION, ETERNAL *See* eternal generation.

GLORIFICATION The final mighty act of God in salvation. Occurring at Christ's return, glorification is both (1) the reembodiment of believers who have died and exist without their bodies in heaven, and (2) the instantaneous change in the bodies of believers on earth. In the first case, their bodies are raised from the dead and transformed; in the second case, their current bodies are immediately transformed. In both cases, the glorified bodies are imperishable (never to wear out or become sick), glorious (beautiful, perhaps radiant), powerful (not superhuman but full strength), and spiritual (dominated by God's Spirit). *See also* resurrection of people; second coming.

GLORY The infinite beauty that is God's because of who he is in his perfections and that is put on display as he manifests himself as God through creation, redemption, and consummation. Furthermore, glory is the brilliant splendor that radiates from God's revelation of his character and mighty acts (Exod. 33:18–19). God created all things for his glory: the heavens and earth, the angelic realm, and people. When created beings encounter the splendor surrounding God's being and activity, they are to engage in praising him, giving him honor, and exalting him—such adoration is what is meant by "giving God glory." *See also* God; heaven.

GLOSSOLALIA From the Greek (*glōssa*, "tongue"; *laleō*, "to speak"), *glossolalia* refers to the spiritual gift of speaking in tongues. A controversial issue is whether its exercise is in human languages or some other type of encoded message. At Pentecost, the disciples spoke in known languages, to attract and to address non-Aramaic speakers (Acts 2:5–13). For Paul, speaking in tongues is directed to God and not people, "for no one understands" (1 Cor. 14:2), implying that the instances in the church of Corinth were not human languages. Indeed, Paul's insistence that tongue speaking must be interpreted requires only that interpreters possess the code to decipher it (1 Cor. 14:5, 27–28). *See also* cessationism; continuationism; miraculous gifts; spiritual gifts.

GNOSTICISM In the early church, a complex group of movements that opposed sound doctrines. Major tenets: (1) a secret knowledge (Gk. *gnōsis*; hence *gnosticism*) is reserved for elite members; (2) spiritual realities are inherently good, while physical realities are inherently evil; (3) thus, the Son of God could not become incarnate (embodied) by taking on material human nature (a body); (4) thus, Jesus only appeared to be a man (docetism). Gnosticism led to two extremes: asceticism and hedonism. The church condemned all forms of gnosticism, insisting that in the incarnation, the Son became a real and fully human being. *See also* asceticism; hypostatic union; Jesus Christ, humanity of; Manicheanism; Platonism.

GOD The supreme being. The one, true, living God eternally exists as Father, Son, and Holy Spirit. His proper name is Yahweh (Exod. 3:14); other names include Adonai/Lord, Lord of Hosts, El Shaddai (God Almighty), and El Kadosh (Holy One). He is the Creator, Sustainer, and King of the universe, and the Savior and Sanctifier of his people. Though spiritual (immaterial) in nature, he discloses himself through general revelation (e.g., creation, human conscience) and special revelation (e.g., Jesus Christ, Scripture). Additionally, the term *God* refers to the Father of the Son, Jesus Christ, in eternal communion with the Holy Spirit. *See also* communicable attributes; incommunicable attributes; Trinity.

GOD, THE ATTRIBUTES OF *See* communicable attributes; incommunicable attributes.

GOD, THE EXISTENCE OF The actuality of the supreme being, whose reality is independent of human consciousness though known through it. Scripture's assumption is that God exists; it gives no proof. Various arguments are offered for God's existence, including the ontological (God as the greatest conceivable being), cosmological (God as the first/efficient cause of the world), teleological (God as the designer), and moral (God as the moral lawgiver) arguments. General revelation manifests God's existence to all people at all times and in all places. Special revelation manifests God's existence to particular people at particular times and in particular places. *See also* cosmological arguments; Five Ways, the; general revelation; moral arguments; ontological arguments; special revelation; teleological arguments.

GOD-BREATHED With respect to the doctrine of Scripture, the attribute regarding its divine origin. Commonly known by the term *inspiration, God-breathed* better captures the Greek (*theopneustos*; 2 Tim. 3:16) and underscores that Scripture is the product of the creative breath of God. This activity was more than just providential care or divine guidance, leading to a heightened religious consciousness. Rather, it was the superintending work of the Spirit bearing along the authors as they wrote. Yet, ultimately, the God-breathed quality is particularly true of Scripture's very words, and all of them: "all Scripture [Gk. *graphē*, the words themselves] is God-breathed" (NIV). *See also* inspiration of Scripture.

GOOD WORKS The loving actions in which Christians are engaged to help others. While good works contribute nothing to salvation, they flow from salvation and are its necessary fruits. As the gospel changes people from self-absorption to self-giving, the good works they do are ordained by God and glorify him, benefit others, and secure future rewards. Good works are not restricted to "spiritual" activities like praying, fasting, and giving to the poor. They also encompass charging a reasonable fee, lending at a fair rate, and working hard to earn one's paycheck (Luke 3:12–14)—for God's glory and not one's own. *See also* grace; merit.

GOODNESS As an attribute of God, the benevolent kindness that characterizes him and his ways. God, who alone is good (Luke 18:19), is good in himself, and all that he does—creation, providence, salvation—is good (Ps. 119:68). The varieties of God's goodness are (1) grace, which is his goodness expressed to those who deserve condemnation; (2) mercy, which is his goodness expressed to those who are afflicted; and (3) his patience, which is his goodness in withholding punishment. The response to God's goodness is praise, trust rather than anxiety, receiving his gifts with thanksgiving, and imitation of his goodness. *See also* grace; mercy; patience.

GOSPEL The good news of Christ for the salvation of sinful people. It is a twofold announcement: (1) The Son of God became incarnate, lived a sinless life, suffered, was crucified and buried, rose again, and ascended into heaven. This is the accomplishment of salvation. (2) Sinful human beings who hear this good news are instructed to repent of their sins and believe in Christ. This is the appropriation of salvation. They are called by God, justified by grace, regenerated by the Spirit, united with Christ, adopted into God's family, and baptized with the Spirit as application of the gospel. See also *kerygma*.

GOVERNMENT The civil office that exercises authority over a people, state, or country. God establishes government for the maintenance of peace, the encouragement of upright behavior, and the punishment of evildoers. Because government functions as a divine servant, its citizens are to submit to its laws, pay their taxes, pray for their leaders, and honor them (Rom. 13:1–7; 1 Tim. 2:1–3). For some Christians, involvement in government is forbidden because it can exercise deadly force (in war and capital punishment), which violates the law of love. For others, such involvement is demanded by the mandate to build civilization (Gen. 1:28). *See also* authority.

GOVERNMENTAL THEORY With respect to the atonement, the theory developed by Hugo Grotius (1583–1645) that God is the governor of the universe whose love for sinful human beings is his highest attribute. In his mercy, God relaxed the demands of his law while remaining holy by still upholding it to some degree. Christ's death emphasized that the law must be respected, but it did not meet the exact requirements of the law (which had been relaxed). Thus, Christ died, not as a full satisfaction for the law's exact penalty, but as a token of God's concern to uphold his law.

See also atonement; *Christus Victor*; moral influence theory; penal substitution theory; ransom to Satan theory; satisfaction theory.

GRACE   As an attribute of God, his goodness expressed to those who deserve condemnation. Highlighted by God himself when he revealed his name, grace is associated with mercy, patience, love, and faithfulness (Exod. 34:6). Grace is God's de-merited favor. This gift is not owed to people derelict in person and duty who engage in good works; rather, God is gracious to whom he will be gracious (Rom. 9:15), and his gracious salvation is appropriated by faith (Eph. 2:8–9). Catholicism views grace as being infused into people through the sacraments, but Protestantism emphasizes the imputation of God's grace through many means. *See also* condemnation; goodness; love; mercy.

GREAT COMMANDMENT   The directive to love God completely and love others as one loves oneself, which Jesus gave to summarize all the commandments (Matt. 22:37–40). As a commandment, it demands obedience. Still, it calls for wholehearted love for God and love of others; thus, it is not a moralistic rule or a behavioral code concerning outward conduct. As the greatest commandment, it demands Christians' primary attention. It also presupposes or directs love of self: as one loves oneself, one is to love others. It is also called "the law of Christ" (Gal. 6:2) and "the law of freedom" (James 2:12 HCSB). *See also* love; obedience.

GREAT COMMISSION   Jesus's directive concerning the church's missional identity and task. As it travels beyond its location, the church is responsible to make disciples of Christ in every corner of the globe (Matt. 28:18–20). This commission is based on Old Testament prophecy (Luke 24:44–49), promising that the worldwide expansion of the gospel of the forgiveness of sins will be fulfilled. It is the mission of God: as the Father commissioned his Son with the mission, the Son in turn commissioned his church with the same mission (John 20:19–23), and the Holy Spirit's power is provided for its accomplishment (Acts 1:8). *See also* gospel; mission.

GREAT TRIBULATION   The global, intense period of suffering associated with Christ's return. The Tribulation will start with the appearance of "the abomination of desolation," also called "the man of lawlessness" (Matt. 24:15; 2 Thess. 2:3–4), who will wreak havoc. This unprecedented time of trouble, which some believe lasts seven years (Dan. 9:27), will feature unmatched Satanic attack, unparalleled human evil, and furious divine wrath. Some hold that the church, which is promised exemption from such suffering, will be removed from the earth prior to the Tribulation period. Others maintain that the church will be present though protected from divine wrath (Rev. 3:10). *See also* antichrist; rapture; second coming.

GREAT WHITE THRONE JUDGMENT   The world-encompassing, public verdict to be rendered at the judgment seat of Christ. Seated on a great white throne (Rev. 20:11–15), Christ will execute this judgment, evaluating the works that people do during their earthly life. According to some, this judgment will occur at Christ's second coming; for others, it will take place at the end of the millennium. Unlike the personal judgment that occurs at death, this judgment for rewards and punishments will be public and all-inclusive: Christ will judge unbelievers and believers. He will demonstrate himself to be the impartial Judge who judges justly. *See also* good works; judgment.

GUILT   The state of a person who has violated a law of one in authority. Guilt is associated with the liability to suffer punishment; unless this guiltiness is rectified, the person will be condemned and punished. Guilt before God means that a person has transgressed a divinely given law; such violation may have been unintentional or intentional (Num. 15:27–31). This violation may be accompanied by a sense of guilt produced by an accusing conscience. Through the mighty act of justification, God declares a law-violating person not guilty but fully righteous instead, because God imputes the righteousness of Christ to that person's account. *See also* condemnation; forgiveness; justification; sin.

H

HAMARTIOLOGY   One of the topics of systematic theology, being the doctrine of sin (Gk. *hamartia*). It treats the definition of sin (e.g., a lack of conformity to the law of God), its elements (e.g., pride, unfaithfulness, disobedience), its origin (the fall of Adam and Eve), and its consequences (e.g., alienation from God, enslavement to sin, broken relationships). Further discussion focuses on controversial matters such as original sin (i.e., the state of guilt and/or corruption into which all people are born) and its elements (e.g., depravity, inability), and the imputation of Adam's sin (with the positions of Pelagianism, Arminianism, and Calvinism).

HEALING   The restoration of that which is fallen or sick. In the first sense, salvation through the forgiveness of sin is the ultimate healing (Mark 2:1–10). Jesus linked the two in his ministry of "proclaiming the gospel of the kingdom and healing every disease" (Matt. 4:23). Indeed, all physical healing is tied to Christ's redemption (Matt. 8:14–17). In the second sense, healing restores sight, walking, health—even life itself (John 11:1–44). Elders engage in healing prayer for the sick (James 5:13–16); healing is also a spiritual gift (1 Cor. 12:9, 28). In the age to come, healing will not be needed.

HEAVEN   The realm of God in his absolute glory surrounded by adoring angels. Though everywhere present, God manifests his supreme majesty in heaven and is appropriately worshiped for his glorious revelation. Heaven is also the state and place of believers who have died and are currently in God's presence, experiencing a direct relationship with him and enjoying eternal blessing. Still, believers in heaven do not experience the fullness of salvation. They are disembodied and await the resurrection of their body, which will take place at Christ's return. At the consummation the present heaven will give way to the new heaven. *See also* glory; God; new heaven and new earth.

HEIDELBERG CATECHISM   *See* Three Forms of Unity.

HEILSGESCHICHTE   German (*heil*, salvation; *geschichte*, history) for "the history of salvation," referring to the saving highlights of the history of Israel and of the church. Employed especially by the twentieth-century biblical theology movement, it is a critical approach that focuses not on Scripture itself but on certain mighty acts of God as being authoritative for theology. These events, like Israel's exodus from Egypt and the death and resurrection of Jesus (the "Christ event"), constitute a "salvation history" that is distinct from history in general. Criticism focuses on *Heilsgeschichte*'s dichotomy between God's saving activity and the rest of history. *See also* biblical theology; theological method.

HELL   The realm of Satan and demons, into which God cast them until the final judgment. Hell is the sphere of punishment for rebellious angels (2 Pet. 2:4). It is also the state and place of unbelievers who have died and are currently suffering misery and torment. Still, unbelievers in hell do not experience the fullness of their punishment. They are disembodied and await the resurrection of their body, at which point God's wrath will be poured out in its fullness. At the consummation the present hell will give way to the second death, the lake of fire (Rev. 20:14–15). *See also* annihilationism; conditional immortality; eternal conscious punishment.

HERESY   Any belief that stands opposed to orthodoxy, or sound doctrine, that which correctly reflects in summary form all that Scripture affirms about any particular doctrine and which the church is bound to believe. Heresy, then, is any belief that contradicts essential teaching. It is false belief that misinterprets Scripture, or that overlooks or ignores some affirmations of Scripture, or that improperly puts together all the affirmations of Scripture on a particular doctrine. Examples of heresy include Unitarianism, modalism, Arianism, Pelagianism, and universalism. The church is called to avoid heresy and to correct its errors (1 Tim. 1:3; Titus 1:9). *See also* doctrine; orthodoxy.

HERMENEUTICS The discipline of interpretation. General hermeneutics sets forth principles for the interpretation of any literary work. These include knowing the meaning of words, grasping the grammar and syntax of sentences, and understanding the genre (e.g., narrative or poetry). Special hermeneutics offers principles for the interpretation of Scripture. These include reading the text in its redemptive-historical context (e.g., as part of old covenant laws or new covenant instruction), recognizing types and antitypes (e.g., Moses lifting up the bronze serpent foreshadowing Christ on the cross; John 3:14), and discerning its christological focus. Hermeneutics is crucial because Scripture must be interpreted rightly.

HETEROOUSIOS In regard to Christology, an affirmation that the Son is of a different nature from that of the Father and thus not fully God. From the Greek (*heteros*, "different"; *ousios*, "nature"), *heteroousios* was coined by proponents of Arianism to express their belief that the Son is not fully divine because of being different in essence from the Father. Because it contradicts scriptural affirmations about the equality in nature of the Father and the Son (e.g., John 10:30; Heb. 1:3), this belief was condemned as a heresy. The church affirms instead that the Son is *homoousios*, of the same nature as the Father. *See also* Arianism; *homoousios*; Jesus Christ, deity of.

HISTORIA SALUTIS *See* history of salvation (*historia salutis*).

HISTORIC PREMILLENNIALISM With respect to eschatology, the position that Christ's second coming will occur before (*pre-*) his one-thousand-year (*millennium*) reign on earth. As the consensus view of the early church, it is called *historic* premillennialism. Key to this position is its interpretation of Revelation 20:1–6: The Great Tribulation punishes the earth, then Christ returns to rule over it (while Satan is bound) for a thousand-year period. At its conclusion, Satan is loosed and then defeated in a futile effort to oppose Christ. The final events are the last judgment, the resurrection of the wicked, and the new heaven and new earth. *See also* dispensational premillennialism; Great Tribulation; millennium; second coming.

HISTORICAL CRITICISM   *See* biblical criticism.

HISTORICAL THEOLOGY   The study of the interpretation of Scripture and the formulation of doctrine by the church of the past. Such accumulated wisdom provides benefits for the church today, including helping to distinguish orthodoxy from heresy; providing sound biblical interpretations and theological formulations; offering stellar examples of faith, love, courage, and hope; protecting against rampant individualism by rooting the church in its historical legacy; encouraging it to express its beliefs in contemporary form; guiding the church to focus on essential matters; and providing assurance that Jesus is building his church today. Historical theology serves in a ministerial, or helping, role. *See also* systematic theology; theological method.

HISTORY OF SALVATION (*HISTORIA SALUTIS*)   The historical events, in space and time, through which God rescues his people. Examples include the creation of the world, grace extended after the fall, the ark of Noah, the call and justification of Abraham, the liberation of the people of Israel through the Passover and exodus, the Davidic kingdom, the exile and return from it, the incarnation of Christ and his work, and the Spirit's descent on Pentecost to establish the church. These events, known through Scripture, are both historical in nature and suprahistorical, in that they are the outworking of God's eternal purpose. *See also* theological method.

HOLINESS   As an attribute of God, his exaltedness above creation and his absolute moral purity. Portrayed as "sitting upon a throne, high and lifted up" (Isa. 6:1), the holy God is completely separated from his creation. Being incomparably exalted, he is worthy of worship. He is proclaimed to be "Holy, holy, holy" (Isa. 6:3), utterly pure and uncorrupted by sin, though he engages with a sinful world (Hab. 1) and acts to render sinners holy (Isa. 6:4–6). The holy God consecrates objects, days, and people for his purposes, and he calls his children to progress in holiness (1 Pet. 1:13–16). *See also* sanctification; transcendence.

HOLINESS OF THE CHURCH   With respect to ecclesiology, one of the four traditional attributes of the church (the others being unity, catholicity, and apostolicity). This attribute signifies that the church is already sanctified, though imperfectly. For the Catholic Church, holiness is especially associated with saints, members (e.g., Mary) who through God's grace have practiced virtue and been faithful, whereby they are models, intercessors, and renewal agents. For Protestants, holiness is threefold: positionally, the church is already set apart from sin for God's use; purposively, the church aims at perfect purity; and instrumentally, the church fosters greater purity by pursuing the holiness of its members. *See also* apostolicity; catholicity; unity.

HOLY ORDERS   One of seven sacraments of the Catholic Church. Conferred by the laying on of hands by bishops, holy orders grants a sacred power such that the ordained minister acts in the person of Christ. It confers an indelible mark (thus, the sacrament is unrepeatable), bestowing an essential difference between clergy and laity. Holy orders has three degrees: two degrees of priestly participation—(1) the episcopate, for bishops (for apostolic succession), and (2) the priesthood, for priests—and one degree of service—(3) the diaconate, for deacons. Ordination for Protestants, while consecrating ministers, is significantly different from this sacrament. *See also* clergy; indelible mark; laity; ordination.

HOLY SPIRIT, PERSON OF THE   The Third Person of the Trinity, eternally existing together with the Father and the Son in the one Godhead. Like those two persons, the Spirit is fully God, possessing the same attributes of independence, eternality, immutability, omnipresence, omnipotence, omniscience, goodness, holiness, justice, love, and so on. Also like the Father and the Son, he is a distinct divine person, distinguished from them by his particular roles in creation, redemption, and consummation and his particular eternal relationship with them. Specifically, the Spirit proceeds from both the Father and the Son, eternally dependent on them for his person-of-the-Spirit. *See also* eternal procession; *filioque*; ontological Trinity; Trinity.

HOLY SPIRIT, WORK OF THE   While the Father, Son, and Spirit work inseparably together, their roles in creation, redemption, and consummation are also distinct. The Spirit's particular works include convicting nonbelievers of sin (John 16:7–11) and regenerating them (John 3:1–8). As the guarantee of God's continuing work (2 Cor. 1:22), the Spirit seals believers (Eph. 1:13), assures of salvation (Rom. 8:16), and sanctifies (1 Pet. 1:2), producing Christlikeness (Gal. 5:22–23). He prays (Rom. 8:26–27), illumines Scripture (1 Cor. 2:12–15), gives spiritual gifts (1 Cor. 12–14), guides (Gal. 5:16–18), and fosters unity (Eph. 4:3). He will give Christians their resurrection bodies (Rom. 8:11). *See also* economic Trinity; Trinity.

HOMILETICS   As a branch of practical theology, the discipline that studies the nature, methodology, preparation, and delivery of sermons or homilies. Homiletics (from Gk. *homileō*, "to speak with") engages both the theory and practice of preaching. Theoretical aspects include ancient and contemporary rhetoric, communication theory, and the art of delivering messages. Practical aspects include exegesis of biblical texts, contextualization of Scripture for an audience, crafting a sermon (e.g., developing an exposition, plotting a narrative), affective engagement with listeners, life application, and evaluation of the message delivered. Because a sermon is a liturgical element, homiletics also engages with liturgical theology. *See also* preaching.

HOMOIOUSIOS   In regard to Christology, an affirmation that the Son is of a similar nature to that of the Father and thus not fully

God. From two Greek words (*homoios*, "similar"; *ousios*, "nature"), *homoiousios* was coined by some proponents of Arianism to differentiate their belief from the condemned view that the Son is of a different (*heteroousios*) nature from that of the Father. Still, *homoiousios* maintains that the Son is not fully divine because of being only similar in essence to the Father. It contradicts scriptural affirmations about the equality of the Father and the Son (e.g., John 10:30; Heb. 1:3) and is a heresy. *See also* Arianism; *heteroousios*; *homoousios*; Jesus Christ, deity of.

HOMOOUSIOS   In regard to Christology, an affirmation that the Son is of the same nature as the Father and thus fully divine. From two Greek words (*homos*, "same"; *ousios*, "nature"), *homoousios* was coined by early church leaders to emphasize the full deity of the Son against two heretical views: the Son is *heteroousios*—of a nature different (*heteros*) from that of the Father—and the Son is *homoiousios*—of a nature similar (*homoios*) to that of the Father. Support includes affirmations that Jesus and the Father are one (John 10:30) and that the Son is "the exact imprint of his [God's] nature" (Heb. 1:3). *See also* Arianism; *heteroousios*; *homoiousios*; Jesus Christ, deity of.

HOPE   The optimistic view and anticipation of the future, based on the conviction that God is sovereignly directing the course of this world to fulfill his promised consummation of all things in Christ. The object of hope is crucial: it cannot be human effort or worldly resources (Ps. 33:17), for hope's object is not seen (Rom. 8:24–25). Rather, hope is placed in God through the gospel, which promises eternal life and future rewards. It flourishes with patience, endurance, and tenacity (Rom. 4:18). Hopefulness results in a diminishing of despair and anxiety about life, and it encourages thanksgiving, joyfulness, and boldness. *See also* theology of hope.

HUMAN BODY   *See* embodiment.

HUMAN NATURE   A complex essence consisting of an immaterial aspect and a material aspect, united into one. As a soul/body unity, human nature possesses the intellectual capacity of a mind/brain, the emotional capacity of feelings and sentiments, the volitional capacity of a will, the social capacity of relationships, the moral capacity of a conscience, the motivational capacity of drives and passions, and the causal capacity of a body. What exactly of these capacities is due to the immaterial aspect, and what is due to the material aspect, is a mystery but points to their inseparable union in this earthly life. *See also* embodiment; humanity / human being; image of God (*imago Dei*); soul.

HUMANISM Originally, a medieval cultural and educational movement that emphasized a return to the classical sources of Western civilization (e.g., Hebrew Scripture, the Greek New Testament, and church fathers like Augustine and Jerome) and eloquence in speech. Humanism contributed to the Reformation, particularly because some of its leaders, such as John Calvin, were humanists; thus, they were dissatisfied with Catholic scholasticism and attentive to the original sources of Christianity. They demanded that church doctrine be derived from properly translated and interpreted Hebrew and Greek texts. In its contemporary form, humanism is a secular movement that dismisses religious belief and theology.

HUMANITY / HUMAN BEING Humanity is the category of creatures that have been created as a body/soul unity in the image of God. Whereas angels are created beings that are immaterial (without a body), humans are created beings with both an immaterial aspect (soul) and a material aspect (body). As created in God's image, human beings have three responsibilities (Gen. 1:26–28): they are to mirror God ("let us make man in our image"); engage in civilization building, which consists of procreation ("be fruitful and multiply and fill the earth") and vocation ("subdue and rule the earth"); and cultivate interpersonal relationships ("male and female he created them"). *See also* embodiment; human nature; image of God (*imago Dei*); soul.

HUMILIATION OF CHRIST   One of three states of Christ, the others being his preexistent state and the state of exaltation. While preexisting eternally, he did not consider equality with God something to be selfishly grasped, so he entered a state of humiliation. Becoming incarnate of the Virgin Mary, he yielded his preexistent glory, took on limited (though sinless) human nature, and submitted himself to God's law. At the end of his earthly life, Christ was betrayed, was accused of blasphemy, was condemned though innocent, suffered, died on the cross, and was buried. His resurrection marked the end of his state of humiliation. *See also* cross/crucifixion; exaltation of Christ; incarnation; virgin birth / virginal conception.

HYPER-CALVINISM   A minority position within Reformed theology whose overemphasis on divine sovereignty minimizes or destroys human freedom and responsibility. For example, hyper-Calvinism accentuates God's sovereign choice of the elect to the eclipse of the church's responsibility to communicate the gospel and unbelievers' responsibility to believe in Christ. Historically, hyper-Calvinism has appeared in some post-Reformers' theology, and it has been criticized by Arminian theologians such as John Wesley and Charles Finney. Most Calvinists also denounce the position, because its hard determinism cannot account for the biblical emphasis on the Great Commission and the necessity of faith in response to the gospel. *See also* Calvinism / John Calvin; determinism; Reformed theology.

HYPOSTASIS   In regard to the doctrine of the Trinity, a mode of being with attributes, capacities, and activities constituting personhood. Three persons—Father, Son, Holy Spirit—constitute the Triune God. Though operating inseparably, they are distinguished by their works in creation, salvation, and consummation. Though sharing in the one divine essence, they are distinguished by their eternal relationships. The Father is characterized by *paternity*: he is the Father of the Son. The Son is characterized by *sonship*: he is the Son in virtue of being eternally generated by the Father. The Holy Spirit is characterized by *procession*: he eternally proceeds from both the Father and the Son. *See also* eternal generation; eternal procession; person/personhood; *substantia*; Trinity.

HYPOSTATIC UNION   In regard to Christology, the joining together (the union) of the two natures—one fully divine, one fully human—in the one person (Gk. *hypostasis*), Jesus Christ. The preexistent Son of God became incarnate by taking on a fully human nature—both a material aspect, or body, and an immaterial aspect, or soul. The man Jesus had no existence prior to the incarnation; he was *anhypostatic* (no personal existence). Rather, the human nature exists in the divine person; it is *enhypostatic* (existing in the Son of God). The hypostatic union stands opposed to Apollinarianism, Nestorianism, Eutychianism, and kenoticism. *See also* Jesus Christ, deity of; Jesus Christ, humanity of.

I

IDEALISM   The philosophical position that reality is not complex but simple, being ultimately immaterial. Idealism contrasts with materialistic monism, which holds that reality, being simple rather than complex, is ultimately material; and dualism, the view that reality is complex, consisting of material and immaterial elements. Examples include (1) the idealism of George Berkeley, who maintained that the physical world exists as bundles of ideas in the mind of God and in human minds; and (2) German idealism, which emphasized the mind-dependent nature of all that exists. People cannot know "things in themselves" but know only as those things appear to them. *See also* dualism; monism.

ILLUMINATION The work of the Holy Spirit by which he enables the understanding of Scripture by enlightening its readers. Illumination is needed because of the spiritual blindness and stubborn ignorance of sinful people. For this insensitivity to divine truth to be overcome, the same Spirit who inspired Scripture opens up its comprehension (1 Cor. 2:10–16). Debate centers on whether the Spirit's work supplies knowledge (an external impartation of the Word) or is a subjective stimulation—an internal enlightening—of the interpreter's mind, will, or both, through the Word. Illumination removes ignorance and error and leads to certainty in the gospel. *See also* Holy Spirit, work of the; perspicuity of Scripture.

IMAGE OF GOD (*IMAGO DEI*) In one sense, human beings as created by God, understood in different ways. Substantive models consider the image to be some attribute—rationality, free will, moral consciousness—that distinguishes humanity from other creatures. Functional models consider it to be some activity—exercising dominion over the creation—in which people engage. Relational models consider the image to be male-female relationships. Eclectic models find the others to be reductionistic and consider the image to be people themselves in the totality of their being and activities. In another sense, Christ as the divine image renders visible the invisible God. *See also* humanity / human being.

IMMACULATE CONCEPTION A Catholic doctrine proclaimed in the encyclical *Ineffabilis Deus* (December 8, 1854): "The most Blessed Virgin Mary was, from the first moment of her conception, by a singular grace and privilege of almighty God and by virtue of the merits of Jesus Christ, . . . preserved immune from all stain of original sin." Born without sin, and remaining sinless throughout her life, Mary was well prepared to become the mother of Jesus. Protestant rejection of this doctrine focuses on Catholic misinterpretations of passages to support it and its contradiction of Scripture's affirmation that all people are sinful. *See also* bodily assumption of Mary; Mariology; Mary; virgin birth / virginal conception.

IMMANENCE   God's personal relatedness to and involvement in creation. He is not removed from the world but actively engaged in everything that comes to pass. The rhythms of nature, the comings and goings of people, and the movements of history are all acts of God, who is present in them; indeed, he dwells "with him who is of a contrite and lowly spirit" (Isa. 57:15). To be avoided is an excessive notion of immanence by which God is equated with creation (pantheism) or contained in it (panentheism). With the right balance, divine transcendence and immanence—God's exaltedness and involvement—are affirmed. *See also* transcendence.

IMMANENT TRINITY   *See* ontological Trinity.

IMMERSION   One of the modes of baptism, the others being pouring and sprinkling. Immersion is lowering a person completely under water and bringing them up out of the water. Support includes: (1) Narratives using the Greek *baptizō*: those baptized were immersed. For example, "when Jesus was baptized [lowered under the water], immediately he went up from the water" (Matt. 3:16). (2) The meaning of baptism. For example, identification with the death, burial, and resurrection of Christ (Rom. 6:3–5) is best portrayed by immersion, as is escape from divine judgment (paralleling escape from the flood waters; 1 Pet. 3:20–21). *See also* pouring; sprinkling.

IMMINENCE   With respect to eschatology, something about to occur. It has special reference to the second coming, understood in two ways: (1) Christ could return *at any moment*: there are no intervening events that must precede his second coming; or (2) Christ could return *at any time*: his second coming is near but not necessarily a short time away, with intervening events needing to occur before it happens. The first view focuses on passages that emphasize preparedness for Christ's return, which will be unexpected. The second view highlights passages that present signs (tribulation, the antichrist) that must precede his return. *See also* second coming.

IMMORTALITY A divine attribute signifying that God is incapable of dying. God's immortality (from Lat. *in-*, "not"; *mortalis*, "death") coincides with his self-existence: God's very nature is to exist, so he cannot die. In a secondary sense, it is a human attribute reflective of divine immortality, by which people, though they die physically, continue to live forever in another condition. Some theologies embrace the immortality of the soul: God creates human beings with souls that are inherently eternal. Other theologies hold to immortality as a divine gift that God imparts to all human beings such that they live forever. *See also* conditional immortality; death; eternal life; immortality of the soul.

IMMORTALITY OF THE SOUL The doctrine that God creates people with an immaterial aspect that is inherently eternal. On this view, when people die physically, they continue to live in a different condition because their soul cannot die. The view has Greek philosophical roots but not biblical support. From the beginning, the tree of life was a divine provision for continued human existence (Gen. 2:9; 3:22), as will be the case in the re-created universe (Rev. 22:2). Moreover, for believers, eternal life is a gift of God (2 Tim. 1:10), and their resurrection body will be immortal (1 Cor. 15:53–54). *See also* eternal life; immortality.

IMMUTABILITY A divine attribute signifying that God is unchanging yet consistently acting. God is immutable in terms of his (1) essence, existing eternally as three persons in one divine nature; (2) perfections, eternally possessing the attributes of omniscience, love, omnipotence, holiness, and so on; (3) decree, having eternally established his purpose for creation, which he is fulfilling with guarantee; and (4) promises, being completely committed to fulfilling his commitments and never reneging on his pledges. God's immutability does not mean that he is unmoving; indeed, God responds to prayer and forgives when people repent, acting consistently with his immutable being and purposes. *See also* independence.

IMPASSIBILITY The divine attribute of being unaffected by external realities: God is unmoved by human decisions, actions, suffering, and more. Impassibility (from Lat. *in-*, "not"; *passibilis*, "experiencing passion") has two forms. (1) Classical: For some, the classical idea came from Greek philosophy that viewed God as the unmoved mover, incapable of emotions. For others, it developed from the biblical attribute of independence: because God is self-sufficient, not dependent on anything external for his nature, knowledge, and will, he is unresponsive to outside factors. (2) Contemporary: This form affirms God's self-sufficiency together with his feeling emotions (e.g., affliction; Isa. 63:9). *See also* independence; suffering.

IMPECCABILITY With regard to Christology, the question of whether Jesus could have sinned. Impeccability (from Lat. *in-*, "not"; *peccare*, "to sin") does not concern sinlessness; Jesus never actually sinned. Rather, the issue is whether he could have sinned. Most believe that Jesus, because of the union of his divine and human natures, could not have sinned. If he were ever poised to yield to temptation, his divine nature would have prevented him from doing so. Some believe that if Jesus could not have sinned, his temptations would not be actual enticements to do what he never could have done. *See also* hypostatic union; Jesus Christ, humanity of.

IMPUTATION In regard to the doctrine of salvation, the divine work of crediting the righteousness of Christ to people who believe in him. God's work of imputing righteousness is exemplified by Abraham, who, before engaging in good works and apart from the law, believed God's promise by faith, and God counted him righteous. The object of faith of fallen people today is Jesus Christ, whose perfect obedience to the law, culminating in his death and rewarded with his resurrection, is imputed to them as righteousness as they trust him. Imputation stands opposed to infusion of grace, emphasized in Catholic theology. *See also* grace; infusion; justification.

"IN, WITH, AND UNDER" With regard to the Lutheran view of the Lord's Supper, the belief that Christ is truly and wholly present in the sacrament. For Martin Luther, the sacrament is Christ's true body and blood, under the elements of bread and wine, given to Christians to eat and drink. Specifically, the body of Christ is "under the bread, with the bread, and in the bread" (*Formula of Concord*, 7:35). This is not transubstantiation, for no change occurs in the bread and wine. Rather, it is consubstantiation, the body and blood of Christ being "in, with, and under" the elements. *See also* consubstantiation; real presence of Christ.

INABILITY, TOTAL   *See* total inability.

INCARNATION   With respect to Christology, the taking on of a fully human nature by the fully divine Son of God. The incarnation (from Lat. *carne*, "flesh" or "body") took place about two thousand years ago through the power of the Holy Spirit. The Son, who is eternally and fully divine, took on a fully human nature consisting of mind, emotions, will, motivations, purposing, and body. Without losing, setting aside, or muffling his divine attributes, the Son became the God-man; he remains so for all eternity. The incarnation was designed to rescue fully human beings who are sinful (Heb. 2:14–18). *See also* humiliation of Christ; hypostatic union; Jesus Christ, humanity of.

INCLUSIVISM   With regard to Christianity and other religions, the position that salvation comes through Christ yet extends beyond Christianity to include adherents of religions like Islam, Buddhism, and Hinduism. Like exclusivism, inclusivism affirms that the person and work of Christ is the ground of salvation; through his life, death, and resurrection, Christ accomplished redemption. Unlike exclusivism, inclusivism denies that faith in his person and work is necessary to experience salvation. While people from non-Christian religions can be saved only by the salvation accomplished by Christ, they may experience salvation apart from faith in Christ. Inclusivism contrasts with exclusivism and pluralism. *See also* exclusivism; pluralism.

INCOMMUNICABLE ATTRIBUTES   With respect to the doctrine of God, his characteristics or perfections, as revealed by Scripture, that God does not communicate, or share, with human beings. These attributes include independence, immutability/unchangeableness, eternity, omnipresence, simplicity, and spirituality/invisibility. Incommunicable attributes underscore the Creator-creature distinction. For example, whereas the Creator is completely self-sufficient, his creatures are completely dependent on him; whereas the Creator is present everywhere and eternal, his creatures are spatially and temporally bound. Incommunicable attributes are distinguishable from communicable attributes, those characteristics (e.g., knowledge, wisdom, truthfulness, faithfulness, love, goodness, holiness, power) that God does communicate, or share, with human beings. *See also* communicable attributes.

INCOMPATIBILISM The position that divine sovereignty and human responsibility cannot be held together. Incompatibilism maintains that the following affirmations are incompatible: (1) God is absolutely sovereign; (2) human beings are morally responsible creatures. Though some texts affirm God's sovereignty and other texts affirm human responsibility, the one set is pitted against the other set: God may be sovereign, but not in an absolute sense. Some limitation is placed on his power, or some limitation is placed on his (fore)knowledge, or both. Additionally, human responsibility is associated with libertarian freedom: nothing can decisively incline human beings in one direction or another. *See also* compatibilism; determinism.

INCOMPREHENSIBLE With respect to the doctrine of God, the reality that God can never be fully understood. In one sense, *incomprehensible* means that something is completely unintelligible; nothing can be known about it. It is not in this sense that God is incomprehensible but in the sense that he can never be completely grasped. Though knowable in the manner and to the degree that he reveals himself, God can never be fully comprehended (Deut. 29:29). God is incomprehensible because finite creatures can never comprehend the infinite God, and because the noetic (intellectual) effects of the fall distort human understanding of him. *See also* apophatic theology; knowability; noetic effect.

INDELIBLE MARK With respect to the sacraments of the Catholic Church, a quality that is uniquely bestowed through baptism, confirmation, and holy orders. When these sacraments are administered, in addition to grace, they confer a sacramental character or seal by which their recipient is made a member of the Church according to different functions. The indelible mark of baptism is belonging to Christ, the mark of confirmation is special strength of the Holy Spirit, and that of holy orders is sacred power to act in the person of Christ. Because of their indelible quality, these sacraments can never be repeated. *See also* baptism; confirmation; holy orders; sacrament.

INDEPENDENCE With respect to the doctrine of God, his attribute of self-existence. God's very nature is to exist; he is not and cannot be dependent on anything or anyone. This attribute underscores the Creator-creature distinction: whereas the Creator is completely independent, creatures are completely dependent, contingent on his will for their existence. Proof that God is self-sufficient is that he "made the world and everything in it" (Acts 17:24). Because he has life in himself (John 5:26), he is able to give "life and breath and everything" to his creatures (Acts 17:25). Though independent, God has designed his people to glorify him. *See also* decree; God; impassibility; predestination.

INDULGENCES "An indulgence is a remission before God of the temporal punishment due to sin whose guilt has already been forgiven" (*Catechism of the Catholic Church*, 1471). There are two types: *plenary* indulgences remit all punishment due to sin, while *partial* indulgences remit part of that punishment. Catholics may gain indulgences through activities prescribed by the Church, which applies the merits of Christ and the saints to relieve punishment. Protestantism condemns this practice: indulgences are superfluous because Christ, through his sufficient sacrifice, has remitted all punishment due to sin. Thus, there is no temporal punishment for forgiven people to face. *See also* merit; purgatory.

INERRANCY   An attribute of Scripture whereby everything that it affirms is true. Inerrancy is characteristic of all of Scripture, not just the parts concerning salvation, faith, and doctrine. It also means that Scripture never contradicts itself. Inerrancy is consistent with the varied writing techniques employed by its authors, including ordinary speech rather than technical language; loose quotations of the Old Testament by the New Testament writers; translations of Jesus's sayings (from the Aramaic that he spoke into Greek); and divergent parallel accounts, which relate the same event but present it with significant differences (e.g., Judas's death; Matt. 27:1–10; Acts 1:15–19). *See also* Chicago Statement on Biblical Inerrancy; infallibility of Scripture; truth.

INFALLIBILITY, PAPAL   In regard to Catholicism and the authority of the pope, *infallibility* refers to the doctrine that when the pope speaks *ex cathedra*—"from the seat (of Peter)"—regarding a matter of doctrine or morality, the Holy Spirit protects him from failure. Thus, his pronouncement is true and guaranteed against error. This dogma was proclaimed by Vatican Council I (1870). Protestantism denies papal infallibility, disputing the Catholic Church's interpretation of biblical texts (e.g., Matt. 16:13–20) to support it and noting that *ex cathedra* pronouncements (e.g., the immaculate conception and bodily assumption of Mary) contradict Scripture and thus are in error. *See also* bodily assumption of Mary; immaculate conception; Vatican Council I.

INFALLIBILITY OF SCRIPTURE   In relation to the doctrine of Scripture, *infallibility* is a term historically used to refer to the Bible's absence of liability to fail. It was often used as a synonym for *inerrancy* and had to do with the truthfulness of Scripture. In the contemporary context, *infallibility* has come to be used in distinction from *inerrancy*, referring to Scripture's inability to fail to accomplish the purpose intended by God. Accordingly, one could affirm the infallibility of Scripture—it never fails to save, correct, encourage, or warn—yet also affirm the errancy of Scripture—it contains actual errors of history, chronology, and science. *See also* Chicago Statement on Biblical Inerrancy; inerrancy.

INFANT BAPTISM   The practice of administering baptism to infants, specifically the children of Christian parents. Also called paedobaptism (from Gk. *pais*, "child"), it is generally of two types. One is baptism for salvation, or baptismal regeneration; for example, Catholic baptism cleanses infants of original sin and regenerates them. Another type is baptism not for salvation but for incorporation into the covenant community. Just as infant boys were circumcised as a seal of membership in the old covenant, so infant children are baptized as a seal of membership in the new covenant and as a promise of grace. It contrasts with believer's baptism. *See also* baptismal regeneration; believer's baptism; Reformed theology.

INFINITE   God's limitlessness with respect to time, space, and knowledge. Regarding God's infinity in relation to time, he is eternal, having no beginning, end, or time sequencing in his being. He is not bound by time, though he does act in time. God's infinity with respect to space means he is omnipresent, existing everywhere with his entire being at the same time. He is not limited by space, though he manifests his presence differently in different places. Regarding God's infinity in relation to knowledge, he is omniscient, knowing all things, past, present, and future, and all possible and actual things. *See also* eternity; omnipresence; omniscience.

INFRALAPSARIANISM   *See* sublapsarianism.

INFUSION   In regard to the doctrine of salvation, the divine work of introducing or adding grace to people who believe. According to Roman Catholic theology, infusion is especially accomplished by means of the seven sacraments. Baptism begins the process, as God's grace is introduced through that sacrament, which removes original sin, brings about regeneration, and incorporates the one baptized into Christ and the Church. The process continues as more grace is added through the Eucharist and, when grace is destroyed through mortal sin, it is reintroduced through penance. Through infusion the faithful's character is transformed. Infusion stands opposed to imputation. *See also* imputation.

INNER TESTIMONY OF THE SPIRIT   This work of the Holy Spirit in believers is of two types. One regards the assurance of salvation: the Spirit bears witness that Christians are truly children of God (Rom. 8:16). The second type, emphasized by John Calvin, addresses how Christians become convinced that the Bible is the authoritative Word of God. The Spirit, who inspired the writers of Scripture, persuades believers that those authors faithfully communicated what God commanded them. This conviction, sealed on believers' hearts, is higher than human reason and above any church affirmation, and it produces absolute certainty of Scripture's authority. *See also* assurance of salvation; Holy Spirit, work of the; perseverance.

INSPIRATION OF SCRIPTURE   The special work of the Holy Spirit by which he superintended the biblical authors as they composed their writings. While these authors employed their own personalities, theological perspectives, writing styles, and so forth, the Spirit ensured that what they wrote was what God wanted them to write: the Word of God, fully truthful and divinely authoritative. Inspiration is plenary (*all* Scripture is God-breathed; 2 Tim. 3:16), verbal (inspiration extends to the *words* of Scripture), and concursive (the Spirit and the human authors *wrote together*). Modes of inspiration include historical research, Spirit-assisted memory, miraculous revelation, and sound judgment. *See also* God-breathed.

INTELLIGENT DESIGN   A movement that critiques evolution and claims that intelligent causes are needed to explain the complexity of life and that these causes can be empirically observed. The intelligent design movement critiques evolution, and the worldview of naturalism undergirding it, by seeking to show its failure to explain the origin of life, the dearth of transitional forms in the fossil record, the development of irreducibly complex organs (e.g., eyes), and more. Intelligent design also seeks ways to establish the fact that God's work in the universe is empirically detectable, with such indications of intelligent causes constituting evidence for an Intelligent Designer, or God. *See also* evolution; evolution, theistic; teleological arguments.

INTERCESSION Prayer directed to the Father by the Son and the Holy Spirit on behalf of Christians. When Christians are perplexed, not knowing how or what to pray, they may rest in the promise that the Holy Spirit intercedes for them. Such prayer is not in human words, nor does it consist of speaking in tongues, but it is effective, being offered according to the Father's will (Rom. 8:26–27). Similarly, Christ, forever exalted to the right hand of the Father, intercedes for Christians (Rom. 8:34), assuring them that he is able to save them completely (Heb. 7:25). *See also* prayer.

INTERMEDIATE STATE With respect to eschatology, the condition of people between their death and resurrection. Because death results in the separation of the material and the immaterial aspects of human nature, the bodies of the deceased are sloughed off and buried or cremated while they continue to exist as disembodied people in the intermediate state, in one of two conditions: at their death, Christians enter immediately into the presence of Christ in heaven (2 Cor. 5:1–9; Heb. 12:23), while non-Christians are plunged into torment in hell (Luke 16:19–31). Both disembodied believers and disembodied unbelievers await the resurrection of their bodies. *See also* death; embodiment; heaven; resurrection of people; soul.

INTERNAL CALL *See* effective/internal call.

INTERNATIONAL COUNCIL ON BIBLICAL INERRANCY *See* Chicago Statement on Biblical Inerrancy.

INTERPRETATION OF SCRIPTURE *See* hermeneutics.

INTERPRETATION OF TONGUES   With respect to spiritual gifts, the gift of interpretation of tongues accompanies the gift of speaking in tongues. Because speaking in tongues involves praise and prayer to God through unintelligible communication (either some foreign language or some other type of encoded message), then the interpreter knows that language, or has the ability to translate it, or holds the key to decode it so that its meaning is disclosed to the church. If Christians are ready to speak in tongues in the church but no one with the gift of interpretation is present, they are to remain silent (1 Cor. 14). *See also* speaking in tongues.

IRRESISTIBLE GRACE   One aspect of the Reformed doctrine of salvation, focusing on the certainty of God's work to effect salvation. Because of sinfulness, people are characterized by total depravity (every aspect of human nature is corrupted) and total inability (human effort is incapable of overcoming sinfulness and meriting God's favor). To the elect, God grants grace—by his favor alone, he calls, justifies, unites to Christ, regenerates, adopts, sanctifies, preserves—and this work is effective. Irresistibility does not mean that people are forced to repent and believe. Rather, the elect are enabled to embrace salvation, which they will certainly do. *See also* Reformed theology; saving grace.

J

JEALOUSY   The divine attribute by which God is protective of his honor. Because God alone is worthy of ultimate allegiance, when his people give themselves to something or someone else, God, "whose name is Jealous" (Exod. 34:14), is provoked to jealousy. The divine attribute is not like the sinful form of jealousy, which is akin to covetousness or envy. But human jealousy may reflect its divine counterpart when, for example, a spouse acts righteously to impede another person from disrupting the marriage covenant. Similarly God's people should be jealous for his honor, standing against those who mock or dishonor God.

JESUS CHRIST, DEITY OF   One of the two natures of the God-man (the other being his humanity). The Son of God, the Second Person of the Trinity, eternally exists with the Father and the Holy Spirit. He is coequal with them in power and glory and shares in the one divine nature characterized by independence, eternality, immutability, omnipresence, omnipotence, omniscience, goodness, holiness, justice, love, and more. In becoming incarnate, he did not change with respect to deity; rather, remaining what he was (fully God, without alteration), he became what he had never been (fully human). The Chalcedonian Creed expresses this doctrine. *See also* Chalcedonian Creed; hypostatic union; Jesus Christ, humanity of.

JESUS CHRIST, HUMANITY OF   One of the two natures of the God-man (the other being his deity). The divine Son of God became incarnate by taking on a real and fully human nature—both a material and an immaterial aspect. His humanity was that of a first-century Palestinian Jew and consisted of a mind, emotions, passions, will, motivations, purposing, and body. Like all human beings, he was born; developed physically, spiritually, relationally, and intellectually; ate, drank, became tired, and slept; expressed emotions like love, joy, and righteous anger; related to other people; and died. The Chalcedonian Creed expresses this doctrine. *See also* Chalcedonian Creed; hypostatic union; Jesus Christ, deity of.

JESUS CHRIST, HYPOSTATIC UNION OF   *See* hypostatic union.

JUDGMENT   An authoritative decision of evaluation and recompense. Judgment often involves a declaration based on an assessment of one's conformity, or lack of conformity, to a will/law, with a corresponding reward or penalty. God is the ultimate judge, and he delegates the responsibility to judge to his Son. Accordingly, all humanity will stand before the judgment seat of Christ to hear his authoritative decision. This decision will reflect his evaluation of their earthly works done either in accordance with God's will or in violation of his law. Obedience and faithfulness will be rewarded, while disobedience and unbelief will be punished. *See also* great white throne judgment.

JUSTICE   Fairly giving people what they are due, especially with respect to the administration of a law. The application of justice means that violators of the law are penalized while its observers are commended. Several varieties: (1) Rectoral justice establishes judgments, determining right and wrong. (2) Distributive justice requires conformity to the standard of right and wrong. This involves both (3) remunerative justice, which rewards conformity to the law, and (4) retributive justice, which punishes nonconformity to the law. (5) Social justice is the fair distribution of economic means, educational prospects, political influence, and other such opportunities within a community.

JUSTICE OF GOD   *See* righteousness.

JUSTIFICATION   A mighty act of God by which he declares sinful people not guilty but righteous instead. He does so by imputing, or crediting, the perfect righteousness of Christ to them. Thus, while they are not actually righteous, God views them as being so because of Christ's righteousness. The first aspect is the forgiveness of sins, resulting from Christ's substitutionary death (Rom. 3:25; 5:9). The second aspect is imputation, resulting from Christ's obedience that makes people righteous (5:18–19). This Protestant view contrasts with the Catholic view that justification is not only forgiveness of sins but also regeneration and sanctification. *See also* forgiveness; imputation; infusion.

K

KANT, IMMANUEL One of history's greatest philosophers (1724–1804), whose profound impact on philosophy and theology continues to be felt today. He transformed epistemology, proposing in place of empiricism and rationalism his transcendental idealism: the mind contains innate categories for processing sense experience. His moral philosophy focused on the categorical imperative: "Act only according to that maxim by which you can at the same time will that it should become a universal law."* He postulated the existence of God based on moral argument. Kant's *Religion within the Limits of Reason Alone* proposed that religion rely not on revelation but solely on reason. *See also* Enlightenment, the; rationalism.

KATAPHATIC THEOLOGY With reference to the doctrine of God, an approach emphasizing the positive ability to talk about God. Also called the *via positiva* ("positive way"), this theological method, while aware of the limitations of human language, insists that it is possible to give descriptions of God, based on divine revelation that affirms his attributes. Indeed, many words used to describe God are positive: God is good (gracious, merciful), love (eternally giving of himself), just (righteous and acting righteously), wrathful (intensely hating all sin), and sovereign (able to accomplish his will). Kataphatic theology stands in contrast with apophatic theology. *See also* apophatic theology; theological method.

KENOSIS/KENOTICISM In regard to Christology, kenoticism is the view that in the incarnation, the Son of God divested himself not of his essential divine attributes but of those attributes that are

---

* Immanuel Kant, *Grounding for the Metaphysics of Morals*, in *Ethical Philosophy*, trans. James W. Ellington, 2nd ed. (1785; Indianapolis: Hackett, 1994), 30.

relative to his activity in the world, that is, omniscience, omnipresence, and omnipotence. After his exaltation, the Son again took up those attributes. The term *kenosis* (Gk. *kenōsis*) derives from the use of the Greek verb *kenoō* in Philippians 2:7, according to which the Son "emptied himself." Kenoticism misunderstands the nature of the incarnation, which did not involve the Son divesting himself of certain divine attributes but entailed him humbling himself by taking on the fullness of human nature. *See also* hypostatic union; incarnation.

KERYGMA   The proclamation of the gospel, or its central message. The *kerygma* (Gk. "preaching") originates with Christ himself, who "came into Galilee, proclaiming the gospel of God" (Mark 1:14). As developed, the core message—the apostolic preaching—includes (1) the announcement that the kingdom of God has arrived (2) through the life, death, burial, resurrection, and ascension of Christ and (3) the descent of the Spirit to inaugurate the new covenant era (4) that will continue until Christ returns. (5) To embrace this gospel, people must repent, believe in Christ for forgiveness of sins, and be baptized. *See also* gospel; preaching.

KESWICK THEOLOGY   Originating in 1875 as a convention promoting holiness in Keswick, England, the Keswick movement became noted for its theology of sanctification. A key tenet is the insistence that the normal Christian life features sustained victory over sin rather than defeat. Additionally, it emphasizes that God provides all the necessary resources for an abundant Christian life, which is appropriated by confession of all known sin, surrender of one's life to Jesus as both Savior and Lord, faith in God's promises, mortification of the self, inner renewal, separation unto God for sanctification and service, and the filling with the Holy Spirit. *See also* filled with the Holy Spirit; sanctification.

KINGDOM   A central theme of Scripture, having to do with the rule of God. The kingdom of God includes (1) the universal reign of the sovereign King over his creation (Ps. 47:7); (2) the people of Israel, whom God graciously chose to be his kingdom people (Exod. 19:5–6); (3) an envisioned future associated with a Davidic king (2 Sam. 7); (4) an inaugurated reality, fulfilled "already" in Jesus, who preached the gospel of the kingdom (Mark 1:14–15), giving rise to kingdom citizens; and (5) a hope for the "not yet" aspects of the kingdom as a future inheritance (Matt. 25:34). *See also* Davidic covenant; gospel; *kerygma*.

KNOWABILITY   With respect to the doctrine of God, the position that because of his self-revelation, God can be known by his creatures. Knowing God in a personal way is a believer's greatest boast (Jer. 9:23–24), is eternal life itself (John 17:3), and comes about only through the Son's revelation of God (Matt. 11:27). Still, unbelievers possess some knowledge of God (Rom. 1:21), and even believers know God only in part now (1 Cor. 13:12). The divine knowability is based on God's free decision to make himself known through both general and special revelation, and the God-given human capacity to know him. *See also* general revelation; incomprehensible; kataphatic theology; special revelation.

KNOWLEDGE   Traditionally, justified true belief. Knowledge consists of a proposition that is believed ("Gregg is married to Nora"), that is true (it corresponds to reality), and for which warrant exists (they have a valid marriage license). While this traditional notion generally holds, it is incomplete in some cases. In theology, knowledge is a divine attribute; indeed, God knows all things. Knowledge is also a human attribute. All people have some knowledge of God, with believers enjoying a personal knowledge of him. All people possess self-knowledge, understanding their own thoughts, emotions, will, and body. They also know other people through relationships. *See also* epistemology; omniscience.

KNOWLEDGE, DIVINE   *See* middle knowledge; omniscience.

L

LAITY   One of two categories of church members or religious organizations, the other being clergy. Laity (from Gk. *laos*, "people") are nonordained people, while clergy (bishops, pastors, elders, priests, deacons, ministers) are ordained. Working in education, business, government, the arts, science, farming, and more, lay people engage in vocations outside the church or religious institutions. Though they may serve in ministry, they are not officially recognized as clergy. According to Catholicism, laity differ in essence from clergy, who have received the sacrament of holy orders. According to Protestantism, the difference between the two is one of office, not essence. *See also* clergy; holy orders; vocation.

LAST JUDGMENT   *See* great white throne judgment.

LAW   A binding rule for conduct established by an authority. For the blessing of his people, God establishes laws prescribing what they are to do (commands) and what they are to avoid (prohibitions). Violations bring curses. Torah was the code of conduct for Israel; it consisted of the Ten Commandments and about six hundred other laws regulating sacrifices, purity, and more. As interpreted by Christ, these laws are either abrogated (dietary restrictions are removed), modified (the sacrifices are fulfilled in Christ's sacrifice), or continued (love God, love others). Combined with new covenant regulations, they compose the "law of Christ" for Christians. *See also* authority; sin.

LAYING ON OF HANDS   With respect to ecclesiology, the act of consecrating people for God's intended purpose. In Scripture, the laying on of hands was for blessing (Gen. 48:8–20; Mark 10:16), healing (Mark 8:22–25; Luke 4:40), transferring of sin to a sacrifice

(Lev. 16:20–22), conferring the Spirit in unusual circumstances (Acts 8:14–18; 19:6), conveying God's directive or gift (Deut. 34:9; Acts 9:17; 2 Tim. 1:6), and ordaining elders (1 Tim. 5:22). Catholicism practices the laying on of hands for its sacraments of confirmation and holy orders. Protestants lay on hands to ordain pastors, commission missionaries, and pray for the sick. *See also* anointing of the sick; ordination; prayer.

LEGALISM   In terms of sanctification, the approach that advocates obeying additional commands and prohibitions beyond biblical norms, for the increase in holiness and/or to merit favor with God. Legalism flows from the human tendency to seek to work for everything one receives, including salvation and God's blessings. It stands in contrast with (1) lawfulness, conforming to and fulfilling the law by obeying divinely given commandments out of love for God (John 14:15), and (2) antinomianism, a rejection of any role for the law. Though following additional rules may appear to enhance one's progress in sanctification, Scripture strongly condemns legalism (Col. 2:16–23). See also *adiaphora*; sanctification.

LIBERALISM   A form of theology that stands in contrast to conservative or traditional theology. Within Protestantism, liberalism developed in the nineteenth century with Friedrich Schleiermacher's attempt to render the Christian faith palatable to its cultured despisers. In the twentieth century, Protestant liberalism crept into Catholic theology. Liberalism was opposed by fundamentalism, Barth's neo-orthodoxy, evangelical theology, and conservative Catholicism. Major tenets: (1) Traditional theology is untenable in an enlightened, scientifically advanced world. (2) Belief in supernatural matters such as angels, demons, and miracles is mere superstition. (3) Christian doctrine needs to be reformulated in light of contemporary cultures, hopes, and aspirations. *See also* evangelicalism; fundamentalism / fundamentalist-modernist debate; neo-orthodoxy.

LIBERATION THEOLOGY   A theological movement, with Marxist tendencies, that arose in the 1960s in Latin America.

Representatives include Gustavo Gutiérrez and Leonardo Boff, and its varieties include black, feminist, and third-world theologies. Major tenets: (1) Sin takes the form of political, social, and economic oppression and is more systemic/cultural than personal in nature. (2) God takes the side of the poor and exploited over against their oppressors, and he encourages the use of violence to counter injustice. (3) Salvation is liberation from repressive tyranny as the kingdom of God introduces a new social order in which justice reigns. *See also* liberalism; theological method.

LIMBO   With respect to traditional Catholic theology, the state of the souls of infants who die without baptism. Because of original sin, these infants bear the guilt of Adam, but they are not subject to eternal punishment because they are not guilty of personal sin. Still, they have not merited salvation and so are not rewarded with eternal happiness. Contemporary Catholic theology, however, notes that this theory is not taught in divine revelation and was never proclaimed a doctrine by the Church; thus, it is only a hypothesis. Accordingly, the Church's current focus is on entrusting unbaptized infants to God's mercy. *See also* baptismal regeneration; infant baptism; original sin.

LIMITED ATONEMENT   The position that Christ died with the intent of actually and certainly saving only the elect. Biblical support includes affirmations that Christ died for the elect (Rom. 8:32; 2 Cor. 5:14–15), a particular group of people—his sheep (John 10:11) and church (Eph. 5:25). Theological support appeals to agreement within the Trinity: those whom the Father purposed to save are the same people for whom Christ came to die and the same people to whom the Spirit applies salvation. The elect alone are in view. Limited atonement stands opposed to unlimited atonement and disagrees with the multiple-intentions view. *See also* atonement; multiple-intentions view of the atonement; unlimited atonement.

LITURGY / LITURGICAL THEOLOGY   Liturgy (from Gk. *leitourgia*, "ministry") is an ordered structure of public worship. It may feature a call to worship, singing of praise and thanksgiving, spoken or recited prayers including confession of sin, the reading and preaching of the Word of God, administration of baptism and the Lord's Supper, and a benediction. Liturgical theology is (1) the discipline that studies the nature, attributes, and works of God using as its source the liturgy of the church; and (2) the discipline that studies the nature, attributes, and ministries of the church, using its liturgy as its source. *See also* normative principle; regulative principle; theological method; worship.

LOGICAL POSITIVISM A twentieth-century philosophical movement that emphasized knowledge is obtained only through the senses. Its major tenet was the verification principle: only statements that can be empirically verified (confirmed by the five senses) are meaningful statements. The result was the dismissal of all metaphysical statements. For example, "God is love" and "the soul survives death" are nonsensical affirmations because there is nothing empirical that can count either for or against them. Of course, the verification principle itself fails to meet its own criterion and is therefore meaningless; there is nothing empirical that can confirm or deny the statement. *See also* epistemology.

LORD/LORDSHIP "Lord" is one of the divine titles of Jesus Christ. In the Old Testament, "Lord" was a frequent reference for God/Yahweh. The New Testament uses the title in a unique way when it takes texts about Yahweh and applies them to Jesus. For example, when Peter (Acts 2:21) and Paul (Rom. 10:13) proclaim, "everyone who calls on the name of the Lord will be saved," the Lord is Yahweh in the Joel (2:32) citation but Jesus in the apostles' promise. This title is particularly ascribed to Jesus in his exalted state (Acts 2:36). Acknowledgment of the lordship of Christ means salvation. *See also* Jesus Christ, deity of.

LORD'S SUPPER An ongoing rite of the Christian faith, one of two ordinances or sacraments of the church. Christ ordained it, instituting the Lord's Supper at his last supper (Matt. 26:26–29).

Observed between the first and second comings of Christ, it involves symbolic elements—bread that is broken (portraying Christ's broken body), a cup of wine / grape juice (portraying Christ's shed blood), and the distribution of both to the church (portraying the church's appropriation of Christ's work). It proclaims the gospel, fosters remembrance of Christ's sacrifice, signals the new covenant relationship, unites Christians with Christ, and portrays unity in the church. *See also* consubstantiation; Eucharist; memorial view; ordinance; real presence of Christ; sacrament; spiritual presence of Christ; transubstantiation.

LOVE   A divine attribute signifying that God gives of himself. The Godhead is an eternally loving community as the Father, Son, and Spirit love one another. From this fullness of self-giving, God created image bearers, whom he loves even when they fall into sin. Again, in his infinite love, God gave his Son to rescue his fallen people. Jesus demonstrated the highest self-sacrificial love for his enemies, who are united in love by the love of the Holy Spirit. In a secondary sense, it is a human attribute reflective of divine love, in which people love God and others. *See also* goodness; grace; mercy.

LUTHERANISM / MARTIN LUTHER   Lutheranism is a major type of Protestant theology that developed in the sixteenth century. Its founder, Martin Luther (1483–1546), was a Catholic monk and theologian whose questioning of the sale of indulgences (*Ninety-Five Theses*) ignited the wrath of the Catholic Church and sparked the Reformation. His emphases on the authority and perspicuity of Scripture (without the Apocrypha), justification by grace through faith alone, the priesthood of believers, reduction of the sacraments from seven to two (baptism and the Lord's Supper), and more, established the framework for Lutheranism. Its two foundational statements are the Augsburg Confession and the Formula of Concord. *See also* Augsburg Confession; consubstantiation; Formula of Concord; magisterial Reformation.

M

MAGISTERIAL REFORMATION One type of Protestant movement that developed in the sixteenth century from Martin Luther, Huldrych Zwingli, and John Calvin. They advocated the centuries-old church-state relationship that accorded magistrates, or secular authorities, a key role to exercise in church life, worship, and government. For example, Frederick the Wise was Luther's protector from the Catholic Church, and Zwingli and Calvin carried out their reformations with the support (and, at times, the interference) of the city councils of Zurich and Geneva. This movement contrasts with the radical Reformation, which denied any role for the civil government in matters of the church. *See also* Anabaptism; radical Reformation.

MAGISTERIUM The teaching office of the Catholic Church. Consisting of the pope with the bishops, the Magisterium bears the responsibility of giving an authentic interpretation of divine revelation, whether in its written form, Scripture, or in the form of Tradition. Correlatively, no individuals, relying on their own judgment, may distort Scripture according to their own understanding and interpret it in a sense contrary to the Magisterium's interpretation. As it focuses on teaching and preserving the Catholic faith, this office—specifically the pope and, with him, the body of bishops—enjoys the gift of infallibility in matters of faith and morals. *See also* infallibility, papal; Roman Catholicism; tradition.

MANICHEANISM A gnostic-like religion that was originated by Mani in Persia in the third century. It proposed a radical dualism between the good, spiritual realm of light and the bad, material realm of darkness. These two equal yet opposite powers are locked in conflict, causing the pitched battle within human beings between their soul and their body. It also promoted heretical ideas about Jesus: he was fully divine but not at all human, and his suffering, death, and resurrection were mystical and in appearance only. Manicheanism drew Augustine under its influence before he became a Christian, and it infiltrated early Christianity. *See also* Augustinian theology; gnosticism; hypostatic union; Platonism.

MARCIONISM   A heretical movement led by Marcion, a teacher in Rome who came under the influence of gnosticism. His "canon" of Scripture consisted of "the Gospel and the Apostle," that is, a mutilated version of the Gospel of Luke and ten letters of Paul (missing the Pastoral Letters). He rejected the Old Testament and the rest of the emerging New Testament that reflected favorably on the Old, because he believed that the god of the Old Testament was evil and the creator of the material world. The church knew Marcion was wrong and was prompted to settle the true canon. *See also* canon of Scripture; gnosticism.

MARIOLOGY   The doctrines associated with Mary. Catholic theology emphasizes (1) Mary's special predestination to become Jesus's mother; (2) her immaculate conception: Mary was conceived without sin; (3) Mary's enduring sinlessness, as seen in her perpetual virginity; (4) her obedience of faith in consenting to the incarnation, which undoes Eve's disobedience; (5) the work of the Holy Spirit in her virgin womb, rendering her *theotokos* (the "bearer of God"); (6) the bodily assumption: when her earthly life ended, Mary's body was taken into heaven; (7) her invocation as Advocate, Helper, Benefactress, and Mediatrix. Besides acknowledging her as *theotokos*, Protestantism denies these doctrines. *See also* bodily assumption of Mary; immaculate conception; Mary; *theotokos*; virgin birth / virginal conception.

MARKS OF THE CHURCH   With respect to ecclesiology, the visible elements that are sufficient and necessary for the existence of a true church. In the Reformation period, these marks underscored the rightness of Protestant churches in contrast to the false Catholic Church. According to Martin Luther, the two marks are "the gospel . . . rightly taught and the sacraments [baptism and the Lord's Supper] rightly administered" (Augsburg Confession, 7). John Calvin concurred: "the Word of God purely preached and heard, and the sacraments administered according to Christ's institution" (*Institutes of the Christian Religion*, 4.1.8). Later Calvinists added a third mark, church discipline (e.g., Belgic Confession). *See also* baptism; church discipline; Lord's Supper; ordinance; preaching; sacrament.

MARRIAGE   The joining together of a man and a woman in a monogamous covenant relationship. Marriage is a creation ordinance: God's explicit design is for the majority of human beings, not just believers, to be married (Gen. 1:28). The two exceptions are singleness for those with the gift of celibacy (1 Cor. 7:7) and those who make themselves eunuchs (Matt. 19:12). The purposes for marriage are creating a new family by uniting a man and woman as one flesh (Gen. 2:24), procreation (Gen. 1:28), pleasure (Song of Songs), comfort (2 Sam. 12:24), and protection against immorality (1 Cor. 7:2, 9). Matrimony is a sacrament in the Catholic Church. *See also* celibacy; divorce; sacrament.

MARY   The mother of Jesus Christ. As a young virgin, Mary was the divinely chosen human agent through whom the incarnation of the Son took place. She is *theotokos*, the one who bore God; moreover, her obedience is exemplary, and she is blessed because her faithfulness brought blessing to everyone. Still, she is a flawed model because she failed to grasp Jesus's identity, at times misapplying her maternal relationship with him. This biblical theology of Mary contrasts with the Catholic Tradition–enriched portrait of her, including her immaculate conception, sinless life, bodily assumption, and roles as Advocate, Helper, Benefactress, and Mediatrix. *See also* bodily assumption of Mary; immaculate conception; Mariology; *theotokos*; virgin birth / virginal conception.

MATERIALISM The philosophical position that reality is simple rather than complex and that reality is ultimately physical. This form of monism contrasts with idealistic monism, which holds that reality, which is simple rather than complex, is ultimately immaterial; and dualism, the view that reality is complex, consisting of two elements, material and immaterial. Materialism is reflected in evolution, which attributes the origin and development of the universe to physical processes. It is supported by neurophysiology, which maintains that rationality, free will, moral consciousness, and faith are intimately tied to material processes. Materialism is hostile to and contradicted by Christian theology. *See also* dualism; embodiment; human nature; monism; neurophysiology; soul.

MATRIMONY *See* marriage; sacrament.

MEANS OF GRACE In respect to ecclesiology, activities by which God's blessings are communicated to his people. Many Protestant churches consider preaching and the sacraments to be means of grace. Preaching communicates the gospel by which salvation comes, and baptism and the Lord's Supper bestow what they signify: forgiveness, identification with Christ, his presence, spiritual nourishment, church membership, and more. Other churches do not restrict the means of grace to these three activities. Still others avoid the language of *means of grace* to avoid association with Catholic theology's position that grace is infused into the faithful through the seven sacraments. *See also* baptism; Lord's Supper; ordinance; preaching; sacrament.

MEDIATOR One who acts as an intermediary to restore peace between conflicting parties. In terms of salvation, "there is one God, and there is one mediator between God and men, the man Christ Jesus, who gave himself as a ransom for all" (1 Tim. 2:5–6). Because of human sinfulness, enmity characterizes the relationship between God and people. To rescue them, Jesus shed his blood as a ransom, died as their substitute, removed the liability for them to suffer punishment, and assuaged the divine wrath against them.

Accordingly, he acted as mediator, removing enmity and restoring peace between God and them. *See also* atonement; Jesus Christ, deity of; Jesus Christ, humanity of; reconciliation.

MEDIEVAL THEOLOGY *See* scholasticism (Catholic).

MEMORIAL VIEW With respect to the Lord's Supper, the position that the emphasis of this ordinance is on remembering what Christ accomplished on the cross. The view is usually identified with Huldrych Zwingli, who interpreted Jesus's words, "This is my body," figuratively to be, "This signifies my body." He further underscored Jesus's following words, "Do this in remembrance of me," concluding that the bread is a symbol of Christ's body to remind Christians that his body was crucified for them. As a memorial of Christ's crucifixion, the Lord's Supper requires faith. Many free churches—for example, Baptist, Bible churches—hold this view. *See also* consubstantiation; Lord's Supper; spiritual presence of Christ; transubstantiation; Zwingli, Huldrych.

MERCY As an attribute of God, his goodness expressed to those who are afflicted. Highlighted by God himself when he revealed his name, mercy is associated with grace, patience, love, and faithfulness (Exod. 34:6). Mercy is seen in God's fatherly compassion for his children, whose weaknesses and failings he knows well (Ps. 103:13–14). It is seen in Jesus's pity toward the miserable, like the blind men who begged, "Have mercy on us" (Matt. 9:27). Because God is merciful, his people are to love their enemies, do good, and lend without expecting repayment—that is, be merciful like God (Luke 6:35–36). *See also* grace; love.

MERIT According to Catholic soteriology, the reward that God grants to the faithful for good works that, through his grace, enable them to gain salvation. God and human beings cooperate so that the merit of good works is owed first to God's grace, then to the faithful. This merit does not pertain to the beginning of salvation, for that grace belongs to God's work alone. But merit enters in when the faithful, through the Holy Spirit and love, earn for themselves and for others the grace needed for gaining eternal life. Protestantism denies any role for merit in achieving salvation. *See also* good works; grace; indulgences.

MESSIAH The "anointed one" (Heb. *mashiach*) who saves God's people. In the Old Testament, the hope of the Messiah centered on a descendant of David (2 Sam. 7) who would reunite the divided kingdom of Israel and defeat its enemies (Ps. 45). The messianic age also included the Gentiles, as the Messiah would bring peace to the world (Isa. 42:6). In the New Testament, *Christ* (Gk. *christos*, "anointed one") became the title for Jesus of Nazareth, the long-awaited messianic hope (Matt. 16:13–20). He fulfilled the messianic prophecies (Acts 4:24–28), performed the works associated with the Messiah (Matt. 11:2–6), and, having accomplished salvation, was exalted as Christ over the world. *See also* Davidic covenant; Jesus Christ, deity of; Jesus Christ, humanity of; kingdom.

METAPHYSICS The branch of philosophy that studies the nature of reality. Two aspects of this discipline are ontology (Gk. *ontos*, "being"), focusing on matters of being, and cosmology (Gk. *kosmos*, "world"), focusing on the origin and nature of the universe. Metaphysics raises and seeks to answer questions such as the following: Why does something exist rather than not exist? Is existence primarily simple (either material or immaterial) or complex (both material and immaterial)? Do only particular things (horses, red balls) exist, or do universals (horseness, redness) exist also? Are time and space real, or do they exist as ideas in one's mind only? *See also* epistemology; ethics.

METHOD IN THEOLOGY *See* theological method.

METHOD OF CORRELATION In terms of an approach to theology, Paul Tillich's answering or apologetic theology that centers on the link, or correlation, between contemporary questions and systematic theology. Philosophy, specifically ontology, presents pressing inquiries and topics, which consistently revolve around the issues of being human and human existence. Systematic theology, based on divine revelation, responds to (correlates with) those unrelenting questions. This methodology is a circle in which the existential questions and theological answers become inseparable. The content cannot come from the inquiries and topics; it comes from revelation. But the form always comes from the questions and issues. *See also* apologetics; theological method.

METHODISM *See* Wesleyanism / John Wesley.

MIDDLE KNOWLEDGE With respect to the doctrine of God, a type of divine knowledge that stands between his natural knowledge and his free knowledge. Natural knowledge is the knowledge that God possesses of all actual things (past, present, and future) and of all possible things (what *could* be). Free knowledge is the knowledge that God possesses of all things he has decreed or ordained must happen (what *will* be). Middle knowledge is the knowledge that God possesses of all things that can take place involving a human decision before God decrees something about them (what *would* be, under different circumstances). *See also* omniscience.

MILLENNIUM With respect to eschatology, either another name for the current church age or a future period in relation to the second coming of Christ. From the Latin (*mille*, "one thousand"; *annum*, "year"), *millennium* finds expression as "a thousand years" in Revelation 20:1–6. The nature of the millennium is debated. Historic premillennialism and dispensational premillennialism hold to Christ's return before (*pre-*) his thousand-year reign on the earth. Postmillennialism views this age as one of peace and prosperity, after (*post-*) which Christ will return. Amillennialism believes there is no (*a-*) future millennium but identifies it with the current church age. *See also* amillennialism; dispensational premillennialism; historic premillennialism; postmillennialism; second coming.

MIND   The intellectual capacity for thinking and other mental activities involved in consciousness. Along with emotions and will, it is one aspect of divine, angelic, and human nature. The mind involves reasoning, reflecting, remembering, and discerning. The divine mind is omniscient; God knows everything. Angelic mind is distinguished between the mind of angels used for good and the mind of demons used for evil. In humans, the mind is associated with the brain. The human mind before the fall was upright, but the fallen mind is corrupt, futile, and blinded by sin. A redeemed mind is being renewed to love God and his ways. *See also* neurophysiology; omniscience; reason; will.

MINISTRY   An act of service to God and/or people. Ministry (from Lat. *ministerium*, "service") takes its cue from Jesus, who "came not to be served but to serve" (Mark 10:45). Jesus himself gives gifted people to his church, "to equip the saints for the work of ministry" (Eph. 4:12); as members minister to one another, the church "builds itself up in love" (Eph. 4:16). Ministry is also directed toward God, as the church's service of worship offers him praise and thanksgiving (Heb. 13:15). God has further entrusted the church with the ministry of reconciliation to nonbelievers (2 Cor. 5:18–21). *See also* church; evangelism; mission; servant/service; spiritual gifts; worship.

MIRACLE   A supernatural, extraordinary event that diverges from observed natural processes. As signs, miracles point to divine activity; as wonders, they astonish onlookers; as mighty works, they express exceptional power (2 Cor. 12:12). Acts such as the feeding of the five thousand and the raising of Lazarus testified to the deity of Jesus (John 20:30–31). His disciples performed healings and other miracles in Jesus's name as derivative uses of his power; these acts confirmed the disciples' status as authoritative messengers of the gospel (Heb. 2:4). The spiritual gift of miracles is the supernatural ability to effect mighty acts through divine power. *See also* omnipotence; providence.

MIRACULOUS GIFTS   Certain kinds of spiritual gifts that require supernatural power to be exercised. These are prophecy, speaking in tongues, interpretation of tongues, word of knowledge, word of wisdom, healings, and miracles (some include exorcisms). In the debate between continuationism and cessationism, the former position believes that the Spirit continues to distribute miraculous gifts today to build up the church. The latter position believes that these gifts were designed to function as confirmation of the gospel and its original messengers in the early church; because these miraculous gifts have served their purpose, the Spirit is no longer distributing them today. *See also* cessationism; continuationism; spiritual gifts.

MISSION   With respect to ecclesiology, the mandate Jesus gave to his church concerning its purpose to make disciples in all nations (Matt. 28:18–20). God himself is a missional God, who originated mission with the creation of image bearers, his permission that they would fall, his election and liberation of the people Israel, and his unfolding plan for global salvation through the Messiah. The Father commissioned the Son to become incarnate and accomplish salvation, and the Son in turn commissioned his church to announce how salvation is appropriated (John 20:19–23). Accordingly, the church's orientation in all that it is and does is missional. *See also* church; evangelism; Great Commission; ministry.

MODALISM   A heresy that maintains that "Father," "Son," and "Holy Spirit" are three names for, or *modes* (thus, *mod*alism) of, one and the same person. They are not three persons. Modalism fails to account for several matters. One is the baptism of Jesus: all three persons of the Trinity were active, as the Father spoke words of commendation about his baptized Son, on whom the Spirit was descending (Mark 1:9–11). Another event is Jesus praying: the Son of God did not direct his prayers to himself but directed them to his Father, who is a person distinct from the Son (John 17). *See also* Monarchianism; Trinity.

MODERNISM/MODERNITY   The period in Western culture from the eighteenth-century Enlightenment to postmodernism in the mid-twentieth century. Its characteristics: (1) the search for an unshakable foundation for universal, objective knowledge; (2) unquestioning trust in reason, science, and technology; (3) human autonomy, expressed in the rejection of divine revelation and religious authority; (4) loss of the supernatural, with a turn toward naturalism; and (5) belief in the unstoppable progress of humanity. Modernity contained within itself the seeds of its own demise: it undermined religious belief, community, and morality, as witnessed by modern atrocities of world wars, the Holocaust, genocide, and more. *See also* Enlightenment, the; postmodernism; premodern.

MONARCHIANISM   An early heresy regarding the Trinity. Monarchianism (from Gk. *monarchia*, "ruler") has two forms. *Dynamic* (from Gk. *dynamis*, "power") *Monarchianism* believed Jesus was an ordinary, though particularly holy, man on whom the Spirit (or Christ) descended at his baptism. This powerful presence made Jesus able to perform miracles, but he was not divine. *Modalistic Monarchianism* (also modalism and Sabellianism) maintained that the members of the Trinity are one and the same person, not three persons. The one God is designated by three different names— "Father," "Son," and "Holy Spirit"—at different times. They are three *modes* (thus, *mo*dalism) of the one God. *See also* adoptionism/adoptianism; modalism; Trinity.

MONASTICISM   A movement that emphasizes the pursuit of personal piety and church renewal, especially through ascetic practices. Monasticism (from Gk. *monastēs*, "solitary") developed in the early church in two forms: hermetic, emphasizing individual withdrawal from the world in pursuit of personal holiness, and communal, promoting collective devotion to God. Ascetic disciplines like eating sparingly, fasting often, and severe treatment of the body were employed to wean adherents from worldly pleasures and promote stellar sanctification. Movements like Irish monasticism and the Franciscans added evangelization as an emphasis. Monasticism is often characterized by the evangelical vows of poverty, chastity, and obedience. *See also* asceticism.

MONERGISM   In regard to the doctrine of salvation, the Protestant position that God alone saves human beings. From the Greek (*monos*, "sole"; *ergon*, "work"), *monergism* refers to a *sole source that works* redemption. God is the single agent that operates the salvation of people. By contrast, *synergism* (Gk. *syn*, "together"; *ergon*, "work") refers to two (or more) sources that *work together* in salvation. God and human beings together operate the rescue of the latter group. Justification exemplifies monergism: one agent, God, justifies the ungodly (Rom. 4:5), who do not / cannot contribute anything. *See also* justification; synergism.

MONISM   The philosophical position that reality is simple rather than complex, with two possibilities: materialistic monism holds that reality is ultimately material, whereas idealistic monism maintains that reality is ultimately immaterial. Monism is contrasted with dualism, the view that reality is complex, consisting of two elements, material and immaterial; the one cannot be reduced to the other. Contemporary materialistic monism affirms that what used to be considered the realm of the soul—rationality, consciousness, morality, faith—is ultimately explained by material processes in the brain and central nervous system. Monism cannot account for the disembodied state of believers in heaven. *See also* dualism; intermediate state; materialism; neurophysiology.

MONOPHYSITISM   With respect to Christology, the denial that the incarnate Christ has two distinct natures—one divine, one human—united in one person. Monophysitism (from Gk. *monos*, "one"; *physis*, "nature") holds that the incarnate Christ has only one nature, that is, a divine nature. His human nature was absorbed by his divine nature, or it was not fully human. Eutychianism was an early expression of monophysitism, but portions of the church continued to affirm the view even after it was contradicted by the Council of Chalcedon (451). The view was again condemned at the Council of Constantinople II (553). *See also* Chalcedonian Creed; Eutychianism; hypostatic union; monothelitism.

MONOTHEISM The belief in and worship of one God. Monotheism (from Gk. *monos*, "one"; *theos*, "god") characterizes Judaism, Christianity, and Islam but contrasts with polytheistic (from Gk. *polys*, "many"; *theos*, "god") religions like Hinduism, Confucianism, and Taoism. The Jewish Shema proclaims, "Hear, O Israel: The LORD our God, the LORD is one" (Deut. 6:4). Jewish monotheism is at the heart of Christianity, which affirms "God is one" (Rom. 3:30), with this qualification: the one God eternally exists as three persons, Father, Son, and Holy Spirit, who in the Godhead are equal in all things, one in essence, power, and will. *See also* Trinity; tritheism.

MONOTHELITISM With respect to Christology, a variation of monophysitism. Monothelitism (from Gk. *monos*, "one"; *thelēma*, "will") holds that the incarnate Christ has only one will, that is, a divine will. The view does not formally contradict the Chalcedonian Creed's insistence that Christ has two distinct natures. But it does reject the idea of Christ possessing two wills as leading to a division in his person. The Council of Constantinople III (680–81) denounced monothelitism, affirming that in the one person of Christ, each nature willed what is proper to itself—miracles by the divine nature, suffering by the human nature. *See also* Chalcedonian Creed; Council of Constantinople (I, II, III); hypostatic union; monophysitism.

MONTANISM An early heretical movement condemned by the church. It was founded by Montanus, a self-proclaimed prophet, who was joined by two prophetesses, Prisca and Maximilla, who called themselves the mouthpiece of the Holy Spirit. Montanism emphasized prophecy, speaking in tongues, visions, asceticism, and other intense, ecstatic religious experiences. It also stirred up hope in the imminent return of Christ and prophesied that the new Jerusalem would descend from heaven to Phrygia (where the movement had originated). The church denounced Montanism and emphasized that the activity of God was concentrated in the institutional church and not in such unrestrained movements.

MORAL ARGUMENTS With respect to the doctrine of God, a category of rational arguments for God's existence. As *a posteriori* arguments, they are based on experience, specifically human moral experience. An example is C. S. Lewis's argument (in *Mere Christianity*) based on the fact of quarrels and the moral law these presuppose (otherwise, people would not make excuses for breaking the moral law): (1) moral obligation exists within every person; (2) a sense of obligation can come only from one to whom moral authority is rightly ascribed; therefore, (3) this obligation must come from a moral lawgiver, who is God. See also *a posteriori / a priori*; cosmological arguments; God; knowability; ontological arguments; teleological arguments.

MORAL INFLUENCE THEORY A model of the atonement, or what Christ's death accomplished, offered by Abelard (1079–1142). Major tenets: (1) People need their love for God to be stimulated. (2) A persuasive exhibition of God's love is necessary to stimulate such love for God. (3) Christ's death provided this demonstration of divine love, which in turn stimulates people to love God. This theory is inadequate because it removes the atonement from an objective reality (what Christ's death accomplished) to a merely subjective influence on people (Christ's death kindles within them a love for God). It also detaches the atonement from forgiveness of sins. *See also* atonement; *Christus Victor*; governmental theory; moral influence theory; penal substitution theory; satisfaction theory.

MORTAL SIN According to Catholic theology, one of two types of sin, the other being venial sin. Mortal sin is a serious violation of God's law, meeting three conditions. (1) Its object is a grave matter, as specified by the Ten Commandments. (2) It is committed with full knowledge of the sinful nature of the act. (3) It is committed with complete consent, by personal choice. Mortal sin results in the destruction of love and the loss of grace. If it is not redeemed and one dies in this state, eternal death is the punishment. It is forgiven through the sacrament of penance. *See also* penance; sin; venial sin.

MORTIFICATION   With respect to sanctification, the ongoing process of considering oneself dead to sin and putting to death one's desire for sinful pleasures. Based on Paul's presentation of the sin nature as the "old self" (Rom. 6:6), mortification rests on the truth that Christians, through their identification with Christ's death, have died to sin (6:2). Their sinful nature was crucified with him, releasing them from enslavement to sin. Accordingly, Christians must consider themselves dead to sin (6:11). Through the Holy Spirit's assistance (Gal. 5:16–17), they kill their craving for sin, its lure gradually weakening as they mortify it. *See also* cross/crucifixion; sanctification; sin.

MOSAIC COVENANT   *See* old covenant.

MULTIPLE-INTENTIONS VIEW OF THE ATONEMENT   The position that God had multiple intentions that he accomplished through Christ's death: Christ died for the purpose of (1) securing the sure salvation of the elect; (2) paying the penalty for the sins of everyone, making it possible for all who believe to be saved; and (3) reconciling all things to God. Support includes the same passages (e.g., Rom. 8:32; Eph. 5:25) used by limited atonement for intention (1), the same passages (2 Cor. 5:17–21; 1 John 2:2) used by unlimited atonement for intention (2), and passages such as Colossians 1:19–20 and Ephesians 1:10 for intention (3). But it rejects some argumentation for limited atonement (no passages say Christ died *only* for the elect) and unlimited atonement (no passages affirm prevenient grace). *See also* atonement; limited atonement; unlimited atonement.

MYSTERY   A truth known originally to God in ages past that has now been disclosed, especially through the gospel, for human beings to embrace. Specific mysteries are God's plan to sum up everything in Christ (Eph. 1:10); the participation of the Gentiles in Christ and their inclusion with the Jews in his body (Eph. 3:6); and Christ in believers as their hope of glory (Col. 1:27). Church leaders are stewards of these mysteries (1 Cor. 4:1), in the sense of "the mystery of the faith" (1 Tim. 3:9), or sound doctrine about Christ (1 Tim. 3:16). *See also* sacrament.

MYSTICISM   An approach to knowing and loving God that bypasses ordinary means and relies on direct access to him. Christian mysticism, which has been around since the early church, emphasizes direct communication and communion with God through contemplation, intuition, and personal union. It may appropriate dreams, visions, and other ecstatic revelations to experience God, at times combining ascetic practices like fasting and solitude. The usual means of relationship with God—reading and meditating on Scripture, participating in the church and sacraments—may be incorporated but are often dismissed because they fail to provide the intimacy of direct encounter with God. *See also* knowability; sanctification.

N

NATURAL HEADSHIP OF ADAM   The doctrine that by God's design in creation, the human race existed physically in Adam; therefore, he is the physical head of all human beings. Also called the realist view, it maintains that all people were seminally present in Adam's body, not as individuals, but as a corporate whole. Thus, when Adam sinned, the entire human race, existing in him, sinned with him. This natural headship explains original sin—people are guilty and corrupt because they sinned in their head, Adam. Support includes the idea that descendants are "in the loins" of their ancestors (Heb. 7:9–10). *See also* Adamic covenant; federal headship; original sin; Reformed theology; representative headship of Adam; sin.

NATURAL LAW The rule, in accordance with God's moral law for human conduct, that is found in human nature. It is known by human beings through reason and enables them to discern right from wrong. For example, just as nothing should inhibit the development of a tadpole into a frog, and just as nothing should inhibit the development of an acorn into a tree, so also should nothing—for example, abortion—inhibit the fertilization and *in utero* development of a fetus into a person living outside the womb. Particularly important in Catholic theology, natural law is embraced cautiously by some Protestants. *See also* general revelation.

NATURAL THEOLOGY The approach to constructing (elements of) the Christian faith through general revelation without appeal to Scripture. It is exemplified in arguments—ontological, cosmological, teleological, moral—for God's existence. Natural theology rests on general revelation, God's manifestation of himself in creation, human reason and conscience, providence, and more. Given this revelation, natural theology can be constructed. Still, it is limited by the general revelation on which it is based; thus, natural theology cannot develop doctrines such as the Trinity, Christ's person and work, and salvation. Karl Barth rejected natural theology, criticizing it as the bankrupt approach of Protestant liberalism. *See also* Barth, Karl; general revelation; liberalism; theological method.

NATURE The entirety of creation as the product of the creative activity of God. It includes inorganic reality (the seas, mountains), the plant world, the animal kingdom, angels and demons, and human beings. As originally created, nature was good. Because of the fall, nature has been corrupted, not pristine and fruitful as before. Still, it reveals the eternal power and divine nature of the invisible God, whose revelation in creation is rejected by sinful people (Rom. 1:18–25). God's redemption of sinful people will ultimately result in the restoration of the entire creation, either through destruction and re-creation, or wholesale renewal. *See also* creation *ex nihilo*; fall; general revelation.

NATURE, DIVINE   *See* communicable attributes; incommunicable attributes.

NATURE, HUMAN   *See* human nature.

NECESSITY   That which must exist or occur. Necessity is one of three modes of existence: something necessary must exist, something impossible cannot exist, and something contingent may or may not exist. The doctrine of God emphasizes that necessary existence is true of God alone; contingent existence is true of everything created. Necessity also refers to that which must occur. The doctrine of the divine decrees underscores that God's purpose—whatever he has predestined to happen—will certainly be realized. That plan will take place not through constraint, forcing people against their will, but of necessity, in accordance with their nature. *See also* decree; God; independence; predestination.

NECESSITY OF SCRIPTURE   An attribute of Scripture (in written form or orally transmitted) whereby it is essential for knowing the way of salvation, for progressing in godliness, and for discerning God's will. Negatively, without Scripture there can be no salvation, growth in holiness, or knowledge of God's will. However, Scripture is not absolutely necessary; indeed, before the Old Testament was written, people were saved, pleased God, and knew his will. Rather, there is a necessity conditioned on God's good pleasure to reveal his truth through a written Word. Without Scripture, people cannot have what God willed to reveal through Scripture. *See also* sufficiency of Scripture.

NEO-ORTHODOXY   The theology that developed from Karl Barth, Emil Brunner, and others in the twentieth century. Based on their disillusionment with Protestant liberalism, this new (*neo-*) approach criticized liberalism's accommodation to contemporary culture and returned to early church and Reformed doctrine (*orthodoxy*). Key tenets: (1) dialectical method, which emphasizes the paradoxical nature of theology; (2) the radical transcendence and freedom of the Triune God; (3) the Word of God as Jesus, the Bible that becomes the Word, and proclamation; (4) the image of God as fundamentally relational; and (5) human sinfulness that can be overcome only by God's sovereign initiative in Christ. *See also* Barth, Karl; dialectical theology; liberalism; theological method.

NESTORIANISM   With respect to Christology, the denial of the hypostatic union, that the incarnate Christ had two natures—one divine, one human—united in one person. Major tenets: (1) In the incarnation, two distinct persons—one divine, one human—worked in conjunction with each other. (2) This is true because a union of divine and human would have involved God in change, which is impossible. Though Nestorius denied that he held this position, the Councils of Ephesus (431) and Chalcedon (451), and the Chalcedonian Creed, condemned Nestorianism: Christ was not divided into two persons, but two natures were united in one person. *See also* Chalcedonian Creed; hypostatic union; Jesus Christ, deity of; Jesus Christ, humanity of.

NEUROPHYSIOLOGY   The science that studies the nervous system, with important implications for the doctrine of humanity. Neurophysiology is producing evidence that what theology used to ascribe to the soul—rationality, free will, moral consciousness, faith—is intimately tied to neurological processes in the brain and central nervous system. Such evidence of a material basis for human existence calls into question what happens after death, or the nonfunctioning of the body. Some Christians have abandoned the traditional belief in disembodied life after death. That scripturally warranted belief demands, however, some type of dualism: human nature consists of both material and immaterial aspects. The latter aspect (soul) continues to exist after the former aspect (body) is sloughed off at death. *See also* dualism; embodiment; human nature; intermediate state; mind; monism; soul.

NEW COVENANT The structured relationship that God established with the church, consisting of typical covenantal features. This covenant (1) is unilateral, initiated by God through the death and resurrection of Christ; (2) creates a structured relationship between God and his partners "from every tribe and language and people and nation" (Rev. 5:9); (3) features binding obligations, including (a) on God's part, his ongoing presence through the Holy Spirit, his preserving power, and so on; and (b) on the church's part, to obey the Great Commandment (Matt. 22:37–40) and the Great Commission (28:18–20); and (4) involves two signs: baptism and the Lord's Supper. *See also* baptism; covenant; Lord's Supper.

NEW HEAVEN AND NEW EARTH With regard to eschatology, the final stage and ultimate state of the age to come. This future reality is envisioned in the last pages of Scripture (Rev. 21–22), and it is the last chapter of the biblical story line of creation, fall, redemption, and consummation. Following Christ's return, (his millennium reign on earth [according to premillennialism]), the resurrection, and last judgment, the present creation will be renewed through destruction, yielding a new heaven and new earth. The glory and blessing of God will be experienced in this eternal state, which is the ultimate hope for which this present reality longs. *See also* consummation; glory; great white throne judgment; heaven; resurrection of people; second coming.

NICENE-CONSTANTINOPOLITAN CREED A confession of faith composed at the Council of Constantinople I (381), as a modification of the Creed of Nicea (325) and, like that confession, a defense of the deity of the Son. Following the resurgence of Arianism, the dominant Christology following Nicea, champions of the Nicene faith finally prevailed. The creed affirms that the Son is "only begotten," "begotten of the Father," and "begotten, not made," signifying that whereas all creatures were made, the Son was not created. The creed also affirms that he is *homoousios*, of the same substance as the Father, and thus fully God. *See also* Arianism; Creed of Nicea; *homoousios*; Jesus Christ, deity of.

NOAHIC COVENANT   The structured relationship that God established with Noah (Gen. 6–9), consisting of typical covenantal features. This covenant (1) was unilateral, initiated by God, who had destroyed the world by flood; (2) created a structured relationship between God and his partners: Noah, his family of seven and later offspring, and animals; (3) featured binding obligations, including (a) on God's part, to never again curse the world because of human sin, nor to destroy all creatures; and (b) on Noah's part, to reproduce and fill the earth; and (4) involved the sign of the rainbow as a reminder of the covenant. *See also* covenant.

NOETIC EFFECT   With regard to the doctrine of sin, the devastating impact of the fall on the human mind. The noetic (from Gk. *nous*, "mind") effect of sin is presented as "a debased mind" (Rom. 1:28; cf. 1 Tim. 6:5), as being "alienated and hostile in mind" (Col. 1:21) and "darkened in their understanding" (Eph. 4:18). This does not mean that human thinking and reasoning is completely destroyed by sin; rather, the effect especially manifests itself as wrong thoughts about God and his ways. This effect is countered, though never completely conquered, through regeneration and renewal of the mind (Rom. 12:2). *See also* incomprehensible; mind; reason; sin.

NOMINALISM   The philosophical view that only particulars exist and universals are conceptual or linguistic. A perennial debate in metaphysics, the philosophy of the nature of reality, is whether universal categories like chair-ness (that which all particular chairs have in common, rendering them chairs) exist, or if those universals are only conceptual or a way of speaking. Realism claims that universals and particulars exist; nominalism claims that only particulars exist. Particular chairs resemble one another because people conceive some similarity between them or talk as though some similarity exists. Nominalism (from Lat. *nomen*, "name") means universals exist in name only. *See also* metaphysics; realism.

NONFOUNDATIONALISM A reactive philosophy that denies any ground or starting point for building knowledge. It stands largely against the classical foundationalism of René Descartes, which proposed a self-evident, indubitable, and incorrigible foundation for knowledge. In place of such a privileged ground or basic starting point, nonfoundationalism holds to (1) coherentism: knowledge consists of propositions that cohere together, or stand in proper relationship to one another, like the many strands of a spider's web; or (2) pragmatism: knowledge consists of propositions that work, bringing about successful practical effects. Christian theology is foundationalist in some sense by building its doctrines on Scripture. *See also* epistemology; postmodernism.

NORMATIVE PRINCIPLE One of two principles (the other being the regulative principle) by which the church determines which elements may be incorporated into its worship service. Major tenets: (1) The church must worship God according to his design. (2) While Scripture regulates certain elements of worship, it leaves other indifferent matters to the church's discretion. (3) The church has authority to decide these matters, yet it cannot decide contrary to Scripture. (4) Thus, a biblical warrant is not required for including an element in worship; rather, only if Scripture prohibits its incorporation may the church not include it in worship. *See also* *adiaphora*; liturgy / liturgical theology; regulative principle; theological method; worship.

NOVATIANISM A movement of churches that separated from the Catholic Church in the mid-third century. At issue was the possibility of the restoration of Christians who had denied the faith during persecution. Novatian, a church leader who contributed to the doctrine of the Trinity, adopted a hard-line stance: it was not possible to restore lapsed believers to church membership. Cyprian, emphasizing church unity, and the Catholic Church took the opposite view: after sufficient confession and penance, fallen believers could be readmitted into the church. Novatianism denounced the Catholic Church for compromising the faith and founded its own rigorist churches. *See also* Donatism.

O

OBEDIENCE   An act expressing submission and conformity to a moral requirement or authoritative call. The conditions for obedience are (1) an authority who commands or prohibits (e.g., God, who encourages eating from every tree in the garden and forbids eating from the one tree; Gen. 2:16–17) and (2) covenant people subject to the authority (e.g., at Moses's reading of the old covenant, the people of Israel affirm their intention to be obedient; Exod. 24:7). Obedience communicates divinely commanded loyalty to the authority (e.g., secular leaders; Rom. 13:1–7) and demonstrates, in the case of Christians, a genuine relationship to Christ (1 John 2:1–6). *See also* authority; covenant; government; submission.

OFFICES OF THE CHURCH   The structures for the church's leadership and service. Three or four offices are acknowledged: (1) apostleship, the authoritative office exercised by the original apostles and designed to provide the church's foundation; (2) bishopric, the authoritative office exercised by bishops who consecrate other bishops and ordain priests and deacons; (3) eldership, the authoritative office exercised by elders (or pastors, priests) who

150

teach, lead, pray, and shepherd; and (4) diaconate, the ministerial office exercised by those who serve in various ministries. Some denominations collapse the distinction between bishopric and eldership, and most deny the ongoing function of apostleship. *See also* apostle; bishop; deacon/deaconess/diaconate; elder/eldership.

OLD COVENANT   The structured relationship that God established with the people of Israel (Exod. 19–24), consisting of typical covenantal features. This covenant (1) was unilateral, initiated by God in his address to Moses as the people's representative; (2) formalized a structured relationship between God and his partners, the massively expanded beneficiaries of the Abrahamic covenant; (3) featured binding obligations, including the Ten Commandments and other laws; and (4) involved the swearing of an oath to obey those laws, together with writing and reading the book of the covenant, and throwing the blood of sacrifices on both an altar and the people. *See also* Abrahamic covenant; covenant.

OMNIPOTENCE   The divine attribute of being all-powerful: God can do everything that is proper for him as God to do. Examples include the creation out of nothing, the exodus, and the incarnation of the Son of God in the Virgin Mary's womb. Though often defined as God's ability to do everything, this idea is incorrect: God cannot do certain things, such as sin, lie, do the logically absurd, die, break a promise, or be thwarted in his plans. Such "inabilities" are part of the perfection of God. Also, God is not constrained to act: "he does all that he pleases" (Ps. 115:3). *See also* miracle; providence; virgin birth / virginal conception.

OMNIPRESENCE   The divine attribute of being all-present: God is present everywhere with his entire being at the same time. He is not limited by space and should not be considered as being enormously big or located in one place rather than another. God is both nearby and far away, filling heaven and earth (Jer. 23:23–24). Though God is present everywhere, he manifests his presence in different ways in different situations, to bless, warn, comfort, rebuke, reward, or punish. There is nowhere people can go to escape God (Ps. 139:7–10), and worship is not confined to one place (John 4:20–24). *See also* infinite.

OMNISCIENCE The divine attribute of being all-knowing: God knows all things. He fully knows (1) himself, his infinite knowledge encompassing his infinite being (1 Cor. 2:10); (2) the past, which is as vivid to him as the present; (3) the present, even the minutest details of life (Ps. 139:1–6); (4) the future, even the free-will decisions and actions of his creatures (Isa. 41:22–23); (5) all actual things, that is, people and events that actually exist and happen; and (6) all possible things, that is, all people and events that could possibly exist and happen but never do (Matt. 11:20–21). *See also* infinite; knowledge; middle knowledge; open theism.

ONTOLOGICAL ARGUMENTS With respect to the doctrine of God, a category of rational arguments for the existence of God. Ontological (from Gk. *ontos*, "being") arguments have to do with the being of God. They are *a priori* arguments, meaning that they are prior to human experience; thus, they focus on thinking about the concept of God and do not appeal to experiences of him. An example is Anselm's ontological argument that defines God as "that being than which nothing greater can be conceived." The claim is that existence is an attribute; thus, the greatest conceivable being—God—must exist. See also *a posteriori / a priori*; cosmological arguments; God; knowability; moral arguments; teleological arguments.

ONTOLOGICAL SUBORDINATION *See* subordinationism.

ONTOLOGICAL TRINITY Perspective on the three persons of the Godhead in terms of the distinctions in their eternal relationships. An eternal characteristic of the Father in relation to the Son is *paternity*. An eternal characteristic of the Son in relation to the Father is *sonship* or *generation*. The eternal generation of the Son means the Father eternally grants him his person-of-the-Son. An eternal characteristic of the Holy Spirit in relation to the Father and Son is *procession*. The eternal procession of the Holy Spirit means the Father and Son eternally grant him his person-of-the-Spirit. *See also* economic Trinity; eternal generation; eternal procession; social Trinity; Trinity.

ONTOLOGY The philosophy concerned with the nature of being. Ontology (from Gk. *ontos*, "being") is a branch of metaphysics, the philosophy concerned with the essential nature of reality beyond (Gk. *meta*, "after") the physical. It is a different concern than epistemology, which is about knowing rather than being. Ontology explores questions such as: What is existence? What can be said to exist? How can existent things be categorized (their whatness, whereness, howness)? Does God exist? Ontology debates such matters as whether universals exist (realism) or are conceptual or linguistic categories only (nominalism), substance and accidents, and determinism and indeterminism. *See also* determinism; metaphysics; nominalism; realism.

OPEN THEISM The view that affirms God's omniscience but denies his exhaustive foreknowledge. God's knowledge corresponds to reality, so God knows everything that can be known. Because the future decisions and actions of his free creatures are not yet reality, God cannot know those matters. Such lack of knowledge is not an imperfection, however, because these matters cannot be known. God still knows everything that can be known. Open theism is criticized for contradicting biblical affirmations that God exhaustively knows the future. Indeed, one characteristic that distinguishes God from so-called gods is his ability to predict the future (Isa. 41:22–23). *See also* foreknowledge; middle knowledge; omniscience.

ORDER OF SALVATION (*ORDO SALUTIS*) The sequence of God's mighty acts in applying salvation, with several proposals. There is agreement about the ordering of some events: calling, regeneration, conversion, justification, union with Christ, and adoption take place at the same time at the beginning of salvation; sanctification continues throughout life; glorification comes at the end. Reformed and Arminian theologies disagree about other matters. For Reformed theology, election is a mighty act from eternity past, regeneration precedes conversion, and perseverance accompanies sanctification. For Arminian theology, prevenient grace initiates salvation, regeneration follows conversion, as does election, and there is no necessary perseverance. *See also* Arminian theology; Reformed theology.

ORDINANCE With respect to ecclesiology, a rite ordained by Christ to be celebrated by his church using a tangible sign or signs. Many Protestants use the traditional term *sacrament* instead. However, unlike the sacraments of the Catholic Church, Protestant sacraments are only two: baptism and the Lord's Supper. Moreover, whereas Catholic sacraments are considered to be valid *ex opere operato* (by their mere administration), Protestant sacraments are effective through the Word of God and faith. To distance these rites from their Catholic associations, many Protestants call them ordinances, because Christ ordained baptism (Matt. 28:18–20) and the Lord's Supper (26:26–29). *See also* baptism; Lord's Supper; new covenant; sacrament.

ORDINATION The church's action of consecrating or officially recognizing certain of its members for ministry. Ordination (from Lat. *ordo*, "governing body") is conferred on clergy, rendering them responsible for preaching, administering the sacraments, leading the church, and more. In the Catholic Church, ordination is bestowed by the sacrament of holy orders, with three degrees: the episcopate, for bishops; the presbyterate, for priests; and the diaconate, for deacons. Many Protestant churches have ordination that functions for the confirmation of a candidate's calling, character, theological and pastoral competencies, and more, as well as for public recognition of the individual's responsibility to minister. *See also* clergy; holy orders; ministry.

ORDO SALUTIS   *See* order of salvation (*ordo salutis*).

ORIGEN   A leading theologian, writer, and biblical scholar of the early church (ca. 185–254). He combated Celsus's attacks against Christianity, pioneered textual criticism (the *Hexapla*), wrote the first Christian systematic theology (*First Principles*), and contributed to matters like the canon of Scripture and hermeneutics, and doctrines such as the Trinity and Christology. He also held controversial positions, including a fanciful allegorical interpretation of Scripture; belief in a pretemporal, spiritual world and the preexistence of the human soul; the ransom to Satan theory of Christ's atoning death; and (possibly) the hope of universal salvation (condemned at the Council of Constantinople II). *See also* Alexandrian School; allegory; preexistence of the soul; ransom to Satan theory.

ORIGINAL RIGHTEOUSNESS   With respect to the doctrine of humanity, the view that Adam and Eve were created in the image of God as upright, holy people. As creatures of integrity, their original human nature was righteous and not evil, oriented toward obedience and faithfulness and without a tendency to sin. Still, they were not perfect; they were able not to sin, but also able to sin. A result of the fall was the loss of this original righteousness: uprightness was replaced with fallenness, and their nature became corrupt. Because of its solidarity with Adam, all humanity inherits this corrupt nature. *See also* corruption; image of God (*imago Dei*); original sin.

ORIGINAL SIN   The state of all people at birth, a condition that consists of (1) original guilt, the liability to suffer eternal condemnation (some theologies deny this element); and (2) original corruption, the sinful nature or tendency toward evil. Some theologies further detail this corruption as consisting of (a) total depravity, meaning that every aspect of human nature is infected with sin, and (b) total inability, referring to the absence of spiritual goodness and the incapacity to reorient oneself from self-centeredness to God. Original sin derives from Adam's originating sin, because of all people's solidarity with Adam and his disobedience. *See also* Adamic covenant; corruption; federal headship; guilt; natural headship of Adam; representative headship of Adam; total depravity; total inability.

ORTHODOX CHURCHES *See* Eastern Orthodoxy.

ORTHODOXY Right doctrine or belief. Orthodoxy (from Gk. *ortho-*, "right/proper"; *doxa*, "opinion") is what the New Testament calls "sound doctrine" (1 Tim. 1:10; Titus 1:9; 2:1; cf. 2 Tim. 4:3), that which properly reflects in summary form all that Scripture affirms and which the church is therefore bound to believe and obey. Such sound doctrine is defined in the early church creeds (e.g., the Nicene-Constantinopolitan, Apostles', and Chalcedonian Creeds, treating the doctrine of the Trinity and Christology) and, for Protestants, in their confessions and statements of faith. Orthodoxy stands in contrast with heresy, which is anything that contradicts sound doctrine. *See also* doctrine; heresy; orthopraxy.

ORTHOPRAXY Right practice or behavior. Orthopraxy (from Gk. *ortho-*, "right, proper"; *praxis*, "practice") emphasizes right behavior, not in terms of moralism, external behavior, or religious legalism, but with respect to conduct befitting the name or gospel of Christ (Eph. 4:1; Phil. 1:27; Col. 1:10). Christians are to be imitators of God (Eph. 5:1), being like him in holiness, mercy, and love. They are to follow Christ's example of forgiving, accepting, and loving others, and bearing up patiently when suffering. They are to walk in the Spirit, exhibiting love, joy, peace, patience, kindness, goodness, faithfulness, gentleness, and self-control (Gal. 5:22–23). *See also* orthodoxy.

OUSIA See *substantia*.

OVER-REALIZED ESCHATOLOGY A view that realities that are reserved for the future, after Christ returns, should be prematurely brought into and actualized in the present. For example, some people insist that because human beings, in the future age, will not be married, they should forego marriage in this present age. A future reality is prematurely brought into and realized in the present. The Corinthian church suffered from over-realized eschatology, as seen from Paul's rebuke: "Already you have all you want! Already you have become rich! Without us you have become kings!" (1 Cor. 4:8). This view is corrected by "already–not yet" eschatology. *See also* consummation; eschatology; second coming.

P

PAEDOBAPTISM   *See* infant baptism.

PANENTHEISM   With respect to the doctrine of God, the position that God is present within everything. Panentheism (from Gk. *pas*, "everything"; *en*, "in"; *theos*, "god") does not mean that God and the creation are identical, such that God is everything, and everything is God; that view is pantheism. Rather, panentheism means that God is the life coursing through the creation. For example, "God" is absolute spirit manifesting itself through created reality, which exists in "God." Though Christianity affirms God's omnipresence and immanence, his presence everywhere and activity within creation is not panentheism, for there is still the Creator-creature distinction. *See also* immanence; omnipresence; pantheism.

PANTHEISM   With respect to the doctrine of God, the position that everything is God, and God is everything. Pantheism (from Gk. *pas*, "everything"; *theos*, "god") means that God and the creation are identical, or that created things are modes of God. Reality is one, a unified being, which manifests itself in everything. Though Christianity affirms God's omnipresence and immanence, his presence everywhere and activity within creation is not pantheism, for there is still the Creator-creature distinction. For pantheism, if there is no creation, then there is no God, and if there is no God, then there is no creation. *See also* immanence; omnipresence; panentheism.

PAROUSIA *See* second coming.

PASSIBILITY *See* impassibility.

PASTOR *See* elder/eldership.

PATIENCE As an attribute of God, his goodness in withholding punishment. Highlighted by God when he revealed his name, patience is associated with mercy, grace, love, and faithfulness (Exod. 34:6). Patience is God's slowness to anger; while he is ready to express his displeasure, he holds off. This temporary stay of punishment should not be misconstrued as God clearing the guilty (Num. 14:18). Rather, it should prompt toward repentance (Rom. 2:4–5). Because God is patient, Christians are to master their life (Prov. 16:32), endure suffering (1 Pet. 2:20), and bear with the idle, the fainthearted, and the weak (1 Thess. 5:14). *See also* grace; love; mercy.

PATRIPASSIANISM With regard to the doctrine of God, an early heresy that held that God the Father became incarnate, suffered, and was crucified. From the Latin (*pater*, "father"; *passio*, "suffering"), *Patripassianism* literally means "the Father suffered." Praxeas, a proponent of this view, maintained that Jesus Christ and the Father are one and the same person, so logically, if Christ suffered, then the Father suffered. The church countered this position by affirming that God is impassible, or incapable of suffering. Only the God-man, by virtue of his human nature, could suffer and die; thus, Christ, not the Father, suffered and died. *See also* impassibility; incarnation; Jesus Christ, humanity of.

PATRISTIC PERIOD The era of the early centuries of Christianity. The patristic (from Lat. *pater*, "father") period extended from the death of the apostles to the beginning of the Middle Ages (about the fifth century). It included the apostolic fathers (hence, *patristic* period), leaders who followed the apostles and wrote about church matters, and the apologists, leaders who defended Christianity against its detractors and clarified misunderstandings about the faith. The period also featured fierce persecution against the fledgling church, and heresies that wreaked havoc within it. Orthodox doctrines like the Trinity and Christology were also hammered out at this time. *See also* Christology; Trinity.

PEACE The attribute of the absence of conflict and the presence of harmony. In the Old Testament, *shalom* (Heb. "peace," "welfare") was human flourishing in this earthly life: health, large family, prosperity, peace with enemies, and innumerable divine blessings. Peace for the righteous stood in contrast with its absence for the wicked (Isa. 48:22). According to the New Testament, justification brings peace with God (Rom. 5:1). Moreover, "God is not a God of confusion but of peace" (1 Cor. 14:33), ruling out unintelligible speech, purposelessness, disorderly conduct, and violations of the authority-submission relationship in the church (1 Cor. 14). Order and decency should reign, with the Spirit giving such peace (Gal. 5:22). *See also* reconciliation.

PELAGIANISM The theology proposed by Pelagius (354–420/440) and condemned by the church. Major tenets: (1) A denial of original sin, because there is no solidarity/relationship between Adam and his sin and the human race. With no guilt and no corruption of nature, people have no tendency to sin and may live without sin. (2) A redefinition of grace as God's assistance for people to do the good, his provision of free will to do the good, and his revelation of right and wrong in the conscience and Scripture. Augustine carefully exposed Pelagius's many errors, and the church denounced Pelagianism. *See also* Adamic covenant; Augustinian theology; corruption; grace; guilt; original sin.

PENAL SUBSTITUTION THEORY A model of the atonement, or what Christ's death accomplished. Major tenets: (1) The atonement is grounded in the holiness of God, who, being perfectly holy, hates and punishes sin. (2) A penalty for sin must be paid. (3) People cannot pay the penalty for their sins and live; rather, the penalty is death. (4) Only God can pay the penalty for sin so humans can live, but he must partake of human nature to pay for human beings. (5) By his death, the God-man, Jesus Christ, atones for human sin. (6) The atonement had to be accomplished in this way. *See also* atonement; *Christus Victor*; governmental theory; hypostatic union; Jesus Christ, deity of; Jesus Christ, humanity of; moral influence theory; ransom to Satan theory; satisfaction theory.

PENANCE With respect to Catholic theology, one of the seven sacraments that communicates divine grace to the Catholic faithful. This sacrament deals with mortal sins committed after baptism—sins by which divine grace is lost—by forgiving those sins, restoring divine grace, and reconciling those who have so sinned with both God and the Church. The penitent makes the acts of contrition (sorrow for and hatred of sin), confession to a priest, and satisfaction (reparation for harm caused). Specific acts—for example, praying, good works of mercy—are prescribed by the priest so that the penitent can make satisfaction for sin. *See also* forgiveness; good works; mortal sin; sacrament.

PENTECOST One of the annual holy convocations of the Jews, this festival was observed on the fiftieth (Gk. *pentēkostē*) day after Passover. It was also known as the feast of weeks, the feast of the harvest, and the day of the firstfruits. Pentecost was celebrated with various offerings that acknowledged God's goodness in providing the harvest for his people and their responsibility to give him the initial percentage of what they reaped. The significance for Christians is that fifty days after Jesus celebrated his last supper, the Holy Spirit descended on Pentecost, inaugurating the new covenant between God and the church. *See also* baptism with/in/by the Holy Spirit; church; new covenant.

PENTECOSTALISM   A movement, beginning in 1906 at the Azusa Street Revival, that gave rise to churches such as the Assemblies of God, the Church of God, and the Foursquare Church. Major tenets: (1) baptism in the Spirit for Christians sometime after conversion; (2) speaking in tongues as a sign of that baptism; and (3) the exercise of all the spiritual gifts, including the miraculous gifts of prophecy, speaking in tongues, interpretation of tongues, word of knowledge, word of wisdom, miracles, and healings. Pentecostalism is a worldwide movement noted for its evangelistic zeal, belief in the miraculous, and energetic church planting. *See also* baptism with/in/by the Holy Spirit; charismatic movement; continuationism; speaking in tongues; third wave evangelicalism.

PERFECTIONISM   With regard to sanctification, the position that Christians may be freed from sin in this life. Associated with John Wesley, Christian perfectionism is defined as loving God completely, implying that no attitudes contrary to love remain; rather, all thoughts, affections, decisions, words, and actions are governed by love. Christians are not absolutely perfect because they are not released from ignorance, mistakes, weaknesses, and temptations. Rather, they are freed from all actual, willful violations of the known law of God; still, they must constantly grow in grace. Support includes biblical affirmations that Christians do not sin (1 John 3:9; 5:18). *See also* sanctification; Wesleyanism / John Wesley.

PERICHORESIS   With regard to the doctrine of the Trinity, *perichoresis* (from Gk. *perichōrēsis*, "rotation") refers to the mutual indwelling of the Father, Son, and Holy Spirit. This interpenetration of divine persons is affirmed in Jesus's prayer for his disciples, "that they may all be one, just as you, Father, are in me, and I in you, that they also may be in us" (John 17:21). This mutual indwelling of the Father and the Son (including the Spirit also) is the ground for the perfect unity of the three persons; it also becomes the foundation for the church's unity and union with God. *See also* ontological Trinity; social Trinity; Trinity.

PERSEVERANCE   The mighty act of God to preserve Christians by his power through their ongoing faith, until their salvation is complete (1 Pet. 1:5). It does not apply to everyone who professes faith but is promised to genuine believers. These Christians, though they may fall into sin temporarily, will certainly persist in engaging in good works and exercising faith. Indeed, the saving faith of genuine Christians includes perseverance as an essential element. Moreover, because perseverance is a continuing work of God, these believers may enjoy the assurance of salvation, the subjective confidence that they will remain Christians throughout their life. *See also* assurance of salvation; saving faith.

PERSON/PERSONHOOD   A person is an individual being with attributes, capacities, and activities constituting personhood. In terms of the divine being, three persons—Father, Son, and Holy Spirit—constitute the Triune God. In terms of human beings, a person is an individual substance of a human nature. He or she consists of a material element (body) and an immaterial element (soul); attributes such as gender, sexuality, and relationality; capacities such as mind, emotions, and will; and activities such as vocation and procreation. The current debate about personhood focuses on being or function: Is a person constituted by the fact of existing or by what the person does? *See also* embodiment; human nature; *hypostasis*; soul; Trinity.

PERSPICUITY OF SCRIPTURE   A property of Scripture whereby it is clear and thus comprehensible to all Christians who possess the normal acquired ability to read texts or understand oral communication (when Scripture is read to them). This clarity is true regardless of their gender, age, education, language, or cultural background, though it does not mean Scripture is necessarily easy to understand. This doctrine is affirmed in the context of the church, to which God has given pastors and teachers to assist members in better understanding Scripture. Moreover, its clarity means that unbelievers can gain some cognition of Scripture in general. *See also* Scripture; special revelation.

PIETISM   An approach to the Christian life that emphasizes personal experience and individual purity. Pietism (from Lat. *pius*, "holy") encourages personal Bible study, prayer, and the practice of spiritual disciplines in the pursuit of holiness. It may be accompanied by a loose affiliation with the institutional church because such involvement contributes little to the individual's purity of life. Pietism as a movement developed in the seventeenth and eighteenth centuries in Europe in reaction to dry, sterile Lutheranism and is closely associated with Philipp Jacob Spener (especially his *Pious Desires*; 1675), August Hermann Franke, and Nikolaus Ludwig, Count von Zinzendorf. *See also* sanctification.

PLATONISM   The philosophy of Plato (about 429/428–347 BC) that influences Western thought and Christian theology. Key tenets: (1) Existing things are imperfect copies of the eternal, perfect forms, with the Good being the highest form. (2) Knowledge of the empirical world through sense perception is misguided and should yield to philosophical truth. (3) Through philosophy the soul grasps the forms, but the body is a hindrance. Salvation consists of the soul's escape from its imprisonment in the body. Both positively and negatively, Platonism influenced the notion of God as the Form of the Good, the doctrine of the immortality of the soul, monasticism, and more. *See also* Aristotelianism; Augustinian theology; realism.

PLENARY INSPIRATION   *See* inspiration of Scripture.

PLURALISM   With regard to Christianity and other religions, the position that salvation comes equally through all religions—Christianity, for Christians; Judaism, for Jews; Islam, for Muslims; Buddhism, for Buddhists; Hinduism, for Hindus; and more. Pluralism stands in contrast with exclusivism and inclusivism. While both of those views insist that salvation comes only through Christ, pluralism denies he is the ground of salvation for people other than Christians. Rather, Judaism, Islam, Buddhism, Hinduism, and more have other ways of salvation (e.g., Moksha for Hinduism, the Noble Eightfold Path for Buddhism) equally as valid for their adherents as Christ is for Christianity. *See also* exclusivism; inclusivism.

PNEUMATOLOGY One of the topics of systematic theology, it treats the person and work of the Holy Spirit. This doctrine affirms the personality and deity of the Spirit (Gk. *pneuma*); his eternal procession from the Father and the Son; his work—together with those two—of creation, providence, redemption, and consummation; and the continuities and discontinuities between his work prior to Christ and his new covenant mission beginning at Pentecost. It further rehearses his many ministries, including conviction of sin, regeneration, sealing, assurance of salvation, prayer, illumination of Scripture, filling, empowerment for evangelism, guidance, distribution of spiritual gifts, and others. *See also* Holy Spirit, person of the; Holy Spirit, work of the.

PNEUMATOMACHIANISM *See* Trinity.

POLYTHEISM *See* theism; Trinity.

POSITIVISM *See* logical positivism.

***POSSE PECCARE* (AND RELATED PHRASES)** With regard to hamartiology, the base term that gives rise to three other Latin phrases that express human ability (*posse*) or inability (*non posse*) with regard to sin (*peccare*). *Posse non peccare* affirms that people are able not to sin, while *posse peccare* affirms that people are able to sin. Both were true of Adam and Eve before the fall. When they exercised their ability to sin, they became *non posse non peccare*—not able not to sin. Salvation renders people *posse non peccare*, but not yet *non posse peccare*: not able to sin will only be true in the intermediate state and in the age to come. *See also* sin.

POSTLIBERALISM   The late twentieth-century theology that stands in contrast to traditional theology and goes beyond classical liberalism. Associated with the Yale School and represented by George Lindbeck, postliberalism maintains doctrines are not expressions of objective truth about God (conservative theology) nor accounts of personal religious experiences with God (liberalism) but ways of speaking about God that govern the church. Just as rules of grammar are neither true nor false but are conventions enabling conversation, so doctrines are rules facilitating life in church community. Postliberalism emphasizes narratives, the community over the individual, and the formative character of context on people. *See also* liberalism; theological method.

POSTMILLENNIALISM   With respect to eschatology, the position that Christ's second coming will occur after (*post-*) an age of peace and prosperity (*millennium*) on the earth. Developed in the modern period, postmillennialism believes that the impact of the gospel will be powerful and very extensive, with much of the world's population becoming Christian. As a result, the world will be Christianized, or dominated by Christian principles. While not a literal one-thousand-year period, the millennium will be an age of righteousness, peace, and prosperity, after which Christ will return, execute the last judgment, and establish the new heaven and new earth. *See also* amillennialism; dispensational premillennialism; historic premillennialism; millennium; second coming.

POSTMODERNISM   Intellectual movement that originated in the late twentieth century in reaction against modernism and its enthronement of human rationality, certainty, objectivity, and comprehensive truth claims. Against these fixtures of modernism, postmodernism insisted there is (1) no metanarrative, or overarching story (e.g., the gospel) that is universally binding; (2) no place on which to stand outside of one's own context to formulate objective rational principles and to make universal truth claims (e.g., Jesus is the only way to God); and (3) no certainty, because reality (e.g., maleness and femaleness) is constructed by people and communities and not established by reason. Christian theology, while influenced by both modernism and postmodernism, embraces the strengths and critiques the errors of both movements. *See also* Enlightenment, the; modernism/modernity; premodern.

POSTMORTEM EVANGELISM The view that after death, (1) people who never heard the gospel while they were living—the unevangelized—will be given the opportunity to hear it, or (2) people who heard the gospel but did not embrace it while they were living—the evangelized—will be given another opportunity to be saved. Postmortem evangelism is contradicted by (1) Scripture's silence on it and the fact that (2) divine judgment follows death (Heb. 9:27), (3) human destiny is fixed at death (Luke 16:19–31), and (4) the basis for the determination of this destiny is belief or unbelief in Jesus Christ during one's lifetime. *See also* evangelism; universalism.

POSTTRIBULATIONAL PREMILLENNIALISM *See* historic premillennialism.

POURING One of the modes of baptism, the others being immersion and sprinkling. Pouring, or affusion, is dispensing a significant amount of water over a person's head. Support includes: (1) Certain biblical rituals employed pouring—for example, Jewish ceremonial washings. (2) The meaning of baptism as purification and cleansing from sin (Ezek. 36:25; Acts 22:16; Titus 3:5) is portrayed well by affusion. (3) Pragmatically, pouring works when there are many people to be baptized, when there is a small supply of water, when the one administering baptism is weak, or when the one to be baptized is weak or paralyzed. *See also* immersion; sprinkling.

PRAISE The expression of approval, respect, and honor in reference to God. Praise is an essential element of worship. As the church worships, it engages in recognizing and describing the worth and glory of the awesome majesty of God and his mighty acts in creation, redemption, and consummation. Specific activities of praise include singing hymns and songs (of various genres, and accompanied by musical instruments, shouts of acclamation, the raising of hands, and more), the reading of psalms of praise, and speaking corporate prayers of adoration and thanksgiving. Praise in another sense is the ascription of admiration for human beings. *See also* glory; worship.

PRAYER The act of communicating with God as an expression of trust in him. The biblical pattern is that prayer is addressed to God the Father, in the name (by the authority) of Jesus Christ, in step with (prompted by) the Holy Spirit. At the same time, specific prayers may be directed to the Son (e.g., thanksgiving for his death) and the Spirit (e.g., requesting his filling). Prayer takes on various expressions: praise and adoration, thanksgiving, confession of sin, petition for oneself, and intercession for others. Christians must pray according to God's will, with faith, in anticipation of God's response. *See also* intercession.

PREACHING The act of proclaiming the gospel. Because Scripture is central to Christianity, preaching is essential to Christian worship, discipleship, and mission. Christian preaching takes its cue from forerunners like Noah, "a herald of righteousness" (2 Pet. 2:5); the prophets who proclaimed "Thus says the LORD"; and Jesus himself, whose ministry included announcing the kingdom of God (Matt. 9:35). The church was birthed (Acts 2:22–41) and expanded through the preaching of the gospel by the apostles and others (Acts 6:2; 11:20). God himself does not preach, but he commissions people to proclaim the gospel so that faith is ignited (Rom. 10:13–17). *See also* gospel; homiletics; marks of the church; unity.

PREDESTINATION God's sovereign, eternal, free, and unchangeable determination of everything that comes to pass. The creation of the universe, the fall of human beings into sin, the crucifixion of Christ and his return—all are included in God's foreordination. With respect to salvation, predestination is God's decision regarding people's eternal destinies. For some theologies, God's purpose in salvation consists of two aspects, election and reprobation. For others, it is limited to election only. Key issues include the relationship between God's foreknowledge and foreordination, the extent of God's determination (all things, or only some), and whether predestination is unconditional or conditional. *See also* conditional election; decree; election; foreknowledge; God; necessity; reprobation; unconditional election.

PREEXISTENCE OF THE SOUL Origen's fanciful proposal for the origin of the soul, with influence from Greek philosophy. Major tenets: (1) Because God is all-powerful, he must have always had a creation that he could rule. Thus, God created an invisible, spiritual world composed of good creatures. (2) Possessing free will, these beings abused their freedom and sinned. (3) To rectify this disaster, God created the visible, material world as a home for some of these fallen creatures, who became embodied as human beings. Thus, a human being consists of a preexistent soul that fell in a pretemporal world and is joined to a body. *See also* Origen; Platonism.

PRELAPSARIAN Anything that is before the fall of humanity into sin. From the Latin (*pre-*, "before"; *lapsus*, "the fall"), *prelapsarianism* refers generally to the prefall state of innocence and specifically to (1) the creation of the heavens and the earth and their existence in an originally good state; (2) the divine image bearers, Adam and Eve, who were originally characterized by a face-to-face relationship with God, an undisguised relationship with each other, a relationship of integrity with their own self, and a fruitful relationship with the created order; and (3) God's providential care of his creation without the intervention of redeeming grace. *See also* creation *ex nihilo*; fall; image of God (*imago Dei*).

PREMILLENNIALISM *See* dispensational premillennialism; historic premillennialism.

PREMODERN The approach to biblical interpretation and doctrine in the patristic, medieval, and Reformation periods, prior to the onset of modernity. Although quite diverse, this era shared certain characteristics: (1) belief in the supernatural, rather than skepticism toward it; (2) a consensus on many doctrines, with opposing positions denounced as heresies; (3) submission to authority, including Scripture, tradition, and the church; and (4) a hermeneutic of belief that emphasized the literal and spiritual senses of Scripture, with typology. Modernity, beginning with the Enlightenment, introduced biblical criticism, comparative religions study, the domination of science, naturalism, and more, largely overturning the premodern approach. *See also* biblical criticism; Enlightenment, the; hermeneutics; modernism/modernity; postmodernism; theological method.

PRESBYTERIANISM A form of church government by elders as representatives of the church. Presbyterianism (from Gk. *presbyteros*, "elder") is governance by elders in ranked authoritative structures. Elders are of two types: teaching elders, who are responsible for preaching, the sacraments, and leading; and ruling elders, who lead with the teaching elder. In a local church, the elders form a session or consistory. The elders in a geographical area form a presbytery or classis (e.g., the presbytery of Philadelphia). The members of the presbyteries or classes in a region form a synod. At the national level is a general assembly. *See also* congregationalism; elder/eldership; episcopalianism.

PRESUPPOSITIONALISM The position that Christian truth must be acknowledged by beginning with belief in certain axioms, or unproved assumptions, upon which the Christian faith is grounded. Examples include the existence of God and the truthfulness and authority of Scripture. Accordingly, a presuppositionalist approach to apologetics shuns the presentation of proofs for the existence of God and evidence for the reliability of the Bible, for these arguments always fail to convince nonbelievers. Their worldview, based on competing presuppositions, must be shown to be inconsistent and unlivable, thus prompting unbelievers to see the correctness of the Christian worldview based on better presuppositions. *See also* faith; fideism; reason.

PRETRIBULATIONAL PREMILLENNIALISM   *See* dispensational premillennialism.

PREUNDERSTANDING   With respect to Scripture, the worldview, cultural framework, theological tradition, religious experience, and more that readers bring to the task of interpreting Scripture. To Bultmann's question "Is exegesis without presupposition possible?" the answer is no. All interpretation involves preunderstanding, which exercises a strong influence on that task. Some elements may help in the interpretive process, leading to a correct grasp of Scripture's meaning. Other elements may hurt the process, resulting in a wrong sense of its meaning. One goal of the process is for Scripture to transform improper elements of preunderstanding into proper ones that aid in correct interpretation. *See also* hermeneutics.

PREVENIENT GRACE   In relation to soteriology, a type of grace that goes before all people to prepare their will, which is unresponsive to God because of sin, to embrace salvation. Prevenient (from Lat. *praevenire*, "to go before") grace is a major element in Arminian theology but is denied by Reformed theology. This grace is universal and preconscious, prompting people's initial desire to seek God, arousing a sense of sin, awakening a longing for salvation, and enabling them to repent of sin, believe in Christ, and continue in the faith. This grace overcomes original sin, and it can be resisted. *See also* Arminian theology; original sin; Reformed theology; saving grace; Wesleyanism / John Wesley.

PRIEST   In many churches, a leader who is responsible for the office of ministry. A priest (from Gk. *presbyteros*, also translated "elder" and "presbyter") is divinely called, meets the qualifications for this office, is ordained by the church, and engages in ministry, including preaching, celebrating the sacraments, and leading the church. In the

Catholic Church, priests are men who are ordained through holy orders and must be celibate. They share in the authority of Christ but not in a supreme degree as do bishops. The Anglican Communion permits its priests to be married, and it ordains women as priests. *See also* celibacy; clergy; elder/eldership; holy orders; ordination.

PRIESTHOOD   The office in which priests serve. Biblical roots include Melchizedek, "priest of God Most High" (Gen. 14:18), and the Levitical priesthood, which mediated between God and his people through praying and offering sacrifices on their behalf (Lev. 8). These priestly types anticipated the coming of the priesthood of Christ, who, as the ultimate High Priest, offered himself as the sacrifice for sin. From his priesthood flows that of Christians, who, composing a royal and holy priesthood, offer sacrifices of praise, thanksgiving, and good works (e.g., supporting the ministry of others; Phil. 4:18) to God (Heb. 13:15–16; 1 Pet. 2:5–9). *See also* priest; priesthood of believers.

PRIESTHOOD OF BELIEVERS   The Protestant doctrine that all Christians stand before God through the High Priest Jesus Christ and without the mediation of other people. In opposition to the mediatorial role of Catholic priests ordained through holy orders, the Reformers affirmed the personal responsibility of all people to hear the gospel and be saved. A corollary is that all church members are divinely appointed and empowered to minister to one another through teaching the Word, praying, and, for some, choosing church leaders. This position does not do away with the office of ministry to which God appoints certain church leaders. *See also* priest; priesthood.

PROCESS THEOLOGY   In regard to the doctrine of God, the view that his nature is dipolar and developing. The dipolar nature consists of (1) an abstract essence: God is absolute, unchanging, independent, and unsurpassable in perfection; and (2) a concrete actuality: God is relative, changing, dependent, and always surpassing himself in perfection. In his concrete actuality, God is constantly growing, responding to his relationships with the world and being enriched by them. Process theology, a type of panentheism, is criticized for violating the Creator-creature distinction and making God at least partially dependent on the world for his being and perfections. *See also* independence; panentheism.

PROCESSION, ETERNAL   *See* eternal procession.

PROFESSION OF FAITH   An acknowledgment of Jesus Christ as Lord. A personal profession is a requisite element of salvation: "If you confess with your mouth that Jesus is Lord and believe in your heart that God raised him from the dead, you will be saved. For with the heart one believes and is justified, and with the mouth one confesses and is saved" (Rom. 10:8–10). This verbal confession of faith is the desired response to the gospel and is prompted by the Holy Spirit and grace (1 Cor. 12:3; Acts 18:27). A visible expression of this confession is baptism (Acts 2:38). *See also* baptism; Baptistic theology; believer's baptism; evangelism; gospel.

PROGRESSIVE REVELATION   God's communication of himself is characterized by development, not in terms of evolutionary advancement or the correction of earlier revelation by later revelation, but in terms of fuller disclosure in successive stages, each building on former ones. An example is instruction for worship, developing from altars to the tabernacle, from the temple to worship in spirit and truth. Acknowledging progressive revelation underscores the structure of promise and fulfillment, and type and antitype. It also cautions against reading New Testament meanings into the Old Testament, while it encourages understanding the Old Testament shadows in light of New Testament fullness. *See also* hermeneutics.

PROLEGOMENON   In relation to theological method, that which must be considered before engaging in doing theology. From the Greek (*pro*, "before"; *legō*, "to say"), *prolegomenon* means literally "to say (something) before" doing something else—preparatory remarks. Matters to be considered before engaging in the theological task include setting forth one's preunderstanding, including one's theological system and epistemology (the approach to knowledge); describing the nature, task, source, scope, and method of theology; explaining one's view of divine revelation; accounting for one's starting point (e.g., Scripture or God); explaining the importance of theology; and outlining the topics in theology (e.g., sin, salvation). *See also* systematic theology; theological method.

PROMISE A pledge of commitment to be or to do something for another. The promise then becomes the ground for a trustful expectation of its fulfillment. God is the divine promise maker, declaring who he will be ("merciful and gracious, slow to anger, and abounding in steadfast love and faithfulness"; Exod. 34:6) and what he will do ("I will hear from heaven and will forgive their sin and heal their land"; 2 Chron. 7:14). God's people, as the recipients of his pledges, are expected to trust his promises—this is faith—and to keep the commitments they make (James 5:12). *See also* faithfulness.

PROPHECY In the Old Testament, a type of divine revelation especially focused on disclosing God's will, denouncing sin, and foretelling the future. According to the New Testament, prophecy, which is a spiritual gift empowered by the Spirit, is the reception and communication of divine revelation for the building up of the church. It consists of two aspects: the reception of a message, which God discloses to the prophet; and the report of that message, which is a communication that is regulated in its exercise and must be evaluated by the church (1 Cor. 14:29–32). Whether prophecy continues today is debated. *See also* cessationism; continuationism; miraculous gifts; special revelation; spiritual gifts.

PROPHET In the Old Testament, one who received divine revelation and communicated it, often with the preface "Thus says the LORD." Prophets and prophetesses would be known to be true if their prophecy were fulfilled; if it did not come about, the false messengers would be stoned. According to the New Testament, a prophet is one who receives divine revelation and communicates it to the church, which is responsible for evaluating it for correct and misunderstood/miscommunicated aspects. Whereas Old Testament prophets and prophetesses were a select group of people, New Testament prophets and prophetesses seem to be common and widespread. *See also* cessationism; continuationism; spiritual gifts.

PROPITIATION   One aspect of the atonement, that Christ's death appeased the wrath of God against sinful people. The Old Testament background is the blood of sacrifices that was sprinkled on the mercy seat, thereby assuaging God's wrath and ensuring mercy instead (Lev. 16:11–17). At the heart of propitiation is retributive justice: because God is just, he must punish sin fully. He may exact such deserved punishment from sinful people. Alternatively, he may mercifully mete out that punishment by pouring out his wrath on Christ as "the propitiation . . . for the sins of the whole world" (1 John 2:2). *See also* atonement; expiation; penal substitution theory.

PROPOSITION/PROPOSITIONALISM   In regard to interpretation of Scripture, *proposition* has two senses. (1) A type of communication. As a statement or assertion, a proposition stands in contrast with a promise, command, expressive (praise), and declaration (pronouncement). (2) The content communicated by all types of communication. For example, the warning "There's a snake in the grass!" communicates the danger of being bitten and poisoned if one goes outside. *Propositionalism* refers to the interpretive practice of distilling all literary kinds (e.g., poems, narratives) into a proposition. An example is the reduction of the poetry of Psalm 139 to the propositions "God knows everything" and "God is everywhere." *See also* hermeneutics; theological method.

PROTESTANT SCHOLASTICISM   *See* scholasticism (Protestant).

PROTESTANTISM   The theological and ecclesiastical movements that arose in the sixteenth century in protest against Roman Catholicism. Major tenets: (1) the material principle of justification by God's grace alone accomplished through the work of Christ alone and appropriated by faith alone; and (2) the formal principle of *sola Scriptura* ("Scripture alone") that the Bible alone is the supreme authority for theology and church practice. Originally developed as several diverse yet related reformations against Roman Catholicism (Lutheran, Reformed, Anglican, and Anabaptist), Protestantism has spawned other movements (e.g., Baptist, Methodist/Wesleyan, Pentecostal). It has also spread missionally into most corners of the globe. *See also* authority of Scripture; justification; Roman Catholicism; *solas* of Protestantism.

PROTOEVANGELIUM *See* gospel.

PROVIDENCE The continuing work of God to sustain this created universe in existence and to direct it toward its end. Providence (from Lat. *providere*, "to provide beforehand") includes (1) preservation, God's work to maintain the creation in existence and functioning as he designed it; (2) cooperation, God's work of collaborating with all created realities as they act and occur; and (3) government, God's work of directing the creation toward its divinely purposed end. Some theologies hold to meticulous providence: God ordains and controls everything that happens. Others hold to general providence: God attends broadly but not exhaustively to what occurs. *See also* concurrence; decree; evil, the problem of; miracle; omnipotence; predestination.

PURGATORY According to Catholic theology, the temporary state of purification of the faithful who were not fully obedient in this life. Bearing the stain of forgiven mortal sins and that of venial sins, these faithful experience the temporal punishment for sin in purgatory. When their purification is completed, they go to heaven. Support includes 2 Maccabees 12:38–45 (an apocryphal writing) and 1 Corinthians 3:15 and Matthew 12:32 (both misinterpreted). The evangelical doctrine of justification renders purgatory superfluous, because Christians have been declared not guilty but completely righteous. As a result, they do not need any final purification for their sins. *See also* indulgences; mortal sin; penance; venial sin.

PURITANISM The expression of Reformed theology and ecclesiology in England and America in the sixteenth and seventeenth centuries. Two protests were raised against the Anglican Church's compromised Protestantism: it should not be governed according to episcopalianism, and it needed doctrinal, liturgical, and spiritual reform according to Scripture alone. The Puritans sought to purify the church: they embraced both presbyterianism and congregationalism and oriented their theology, worship, and spirituality according to Calvinism. This Puritan renewal followed the colonists to America and became influential in New England. Key contributors and contributions included John Owen, Jonathan Edwards, and the Westminster Confession of Faith. *See also* Anglicanism; Reformed theology.

QUESTS FOR THE HISTORICAL JESUS With regard to Christology, several historical-critical approaches to discovering the "real" Jesus behind the Gospel accounts. The first quest sought to extract Jesus from his first-century Palestinian world and to demonstrate that the faith of the church was not based on the real Jesus. The second quest focused on Jesus as an eschatological prophet whose radical call to commitment, when stripped of its first-century trappings, could be reshaped to accommodate many viewpoints. The current third quest treats seriously Jesus's historical context, seeking to interpret him and his claims to messiahship as historically relevant and real. *See also* biblical criticism; Christology; theological method.

QUMRAN The central location for the Essenes, a sect of Judaism, in which the Dead Sea Scrolls were discovered. Founded in the second century BC near the Dead Sea, the community of Essenes at Qumran was characterized by severe asceticism. In the war between the Romans and the Jews, the Essenes sided with the insurgents. Before the Romans could conquer Qumran (AD 68), the Essenes hid scrolls containing their religious texts in caves in the hillside. In 1947 some Bedouin shepherds stumbled on those scrolls hidden in jars in a cave. The Dead Sea Scrolls are invaluable for the text of the Hebrew Bible.

QUR'AN The sacred text of Islam. The Qur'an (from Arabic *qara'a*, "the recitation") was revealed by Allah to the prophet Muhammad through the angel Gabriel between AD 609 and 632. Muhammad received and memorized and then recited to others the verbal revelation, and Islam claims that Allah protected the copying of the Qur'an so that it has been perfectly preserved. Major tenets: (1) monotheism: the one God created all that exists, which is therefore completely dependent on him; (2) eschatology: on the Day of Judgment, God the judge will evaluate and reward the good and the evil according to their deeds.

R

RADICAL REFORMATION One type of Protestant movement that developed in the sixteenth century from Conrad Grebel, Balthasar Hubmaier, and Menno Simons. The radical Reformation denied any role for the civil government in matters of the church. Indeed, it broke from the centuries-old church-state relationship, insisting instead that churches be free of state influence and control. It stands in contrast to the magisterial Reformation, which continued to accord magistrates, or civil authorities, a key role in church life, worship, and government. Closely associated with Anabaptist movements, the radical Reformation also denounced infant baptism and instituted believer's baptism in its place. *See also* Anabaptism; believer's baptism; infant baptism; magisterial Reformation.

RANSOM TO SATAN THEORY An early model of the atonement, or what Christ's death accomplished. Major tenets: (1) Satan usurped God's rightful ownership of human beings; thus, they belong illegitimately to Satan. (2) Christ's death was the ransom that was paid to free people from this situation, and it was paid to Satan. (3) Although he demanded Christ for a ransom, Satan did not anticipate the consequences of this exchange, for once Satan possessed Christ, he was forced to let Christ go free. This theory fails, having no biblical basis. *See also* atonement; *Christus Victor*; governmental theory; moral influence theory; Origen; penal substitution theory; redemption; satisfaction theory.

RAPTURE An event associated with the return of Christ. The rapture (from Lat. *rapere*, "to catch up") is a catching up of the church on earth preceding Christ's return. For some, the rapture occurs before the seven-year period of tribulation preceding Christ's return. The purpose is to remove the church and bring it to heaven so that it will be spared the evil and punishment of the tribulation. For others, the rapture occurs immediately before Christ's return for the purpose of catching up the church to meet Christ as he descends from heaven on his return to earth. *See also* dispensational premillennialism; Great Tribulation; historic premillennialism; second coming.

RATIONALISM The philosophy that emphasizes human reason above other ways of knowing. Though related to reason—the intellectual capacity to engage in thinking, to understand, to make judgments, and more—rationalism claims this capacity is the most important and sure means of knowing (above, e.g., sense perception). As a movement, rationalism is associated with the Enlightenment and modernism; it claims that supernatural explanations of reality—God, angels, the soul, miracles, divine providence—are unwarranted and unnecessary. Indeed, rationalism means that reason reigns above divine revelation (Scripture) and religion (the church, and its doctrines and traditions), challenging the Christian faith. *See also* Enlightenment, the; Kant, Immanuel; liberalism; modernism/modernity; reason.

REAL PRESENCE OF CHRIST   With respect to the celebration of the Lord's Supper, the position that in some way Christ is physically present. One form of this position is Catholic theology's transubstantiation: the bread and the wine of the Eucharist are supernaturally changed in substance into Christ's body and blood, so he is physically present. Another form is Lutheran theology's consubstantiation: Christ is physically present "in, with, and under" the bread and wine. These positions are countered by the spiritual presence view—Christ is spiritually, not physically, present—and the memorial view that the Lord's Supper is a remembrance of Christ's death. *See also* consubstantiation; Eucharist; "in, with, and under"; Lord's Supper; memorial view; spiritual presence of Christ; transubstantiation.

REALISM   The philosophical view that universals are real, not merely conceptual. A perennial debate in metaphysics, the philosophy of the nature of reality, is whether universal categories like dog-ness (that which all particular dogs have in common, rendering them dogs) or beauty-ness (that which all particular beautiful people have in common, rendering them beautiful) exist, or if those universals are only conceptual. Realism claims that universals and particulars exist; nominalism claims that only particulars exist. Particular dogs resemble one another because they share universal dog-ness; particular beautiful people resemble one another because they share universal beauty-ness. Platonic philosophy exemplifies realism. *See also* metaphysics; nominalism; Platonism.

REASON The capacity of the mind to engage in logical thinking, investigate facts and draw conclusions, and relate ideas together and make value judgments. Some theologies hold that creation in God's image has particular reference to human reason: to be made in the divine image is to be rational beings. Even the fall into sin did not devastate reason. Other theologies reject this illegitimate reduction of the image to rationality and/or dismiss the idea that sin has not wreaked complete havoc with reason. Importantly for Christians, faith and reason are not in opposition, as "faith seeking understanding" is properly pursued. *See also* faith; fideism; *fides quaerens intellectum*; mind.

RECONCILIATION With respect to the doctrine of salvation, one aspect of the atonement of Jesus Christ. Reconciliation is set against the backdrop of enmity: because of human sin, there is hostility between God and his human creatures. The need is for someone to remove that antagonism and restore peace between these two warring parties. God acted "through him [Christ] to reconcile to himself all things, whether on earth or in heaven, making peace by the blood of his cross" (Col. 1:20). Having reconciled the world to himself, God sends his friends to announce the gospel of reconciliation (2 Cor. 5:18–21). *See also* atonement; mediator; peace.

REDEMPTION With respect to the doctrine of salvation, one aspect of the atonement of Christ. Redemption is set against the backdrop of enslavement: human beings are captive to the slavery of sin. The need is for someone to pay a ransom and set slaves free from such bondage. Christ gave "his life as a ransom" for sinners (Mark 10:45); thus, "in him we have redemption through his blood, the forgiveness of our trespasses, according to the riches of his grace" (Eph. 1:7; cf. 1 Pet. 1:18–19). Redemption, which begins in this life, ultimately includes the resurrection of the body (Rom. 8:23). *See also* atonement; forgiveness; ransom to Satan theory; sin.

REFORMATION   *See* Protestantism.

REFORMED THEOLOGY   The theological tradition of Protestants who closely follow Augustine and the Reformers, especially Huldrych Zwingli and John Calvin, and whose churches include Presbyterian, Reformed, and Reformed Baptists. Major tenets: (1) the three foundational covenants of redemption, of works, and of grace; (2) a view that sees more continuity than discontinuity between the Old and New Testaments; and (3) an emphasis on the supremacy of the sovereignty and glory of God. In its most succinct expression, Reformed theology holds to the five points of Calvinism (TULIP): *t*otal depravity, *u*nconditional election, *l*imited atonement, *i*rresistible grace, and *p*erseverance of the saints. *See also* Arminian theology; Augustinian theology; Calvinism / John Calvin; order of salvation (*ordo salutis*).

REGENERATION   The mighty work of God by which unbelievers are given a new nature, being born again. Regeneration is particularly ascribed to the Holy Spirit (John 3:3–8) working through the gospel (James 1:18; 1 Pet. 1:23–25). It is both (1) the removal of one's old, sinful nature, and (2) the imparting of a new nature that is responsive to God. Unlike conversion, which is the human response to the gospel, regeneration is completely a divine work, to which human beings contribute nothing. Reformed theology holds that regeneration precedes conversion. Arminian theology maintains that conversion, enabled by prevenient grace, precedes regeneration. *See also* Arminian theology; conversion; gospel; Holy Spirit, work of the; prevenient grace; Reformed theology.

REGULATIVE PRINCIPLE   One of two historical principles (the other being the normative principle) by which the church determines which elements may be incorporated into its worship service. Major tenets: (1) The church must worship God according to the way he finds acceptable. (2) Scripture regulates specific elements of worship, insisting that it must be intelligible, purposeful, orderly, and proper (1 Cor. 11:2–16; 14:26–40). (3) Thus, a biblical warrant (e.g., a command) is required for including an element in worship, and if no such warrant exists for it, that element must be excluded. The regulative principle is associated with Reformed theology. *See also* liturgy / liturgical theology; normative principle; Reformed theology; theological method; worship.

RELATIVISM The position that truth and meaning are qualified according to each person, culture, situation, and time period; no universal, objective truth and meaning exist. Furthermore, all knowing is relative to the knower, all ethical norms (good and evil) are relative to the culture and context, and all realities (e.g., human nature, gender) are relative to those experiencing them. While acknowledging the situatedness of people, culture, and context, theism rejects relativism. It underscores the givenness of the world and its reality as created by God and emphasizes that the objective claim that there is no objective meaning and truth is self-contradictory. *See also* logical positivism; postmodernism.

REPENTANCE One aspect of conversion (the other being faith), which is the human response to the gospel. Repentance is changing one's mind and life. It involves an acknowledgment that one's thoughts, words, and actions are sinful and thus grievous to God; a sorrow for one's sin; and a decision to break with sin. Though a fully human response, repentance is not merely human because it is prompted by grace. For some, prevenient grace is given to all people, enabling them to repent. For others, saving grace is given only to the elect, enabling them to repent when hearing the gospel. *See also* conversion; faith; prevenient grace; saving faith; saving grace.

REPRESENTATIVE HEADSHIP OF ADAM The doctrine that by God's design in creation, the human race was constituted in Adam, who was appointed the representative head of all human beings. Also called federal headship, it maintains that Adam stood before God as humanity's representative: as he would go, so it would go. Thus, when Adam sinned, the entire human race, whom he represented, sinned. This representative headship explains original sin—people are guilty and corrupt because when Adam fell, they fell as well. Support includes the parallelism of Adam and Christ as the two heads of the human race (Rom. 5:12–21). *See also* Adamic covenant; fall; federal headship; natural headship of Adam; original sin; Reformed theology; sin.

REPROBATION In terms of the doctrine of salvation, one aspect of predestination (the other being election), or God's decree regarding the eternal destinies of people. Reprobation is the sovereign, eternal purpose of God not to save certain people but to give them over to their sins, for which he justly punishes them. This divine decision is not based on foreknowledge of people's unbelief and evil deeds. Still, though the divine decision is not favorable for the reprobate, they willingly sin and are held accountable for it, and they are rightly punished. Reformed theology holds to reprobation; Arminian theology rejects it. *See also* Arminian theology; decree; election; foreknowledge; predestination; Reformed theology.

REST Intentional suspension of ordinary work for the purpose of refreshment and relaxation. Such repose is not the cessation of activity but the purposeful substitution of one activity for another. Varieties include: (1) rest from having to achieve favor before God through one's best human works, because Christ's righteousness is imputed through faith; (2) rest from worrying about life's necessities, because one trusts that God provides for one's needs; (3) rest from humanly imposed legalism that acts as a straitjacket, enjoying instead freedom in Christ; (4) future rest from wearying labor for Christ in the rewards of the life to come. *See also* justification; legalism; Sabbath/Sabbatarianism.

RESURRECTION OF CHRIST Jesus's return to bodily existence three days after his crucifixion. Jesus's death involved the separation of his soul and body; his body was placed in a tomb while he, being disembodied, continued to exist. After three days, he rose from the dead, returning to earthly life with a glorified body. His grave clothes were laid aside, and his body had features of both continuity (it bore the marks of his crucifixion) and discontinuity (it could pass through doors). This resurrection was a work in which the Father (Acts 2:24), Son (John 10:17–18), and Spirit (Rom. 8:11) participated. *See also* Christology; exaltation of Christ; humiliation of Christ.

RESURRECTION OF PEOPLE   Rising again, with reembodiment, after death. The Old Testament envisions this hope (Dan. 12:1–2), and Jesus highlighted it. He called himself "the resurrection and the life," promising to his disciples a return to life with reembodiment (John 11:25). The apostles testified to Jesus's resurrection, which is an essential part of the gospel. Christ's resurrection paves the way for the general resurrection. Bodies in their earthly existence are perishable, shameful, weak, and natural. At Christ's return, disembodied believers in heaven will receive imperishable, glorious, strong, Spirit-dominated bodies (1 Cor. 15:42–44), as will living believers through an immediate transformation of their earthly bodies. Unbelievers in torment will be resurrected to eternal condemnation. *See also* death; embodiment; glorification; resurrection of Christ.

REVELATION, GENERAL   *See* general revelation.

REVELATION, SPECIAL   *See* special revelation.

REVIVALISM   A movement distinguished by widespread conversion to Christ and renewal of the church. Historically, the church has experienced times of revival, as seen in monasticism, the Reformation, pietism, Puritanism, the Great Awakening, eighteenth- and nineteenth-century revivals, Pentecostalism / charismatic movement, the Jesus movement, and more. Characteristics of revivalism: (1) a deep sense of repentance for the carnal state of the church; (2) intense, expectant prayer for God to send renewal; (3) preaching the gospel to large numbers of people, many of whom are converted; (4) flourishing of churches in terms of worship, devotion to Christ, sanctification, and missional and social engagement. *See also* evangelism; mission.

RIGHTEOUSNESS   As an attribute of God, his uprightness of person, ways, standards, and judgments. God himself is perfectly righteous, as are his ways in creation, providence, salvation, and consummation (Deut. 32:4). As righteous himself, God establishes moral standards that reflect his nature, and he requires conformity to those standards. His judgments of his creatures are righteous: he always and justly rewards obedience to his standards, and he always and justly punishes disobedience to them. Because God is righteous, his people should be fair and impartial in their judgments, and they should champion what is right and abhor what is wrong.

ROMAN CATHOLICISM The branch of Christendom led by the pope. The initial division between Catholic and Orthodox churches occurred in 1054; Protestantism separated from Catholicism during the Reformation. Key differences between the latter: (1) revelation: Catholicism affirms two aspects, Scripture and Tradition; Protestantism embraces Scripture alone; (2) justification: Catholicism considers justification to include forgiveness, regeneration, and sanctification; Protestantism restricts justification to the declaration of being not guilty but righteous instead; (3) grace: Catholicism maintains grace is infused through the sacraments, rendering the faithful capable of cooperating with it to merit eternal life; Protestantism considers grace to be imputed through faith. *See also* Eastern Orthodoxy; imputation; infusion; merit; Protestantism; transubstantiation.

S

SABBATH/SABBATARIANISM The Sabbath is the seventh day, on which God rested and which he then consecrated for his people's benefit. The Sabbath was a day for Israel to cease its normal work, patterned after divine creation and rest and in remembrance of the exodus. Jesus observed the Sabbath but liberated it from the suffocating regulations imposed on it. Insistence that one day per week be set aside for worship and rest is called Sabbatarianism. Grounded in the creation ordinance, and transferring Sabbath instructions from the seventh to the first day of the week because of Jesus's resurrection, Christian Sabbatarianism prescribes Sunday as the church's consecrated day. *See also* rest; vocation; worship.

SABELLIANISM   *See* Monarchianism.

SACERDOTALISM   The doctrine that priestly mediation between God and sinful people is necessary for salvation to occur. Sacerdotalism (from Lat. *sacerdotale*, "priestly") is especially associated with Catholicism, Orthodoxy, and Anglicanism. The authority to act as mediators between God and people is conferred on priests through a sacrament of consecration; for example, holy orders in the Catholic Church bestows on priests a sacred power to act in the person of Christ the head. Following Paul's affirmation that Christ is the only mediator between God and people (1 Tim. 2:5), most Protestants denounce sacerdotalism and champion the priesthood of all believers. *See also* holy orders; mediator; ordination; priesthood; priesthood of believers.

SACRAMENT   A rite or ordinance of Christianity. From *sacramentum*, used in Latin Bibles to translate the Greek word *mystērion* ("mystery"), *sacrament* was associated with mystery; sacraments were mysteries of the Christian faith. Augustine's definition became standard: a sacrament is a visible sign of an invisible grace. The Catholic Church has seven sacraments: baptism, confirmation, the Eucharist, penance and reconciliation, extreme unction, holy orders, and matrimony. Protestant churches have two: baptism and the Lord's Supper. This reduction in number was because (1) Jesus ordained only these two rites (baptism, Matt. 28:19; Lord's Supper, Matt. 26:26–29), and (2) they have tangible signs (water, bread and wine) associated with them. *See also* baptism; Lord's Supper; marriage; mystery; ordinance.

SACRIFICE *See* atonement.

SAINTS Holy people, consecrated to the Lord. Scripture addresses "those sanctified in Christ Jesus, called to be saints" (1 Cor. 1:2), an address not limited to certain leaders but made to all Christians. The saintliness of saints is (1) positional, because they are righteous in Christ; (2) purposive, the goal of greater holiness toward which they strive; and (3) instrumental, the maturing process by which they become more saintly. According to Catholic theology, certain Christians have lived virtuously and faithfully by grace and are canonized as saints, models whom Catholics venerate by invoking their prayers, help, and blessings. Protestants do not venerate saints. *See also* holiness of the church; sanctification.

SALVATION Rescue from sin and condemnation through the divine intervention of forgiveness and the gift of eternal life. Salvation has two aspects: (1) It was accomplished through the perfect obedience, sacrificial death, and resurrection of Christ. (2) It is announced in the gospel and appropriated by people through repentance and faith in Christ's saving work. A major division between Catholicism and Protestantism is whether salvation is appropriated by divine grace through faith, which enables the faithful to cooperate with grace infused through the sacraments so as to merit eternal life (Catholicism), or if it is received by faith alone (Protestantism). *See also* gospel; merit; saving faith; saving grace; *solas* of Protestantism; soteriology.

SANCTIFICATION The cooperative work of God and Christians (Phil. 2:12–13) by which ongoing transformation into greater Christlikeness occurs. Such maturing transpires particularly through the Holy Spirit (2 Cor. 3:18; Gal. 5:16–23) and the Word of God (John 17:17). Unlike other divine works, which are monergistic (God alone works), sanctification is synergistic. God operates in ways that are proper to his divine agency (e.g., convicting of sin, empowering by the Spirit, willing and working to accomplish his good pleasure), and Christians work in ways that are proper to their human agency (e.g., reading Scripture, praying, mortifying sin, yielding to the Spirit). *See also* filled with the Holy Spirit; Keswick theology; monergism; mortification; perfectionism; saints; synergism; Wesleyanism / John Wesley.

SATAN   As "the prince of this world" (John 12:31 NIV) and "the god of this age" (2 Cor. 4:4 NIV), Satan is the head of the realm of demons. Though originally created good with all the angels, Satan fell from his lofty position as the supreme angel by rebelling against God, being cast down to earth, on which he now opposes God as the "evil one." His names indicate his evil activities with regard to humans: as Satan, he is the "adversary" (Heb. *satan*); as the Devil, he is the "slanderer" (Gk. *diabolos*); as Apollyon, he is the "destroyer" (Gk. *apollyon*); as the "ancient serpent" (Rev. 12:9), he is the liar and slayer of life. *See also* demons.

SATISFACTION THEORY   A model of the atonement, or what Christ's death accomplished. Major tenets: (1) Sin is robbing God of his honor. (2) People must render satisfaction for their sin: they must repay—actually, pay more than—the honor they have stolen from God. (3) People cannot pay their debt, for whatever they could pay is owed already to God. (4) Only the God-man can offer satisfaction. (5) By dying, Jesus gave something that he did not owe to God—the obligation to die—and thus obtained a reward. (6) Christ gave this reward to provide satisfaction for people's sin. *See also* atonement; *Christus Victor*; governmental theory; moral influence theory; penal substitution theory; ransom to Satan theory.

SAVING FAITH   One aspect of conversion (the other being repentance), which is the human response to the gospel. Saving faith, which is belief and personal trust prompted by God's grace, involves an understanding of the gospel, an assent to one's need for forgiveness, and a decision to trust Christ to personally save. It contains perseverance as an essential element. Saving faith stands in contrast with bogus faith, which is mere intellectual understanding or assent. Examples include temporary faith (Matt. 13:20–21) or apparent faith (Heb. 6:4–10). It differs also from prevenient grace, which enables people to believe but may not endure. *See also* Arminian theology; conversion; faith; perseverance; prevenient grace; Reformed theology; repentance.

SAVING GRACE The favor that God grants to save, sanctify, and glorify believers. It is termed "saving" to distinguish it from "common" grace, which is God's favor shown to both believers and unbelievers alike. Common grace is not designed to rescue sinful people. That is the purpose of saving grace, which calls, justifies, unites to Christ, regenerates, adopts, sanctifies, preserves, and glorifies those whom God elects to be saved. It is also called "saving" (in Reformed theology) to distinguish it from "prevenient" grace (in Arminian theology), which is divine favor that goes before all people, preparing them to embrace salvation. *See also* Arminian theology; common grace; prevenient grace; Reformed theology.

SCHLEIERMACHER, FRIEDRICH The father of liberal Protestant theology. Seeking to explain the Christian religion in a way that would appeal to his sophisticated friends, he authored *On Religion: Speeches to Its Cultured Despisers* (1799). Breaking with Kant's proposal that God is completely transcendent, Schleiermacher reenvisioned religion as the feeling of absolute dependence on the world spirit. His *Christian Faith* (1821/1822) is a reformulation of Christian doctrines around his idea of religion as an intuition of immediate self-consciousness. Schleiermacher also significantly developed the field of philosophical hermeneutics. His liberal theology prompted strong reaction from theologians like Karl Barth and Emil Brunner. *See also* Barth, Karl; hermeneutics; liberalism; theological method.

SCHLEITHEIM CONFESSION The confessional document that defined the original Anabaptist movement in Switzerland and southern Germany. Written in 1527, it addressed seven concerns: (1) baptism administered to those who have repented, believed in Christ for the forgiveness of sins, and walk in him (i.e., believer's, not infant, baptism); (2) the exercise of church discipline, including excommunication; (3) the Lord's Supper administered only to those who have first undergone believer's baptism; (4) separation from all evil, including Catholic and Protestant churches; (5) qualified pastors for leading the church; (6) separation of church and state, which prohibited involvement in civil government; and (7) the prohibition of swearing of oaths. *See also* Anabaptism; believer's baptism; church discipline; infant baptism; Lord's Supper; radical Reformation.

SCHOLASTICISM (CATHOLIC) The scholarly approach and method employed by theologians in the latter part of the Middle Ages. The scholastic (from Lat. *scholasticus*, "learned") approach joined Christian theology and classical philosophy (especially that of Aristotle) and sought to demonstrate the compatibility of faith and reason. Indeed, theology developed as "faith seeking understanding." The scholastic method featured composing lists of contradictory statements from various authoritative sources and then applying logic to discover their agreement. Important scholastic figures included Anselm, Abelard, Duns Scotus, William of Ockham, Bonaventure, and Thomas Aquinas. After the Reformation, scholasticism emerged in Protestant form and influenced that theology. *See also* Aristotelianism; scholasticism (Protestant); theological method; Thomism / Thomas Aquinas.

SCHOLASTICISM (PROTESTANT) The theological approach and framework of classical Protestant orthodoxy. Protestant scholasticism (from Lat. *scholasticus*, "learned"), drawing upon its Catholic predecessor, was an attempt to preserve the heritage of the Reformation in the two centuries following Luther and Calvin. Though often criticized as an intellectualistic distortion of their theology, scholasticism closely followed the Reformers' doctrine. It also was concerned for the purity of Lutheran and Reformed theology against a revived Catholicism and the Socinian heresy. Theologians like the Lutherans Hollaz and Quenstedt, and the

Reformed Witsius and Turretin, produced important theological works, often polemical in nature. *See also* Lutheranism / Martin Luther; Reformed theology; scholasticism (Catholic); theological method.

SCRIPTURE The written revelation of God concerning himself and his ways. Composed over many centuries through the collaborative work of the Holy Spirit (inspiration) and human authors (e.g., prophets, apostles), this progressive revelation presents a story line of creation, fall, redemption, and consummation. Divinely inspired Scripture is authoritative, possessing the supreme right to command faith and obedience; truthful, always affirming the truth; sufficient, providing wisdom leading to salvation and instruction for pleasing God fully; necessary, being the ultimate way of divine communication; clear, written so as to be understood; and powerful, effecting salvation and transformation of life for those who obey it. *See also* authority of Scripture; God-breathed; inerrancy; infallibility of Scripture; inspiration of Scripture; necessity of Scripture; perspicuity of Scripture; sufficiency of Scripture.

SECOND COMING With respect to eschatology, the future return of Jesus Christ. At his first coming two thousand years ago, Christ's purpose was "to bear the sins of many." He "will appear a second time, not to deal with sin but to save those who are eagerly waiting for him" (Heb. 9:28). Christ will return personally, bodily, suddenly, and triumphantly. Though the time of this return is established, human beings cannot know it (Matt. 24:36). Two key debates are (1) whether the second coming will be preceded by the rapture of the church before the seven-year period of Great Tribulation, and (2) its relationship to the millennium. *See also* amillennialism; dispensational premillennialism; Great Tribulation; historic premillennialism; postmillennialism; rapture.

SECOND HELVETIC CONFESSION The most widely received Reformed confession of faith of the sixteenth century. It was written by Heinrich Bullinger in 1566 to explain Reformed theology in German-speaking Switzerland (Lat. *Helvetia*) and Germany. Whereas the First Helvetic Confession united the Reformed movements in Switzerland, the Second Confession was also adopted by the Reformed movements in France, Hungary, Poland, and Scotland. It addresses the doctrines of Scripture and its interpretation, the Trinity, providence, creation, the fall, free will and regeneration, predestination, Christ and the atonement, and salvation. It also discusses the church and its ministry, sacraments, and relationship to the state. *See also* Reformed theology.

SECULARISM A movement that promotes the consideration of human existence and experience from a natural, nonreligious viewpoint. Secularism (from Lat. *saeculum*, "of this age") rejects a religious orientation to life, maintaining that the reality of this world is shaped, and can be completely explained, by natural, rather than supernatural, causes. A criticism is secularism is too simplistic, ignoring the evident work of God in revelation, the incarnation, and transformation of people. When infected with secularism, theology attempts to reduce Christianity to a promotion of natural human feelings and hopes. The sacred-secular divide wrongly limits God to partial lordship. *See also* Enlightenment, the; modernism/ modernity.

SEMI-PELAGIANISM Various theological systems situated between Pelagianism and Augustinianism. Varieties include the fifth-century theology of John Cassian. Key tenets: (1) the human will is free to do good and not only evil, either by creation or through prevenient grace; (2) prevenient grace is given to all people, restoring to them the ability to repent and believe in Christ; (3) by giving his grace, God cooperates with people in salvation; and (4) God predestines people according to his foreknowledge of their faith in Christ and continuation in salvation. *See also* Arminian theology; Augustinian theology; conditional election; foreknowledge; Pelagianism; prevenient grace; synergism; Wesleyanism / John Wesley.

SERAPHIM In regard to angelology, an order of immaterial/spiritual beings (creatures that have been created without a body) presented only once in Scripture. A seraph is described as having "six wings: with two he covered his face, and with two he covered his feet, and with two he flew" (Isa. 6:2). The seraphim are pictured as standing above the throne of God, and together they engage in continuous worship of God by calling out to one another, "Holy, holy, holy is the LORD of hosts; the whole earth is full of his glory!" (6:3). Their relationship to angelic beings is unknown. *See also* angels.

SERVANT/SERVICE A servant is one who has been created, saved, and called to minister in gospel-centered ministry. Service is directed to the expansion of God's glory, the growth of Christians and the church, and the fulfillment of the Great Commission. Jesus, who forever serves, is the prototypical servant: he "came not to be served but to serve" (Mark 10:45). His disciples are commissioned with gospel ministry; thus, they are stewards, ambassadors who bear the responsibility to carry out the mission of God. As they faithfully serve through his gifts and empowerment, the church grows through divine resources and Spirit-assisted human effort (Eph. 4:11–16). *See also* deacon/deaconess/diaconate; ministry.

SESSION OF CHRIST One aspect of Christ's state of exaltation. Following his preexistent state and state of humiliation, Christ's state of exaltation began with his resurrection and ascension. Elevated to the right hand of God—the position of authority—Christ sat down (*session*, or seating) as Lord (Eph. 1:20–21). Prophesied of the Messiah (Ps. 110:1), his session confirmed his completed work of salvation, initiated his ministry of eternal intercession for his followers (Rom. 8:34; Heb. 7:25), and gave him authority both to send the Holy Spirit to inaugurate the church (Acts 2:33) and to charge it with the Great Commission (Matt. 28:18–20). *See also* Christology; exaltation of Christ; humiliation of Christ; intercession.

SEX/SEXUALITY Sex is the act of intercourse involving the genitals, and sexuality is the desire for and habit of engaging in such acts. God, being immaterial, is nonsexual, without sexual characteristics. He has created embodied human beings with male and female characteristics and thus as sexual beings. To them God has given the mandate for procreation: "Be fruitful and multiply and fill the earth" (Gen. 1:28). As designed by God, sex is (1) between a husband and a wife, good, monogamous, and (2) intended for pleasure, physical and relational oneness, comfort, procreation, and protection against sexual immorality. Sexuality should be expressed in God-glorifying and spouse-honoring ways. *See also* embodiment; gender; human nature; humanity / human being.

SHAME   A condition provoked by a sense of failure to obey or to meet expectations. Shame is related to guilt, as seen with naked Adam and Eve's unashamed transparency that gave way after the fall to a feeling of shame that prompted them to hide their nakedness (Gen. 2:24; 3:7). It may be related to humiliation and regret, illustrated by the Christian who hides their family's addictions and poverty. "To shame" is to direct that sense at others by exposing their defects, as Christ did to his enemies (Col. 2:15). A false sense of shame leads to self-scolding and self-recrimination. *See also* guilt.

SIN   Any lack of conformity to the moral law of God. Such nonconformity applies to one's (1) being: the "sin nature," or tendency to sin; (2) actions: evil deeds like idolatry and murder; (3) attitudes: wrong mind-sets like envy and pride; (4) words: inappropriate communications like gossip and slander; and (5) motivations: disoriented purposes like self-glorification and people pleasing. Elements included in sin are unfaithfulness, disobedience, pride, rebellion, deception, indifference, and hopelessness. Original sin is the state of all human beings at birth, consisting of guilt and/ or corruption. This sinful tendency is the root of actual sins that violate God's law. *See also* concupiscence; law; mortal sin; original sin; sin nature; venial sin.

SIN, ORIGINAL   *See* original sin.

SIN NATURE   The corrupt essence that characterizes all human beings from the moment of their conception. While some theologies reject the doctrine of original guilt (the liability to suffer condemnation because of Adam's sin) as one aspect of original sin, they all agree with this aspect of original corruption, the sinful nature with its tendency toward evil. Some theologies further detail this corruption as consisting of total depravity, the infection of every element of human nature with sin, and total inability, the incapacity to reorient oneself from self-centeredness to God. The sin nature is the source of all actual sins. *See also* corruption; guilt; original sin; sin; total depravity; total inability.

SINLESSNESS OF CHRIST   *See* impeccability.

SOCIAL TRINITY   The perspective on the Godhead that emphasizes that the Father, the Son, and the Holy Spirit are intimately and dynamically related to each other in a divine community or society (hence, *social*). As three distinct persons, they are characterized by three centers of consciousness, equal in essence and expressing love, glory, will, and purpose. At the same time, the three are personally related and perfectly united in harmony because of the divine perichoresis, or mutual indwelling, of the Father in the Son, the Son in the Father, the Father in the Spirit, and so on. They are three "persons-in-community." *See also* economic Trinity; ontological Trinity; *perichoresis*; Trinity.

SOCINIANISM   A heretical movement founded by Faustus Socinus (1539–1604) and his uncle, Lelio Socinus (1525–62). Its major tenets, as set forth in the Racovian Catechism (published in Rakow, Poland, in 1605), include (1) an emphasis on reason over divine revelation, (2) a denial of the deity of Christ, (3) a repudiation of original sin and the predestination of the elect and the reprobate, (4) a criticism of the satisfaction theory of the atonement, and (5) a denial of the Trinity. Socinianism was combated by both Roman Catholicism and Protestantism. Despite this resistance, Socinianism had a significant liberalizing influence throughout Europe.

SOLAS OF PROTESTANTISM   Five principles by which Protestantism defined itself against Catholicism. *Sola fidei* refers to the appropriation of salvation by "faith alone," not faith plus works meriting eternal life. *Sola gratia* refers to the accomplishment of salvation being by "grace alone" without human cooperation. *Sola scriptura* refers to the foundation of the faith being "Scripture alone," not Scripture plus Tradition. *Soli Deo gloria* refers to giving "glory only to God" for salvation and not giving special honor, for example, to Mary. *Solus Christus* refers to salvation being wrought by "Christ alone," without the merits of Mary and the saints.

SON OF GOD   One of the divine titles of Jesus Christ. At twelve, Jesus already had a consciousness of being uniquely related to his Father (Luke 2:41–49). Still, it awaited his baptism for his Sonship to be publicly announced by the Father (Mark 1:9–11). As Jesus lived and ministered, Satan and the demons acknowledged his identity as the Son of God (Matt. 4:1–11; 8:28–34), his disciples began to understand through revelation and Jesus's miracles (Matt. 16:13–20; 14:28–33), and his enemies charged him with blasphemy (Matt. 26:63–66). He died, rose, and lives forever as the unique Son of God (Rom. 1:4). In a derivative sense, Adam, Israel, David and his kingly descendants, and Christians (Gal. 4:4–7) are "sons" of God. *See also* Christology; Jesus Christ, deity of.

SON OF MAN   One of Jesus's divine titles. In the Old Testament, the expression referred to a heavenly being who would appear gloriously in the future as ruler over an eternal kingdom (Dan. 7:13–14). One of Jesus's preferred titles for himself, "Son of Man" became associated with Jesus's incarnation and ascension (John 3:13; 6:62). His use of this divine title was not lost on his enemies: when Jesus claimed to be the Son of Man, "the high priest tore his robes and said, 'He has uttered blasphemy'" (Matt. 26:65). He will return as the triumphant Son of Man (Rev. 14:14). *See also* Christology; Davidic covenant; Jesus Christ, deity of; second coming.

SOTERIOLOGY   One of the topics of systematic theology, being the doctrine of salvation (Gk. *sotēria*). It encompasses all the mighty acts of God in delivering people from sin and condemnation and bringing them salvation. These acts include election (God's gracious choice of his people), effective calling (God's summons to salvation), regeneration (new birth by the Spirit), conversion (the human response of repentance and faith), justification (God's declaration of forgiveness and the imputation of Christ's righteousness), adoption (inclusion in God's family), union (identification) with Christ, sanctification (progress in salvation), perseverance (God's work to retain Christians in salvation), and glorification (completion and fullness of salvation). *See also* gospel; salvation.

SOUL   The immaterial aspect of human nature, which also includes a material aspect, or body. Commonly, the soul is considered to be the mind/reason, feelings, will, motivations, purposing, and the capacity for relationship with God and others. Some distinguish between soul and spirit, the former encompassing intellect, emotions, and will, and the latter being the relational capacity. Traditionally, discussions of the soul's origin have focused on either creationism (God creates the soul) or traducianism (it is derived from parents). With the rise of neurophysiology, this classical debate has yielded to models that treat human nature as an intimate body-soul unity. *See also* creationism; embodiment; human nature; humanity / human being; intermediate state; mind; neurophysiology; traducianism.

SOUL SLEEP   With regard to eschatology, the unorthodox view that people exist in an unconscious condition in the intermediate state, the period between their death and bodily resurrection. Support includes the biblical descriptions of death as "sleep," which is characterized by the absence of memory, praise, and hope (Pss. 6:5; 115:17; Isa. 38:18). But Scripture uses "sleep" as a euphemism for death, pictures a shadowy existence in Sheol ("shades" in the Old Testament; 1 Sam. 28; Isa. 14:9), and presents deceased believers alive in the presence of Christ (2 Cor. 5:1–9; Phil. 1:21–23) and deceased unbelievers in torment (Luke 16:19–31). *See also* death; intermediate state.

SOVEREIGNTY   The divine attribute of being all-powerful as the King and Lord who exercises supreme rule over all creation. Examples include (1) the divine decree regarding creation, providence, redemption, and consummation; (2) the infallible, meticulous outworking of that plan in each and every aspect of it; and (3) the sure salvation of genuine Christians. How divine sovereignty and human freedom and responsibility can be held together is a perennial question; two common proposals are compatibilism and incompatibilism. The issue of how God, who is all-good, can exercise his sovereignty while sin and tragedy abound raises the perplexing problem of evil. *See also* compatibilism; decree; evil, the problem of; incompatibilism; miracle; providence.

SPEAKING IN TONGUES   A gift of the Holy Spirit involving communication in languages or encoded speech. On Pentecost, speaking in tongues was the result of Spirit baptism and manifested itself in the disciples' rehearsing the mighty works of God in languages they had never spoken before (Acts 2:11; 10:46). Speaking in tongues also consists of uttering mysteries that no one understands (1 Cor. 14:2, 9) and expressions of prayer that bypass one's mind (1 Cor. 14:13–17). Such communication, because of not being understood, has limited value. But when combined with interpretation, it is valuable for edifying the church (1 Cor. 14:5). *See also* baptism with/in/by the Holy Spirit; interpretation of tongues; miraculous gifts; Pentecost; Pentecostalism; spiritual gifts.

SPECIAL REVELATION   God's communication of himself to particular people at particular times and in particular places, especially for salvation and to disclose specific knowledge of his nature and attributes, moral law, promises, and ways. Special revelation has five modes: the mighty acts of God, such as the exodus from

Egypt and the conquest of the promised land; dreams and visions, like those he gave to Joseph and Daniel; divine speech, by which God communicated to Adam, Abraham, Moses, and many more; the incarnation, by which God revealed himself in human nature; and Scripture, which is God's written revelation of himself. *See also* general revelation; incarnation; Scripture.

SPEECH-ACT THEORY A philosophy of language that emphasizes that words do things. Pioneered in the twentieth century by John Austin and John Searle, speech-act theory considers every utterance to consist of three interrelated parts: (1) the locution, the content that is communicated ("be anxious for nothing"; "I will come again"); (2) the illocution, the force or intention with which it is communicated (a command; a promise); and (3) the perlocution, the response of the hearer of the speech act (obedience; trust). Applied to the words of God, each divine utterance is a speech act consisting of a locution and an illocution, and which calls forth a perlocution. *See also* Scripture; theological method.

SPIRATION *See* eternal procession.

SPIRIT The immaterial aspect of human nature, which also includes a material aspect, or body. In Scripture, *spirit* is used interchangeably with *soul* (e.g., Luke 1:46–47) and refers to capacities other than bodily ones. Some distinguish between soul and spirit, the former encompassing intellect, emotions, and will, and the latter being the capacity for relationships with God and others. Contemporary discussions focus on human nature as a body-spirit/soul unity. Additionally, *spirit* can refer to a demon, or "unclean" spirit, that oppresses a human being (e.g., Mark 1:23–28). Moreover, *spirit* can refer to the realm of God rather than the realm of the flesh (John 3:6) and can be personalized to refer to the Holy Spirit. *See also* demons; human nature; humanity / human being; soul.

SPIRITUAL GIFTS The Holy Spirit's endowments to believers. The primary purpose of the gifts, such as teaching, leading, exhorting, and giving, is to foster the church's growth, especially by equipping its members for ministry. Other purposes include the confirmation of the gospel and its messengers, provision of a foretaste of the fuller future work of the Spirit, and manifestation of Christ's victory over his enemies. Disagreement exists between cessationists, who believe that some gifts—prophecy, speaking in tongues, interpretation of tongues, word of knowledge, word of wisdom, healings, miracles—have ceased, and continuationists, who believe that all the gifts continue today. *See also* cessationism; continuationism; miraculous gifts.

SPIRITUAL PRESENCE OF CHRIST   With respect to the celebration of the Lord's Supper, the position that Christ is spiritually present. The bread and wine are symbols, but not empty symbols, manifesting Christ's presence. Though Christ's body is in heaven, and thus cannot be present when the church celebrates the Lord's Supper, the Holy Spirit unites heaven and earth. Thus, the church soars up to heaven to be with Christ, or Christ descends to the church, by the Spirit's power. This position opposes real-presence views—transubstantiation and consubstantiation—and goes beyond the memorial view emphasizing a remembrance of Christ's death. *See also* consubstantiation; Eucharist; Lord's Supper; real presence of Christ; transubstantiation.

SPRINKLING   One of the modes of baptism, the others being immersion and pouring. Sprinkling is dispensing a small amount of water over the head of a person. Support includes: (1) Certain biblical rituals employed sprinkling—for example, sprinkling with the blood of bulls and goats (Heb. 9:13). (2) Because baptism symbolizes inward cleansing from sin (Acts 22:16; cf. Ezek. 36:25), sprinkling portrays it well. (3) When infant baptism became the practice of the church, sprinkling became the accepted mode. (4) As is true for pouring, sprinkling works well practically when, for example, the one to be baptized is weak or paralyzed. *See also* immersion; infant baptism; pouring.

STEWARDSHIP A responsibility delegated from one person to another, coming with the authority to discharge the responsibility and the accountability to do so. As God created people in his image, he made them stewards of his creation, charging them with the responsibility to build civilization through procreation and vocation (Gen. 1:26–28). Generally, people are responsible for managing well their resources, gifts, time, and more. Additionally, Christians are given the stewardship of the Great Commandment to love God and others (Matt. 22:34–40) and the Great Commission (28:18–20), being designated as Christ's ambassadors to carry out the ministry of reconciliation (2 Cor. 5:17–21). *See also* humanity / human being; person/ personhood; vocation.

SUBLAPSARIANISM Also called infralapsarianism, one of two Reformed positions regarding the order of God's decrees, the other being supralapsarianism. The issue concerns whether logically, not temporally, God's decree to save people came before (Lat. *supra*) or after (*sub/infra*) his decree to permit the fall (*lapsus*). Sublapsarianism holds this order: (1) God decreed to create people; (2) he decreed to permit the fall; (3) he decreed to elect some to embrace salvation and pass by others. This latter element is an election of sinful humanity. Most Reformed theologians hold to sublapsarianism/infralapsarianism. *See also* decree; election; fall; reprobation; supralapsarianism.

SUBMISSION An act of yielding to those in authority. Ultimate submission is owed to God; allegiance to him takes precedence over obedience to human authorities that contradict him (Acts 5:27–32). Still, submission to rulers is required, for God institutes them and grants them authority (Rom. 13:1–7). Within the family, wives are to submit to their husbands (Eph. 5:22–25) and children are to obey their parents (Eph. 6:1). Within the church, members are to submit to their pastors (Heb. 13:17), who in turn lead in submission to Christ the head. In reverence of him, members submit to one another (Eph. 5:21). *See also* authority; government; obedience.

SUBORDINATIONISM The view of the dependence within the Trinity. Three varieties: (1) Eternal functional subordinationism maintains the Son and the Spirit are eternally dependent on the Father for their personhood—the person-of-the-Son (eternal generation), the person-of-the-Spirit (eternal procession)—though not for their deity. Though differences of relationships and roles exist, the three are completely equal in nature. (2) Economic subordinationism believes the Son was dependent on the Father only during his incarnation. (3) Ontological subordinationism, a heresy, holds the Son and the Spirit are dependent on the Father for their deity and thus inferior to him in nature. *See also* eternal generation; eternal procession; incarnation; Trinity.

SUBSTANCE That which makes something what it is. A substance is something that has attributes, which are of two types: (1) essential attributes are its core and cannot be lost without changing the thing itself; (2) accidental attributes are not its core and can be lost without changing the thing. Some of these accidents—appearance, taste, smell, sound, texture—are perceived by the senses. The term developed importance for Catholicism's doctrine of the Eucharist: in transubstantiation, the accidents of the bread and wine remain the same, but the substance with its essential attributes is transformed into Christ's body and blood. *See also* Aristotelianism; Eucharist; *substantia*; transubstantiation.

SUBSTANTIA In regard to the doctrine of the Trinity, the one essence (that which makes something what it is) that is shared in common by the three persons. Because the early church expounded its doctrine in both Greek and Latin, a correspondence between those parallel developments is needed. The Greek development employed *ousia* for "substance" or "essence" (that which makes something what it is) and *hypostasis* for "person" (a mode of being with attributes, capacities, and activities). The Latin development

used *substantia* for "substance" or "essence" and *persona* for "person."
So, *ousia* corresponds to *substantia* and refers to the one identical
essence of the Godhead shared commonly by the three *hypostases*:
the Father, the Son, and the Holy Spirit. See also *hypostasis*; person/
personhood; substance; Trinity.

SUFFERING Tribulation and tragedy, often resulting from persecution for the Christian faith. It may also refer to the common
afflictions of human existence due to moral evil (e.g., murder, slander, theft) and natural evil (e.g., earthquakes, flooding). As Jesus
experienced suffering, so Christians should expect to undergo it
because of their faithfulness to him (John 16:33). Suffering, though
difficult, is purposeful, used by God to strengthen his people in
holiness, character, and persevering hope (Rom. 5:3–5; James
1:2–4). Christians are to anticipate divine deliverance from suffering (2 Cor. 4:7–12), if not in this life, then surely in the age to
come. *See also* evil, the problem of.

SUFFICIENCY OF SCRIPTURE An attribute of Scripture (in
written form or orally transmitted) whereby it provides everything that people need to be saved, and everything that Christians
need to please God fully. However, Scripture is not absolutely sufficient; indeed, there is much about God that he chose not to
reveal (Deut. 29:29). Rather, the sufficiency of Scripture is restricted to its purpose, which is instructing nonbelievers about
salvation and training believers to be "equipped for every good
work" (2 Tim. 3:16–17). Scripture's sufficiency and the principle
of *sola Scriptura*—"Scripture alone"—are intimately connected
and contradict the need for Catholic Tradition. *See also* necessity
of Scripture; Scripture; *solas* of Protestantism; tradition.

SUMMA THEOLOGICA Authored by Thomas Aquinas (1225–
74), this "summary of theology" is one of the most important
works of all time. Its topics include: doctrine and Scripture's
multiple senses; arguments for God's existence; the Trinity;
creation; angels and demons; human nature, virtues, and vices;

Christology; the sacraments, including Aquinas's philosophical foundation for transubstantiation; and eschatology (unfinished). Its format: a question, objections to Aquinas's position (yet to be stated), an "on the contrary" section offering his counterproposal, Aquinas's arguments for his position, and responses to the earlier objections. Designed for training theology students, the *Summa* became foundational for all Catholic theology. *See also* scholasticism (Catholic); systematic theology; theological method; Thomism / Thomas Aquinas.

SUNDAY   The first day of the calendar week, set aside for Christians to gather together to worship God. Sunday (from Old English, "day of the sun") is also called "the Lord's day" (Rev. 1:10). The early church inherited the Jewish Sabbath, which went from sundown Friday to sundown Saturday. Because Christ's resurrection was on the first day of the week (Luke 24:1), the church switched its worship from the Jewish Sabbath to the Christian Sunday. Throughout its history, the church has dedicated this day to corporate worship services, feasting, thanksgiving, rest, fellowship with believers, and visiting the sick. *See also* Sabbath/Sabbatarianism; worship.

SUPRALAPSARIANISM   One of two Reformed positions regarding the order of God's decrees, the other being sublapsarianism. The issue concerns whether logically, not temporally, God's decree to save people came before (Lat. *supra*) or after (*sub*) his decree to permit the fall (*lapsus*). Supralapsarianism holds this order: (1) God decreed to elect some people and condemn others; (2) he decreed to create both the elect and the reprobate; (3) he decreed to permit the fall of both groups. Election and reprobation, then, refer to people not yet created or fallen into sin. *See also* decree; election; fall; reprobation; sublapsarianism.

SYNCRETISM   Overcontextualization. Because the church is missional, engaging with cultures of all types, it must contextualize the gospel, and the expression of its worship and discipleship, in the different settings into which it expands. The path to proper contextualization is fraught with pitfalls, one of which is over-contextualization, or syncretism. This missional approach is the substitution or dilution of biblically sound worship, theology, and/or practice by means of the incorporation of unbiblical elements. An example is converts from Islam who continue to identify themselves as Muslims rather than as Christians and continue to engage in Islamic worship and religious duties. *See also* contextualization; mission.

SYNERGISM   In regard to the doctrine of salvation, the position that God and human beings together operate the rescue of the latter group. From the Greek (*syn*, "together"; *ergon*, "work"), *synergism* refers to sources that *work together* in salvation. By contrast, *monergism* (Gk. *monos*, "sole"; *ergon*, "work") refers to a *sole source that works* redemption. God is the single agent that operates the salvation of people. Catholic theology, holding to synergism, emphasizes that God has designed salvation to include the participation and empowerment of the faithful in meriting eternal life by grace communicated through the sacraments. *See also* infusion; merit; monergism.

SYSTEMATIC THEOLOGY   The discipline that sets forth God and his relationship to the created world in general and to human beings in particular, as that truth is set forth in all of Scripture. It is an orderly, coherent presentation of this truth, covering all doctrines of the Christian faith—revelation, Scripture, God, angels, humanity, sin, Christ, Holy Spirit, salvation, church, and eschatology. Systematic theology works in conjunction with exegetical, biblical, historical, philosophical, and practical theology. Its task is to answer the question: What are Christians to believe, do, and be today, in light of all that Scripture affirms regarding any particular doctrine? *See also* biblical theology; doctrine; exegesis / exegetical theology; historical theology; theological method.

T

TEACHING   The act of instruction, and what is taught. As the communication of the faith, teaching is an important responsibility of parents (Deut. 6:7), those with the gift of teaching (1 Cor. 12:28–31), pastors (Eph. 4:11; 1 Tim. 5:17), the whole church (Col. 3:16), and especially its mature members (Titus 2:3–5). In terms of what is taught, Scripture is central as it is "profitable for teaching" (2 Tim. 3:16). This has reference to the entire Bible (Matt. 5:19), especially to sound doctrine (1 Tim. 4:6). Teachers are to be well supported (Gal. 6:6) and will be strictly judged (James 3:1). *See also* disciple/discipleship; doctrine; Scripture.

TELEOLOGICAL ARGUMENTS   With respect to the doctrine of God, a category of rational arguments for God's existence. Teleological (from Gk. *telos*, "purpose") arguments have to do with the design evident in this world. As *a posteriori* arguments, they are based on experience, specifically the experience of design and purpose. An example is William Paley's argument from analogy: (1) a watch shows it was designed for a purpose; (2) the world shows even greater evidence of design than does a watch; (3) therefore, if a watch calls for a watchmaker, then the world demands an even greater designer, who is God. See also *a posteriori / a priori*; cosmological arguments; Five Ways, the; God; knowability; moral arguments; ontological arguments.

TEN COMMANDMENTS   The commands and prohibitions that constitute the core of the laws that God gave to his people under the old covenant. Also called the Decalogue (Gk. *deka*, "ten"; *logos*, "word"), the Ten Commandments treat monotheism, idolatry, dishonoring God's name, Sabbath rest, honoring parents, murder, adultery, stealing, bearing false witness, and coveting (Exod. 20:1–17; Deut. 5:1–21). Jesus summed up these and other laws in two commandments: love God, and love others (Matt. 22:35–40). Key debates concern the relationship of these ten with the other divine commands and whether the Ten Commandments are binding for Christians under the new covenant. *See also* dispensationalism; law; new covenant; old covenant.

THANKSGIVING   An expression of gratitude to one who has shown favor. Believers offer thanksgiving to God for his triune nature; his attributes of goodness, love, faithfulness, justice, and more; and his mighty works of creation, providence, redemption, and consummation. Gathered together, the church expresses gratitude through songs and prayers of thanksgiving, celebrating the Lord's Supper (or Eucharist; literally, "thanksgiving"), financial giving, speaking "Amen," rehearsing evidences of grace, and whole-hearted devotion. Believers give thanks to other people for their acts of mercy and kindness, financial help extended, the Word that is taught, and more. Thanksgiving in all circumstances glorifies God. *See also* Eucharist; liturgy / liturgical theology; worship.

THEISM   The worldview that God or some divine being exists. Theism (from Gk. *theos*, "god") comes in various types: Monotheism is belief in one God or supreme being. Polytheism is belief in many gods. Unitarian monotheism is belief that God is one person. Trinitarian monotheism is belief that the one God exists as three persons. Theism stands in contrast to atheism, the view that God does not exist, and agnosticism, the view that one cannot know if God exists. Scripture assumes God exists and acclaims the God of Israel and of the church to be the one true God. *See also* agnosticism; atheism; monotheism; tritheism; Unitarianism.

THEISTIC EVOLUTION   *See* evolution, theistic.

THEODICY   A solution for the problem of evil, or a defense of God's omnipotence and goodness in the face of evil. A theodicy (from Gk.

theos, "god"; *dikē*, "justification") offers the actual reason God has for allowing evil in the world, while a defense offers only a possible reason God might have for not removing evil. The problem of evil it addresses asserts that the propositions "God is all-powerful," "God is all-good," and "evil exists" are mutually contradictory: two of the three may be embraced, but not all three. A theodicy demonstrates that the three are not contradictory. *See also* evil, the problem of.

THEOLOGICAL METHOD   How one approaches and engages in the formulation of doctrine. Theological method treats the nature of theology (the discipline that studies God), its source (Scripture) or sources (general revelation, tradition, experience, reason), its importance (theology provides an orderly presentation of divinely revealed truth), and its procedure. Some examples include "faith seeking understanding" (faith is the starting point for seeking a reasoned understanding of doctrine), scholasticism (the application of logic to discover agreement among contradictory statements), the "scientific" method (formulating general theological principles from an inductive study of the biblical data), and an interdisciplinary approach combining exegetical, biblical, systematic, historical, philosophical, and practical theology. *See also* biblical theology; exegesis / exegetical theology; *fides quaerens intellectum*; historical theology; scholasticism (Catholic); scholasticism (Protestantism); systematic theology.

THEOLOGY   Both a topic in the discipline of systematic theology and that discipline itself. Theology (from Gk. *theos*, "god"; *logos*, "study") is the study of God, in two senses. In its strict sense, theology is one topic of systematic theology, often called theology proper. This is the doctrine of God himself: his existence, incomprehensibility, knowability, attributes, triune nature, decrees, and works. In its broad sense, (systematic) theology is the discipline that sets forth God and his relationship to the created world in general and to human beings in particular, as that truth is set forth in all of Scripture. *See also* God; systematic theology.

THEOLOGY OF GLORY (*THEOLOGIA GLORIAE*) One of two ways of doing theology (the other being a theology of the cross), as expressed by Martin Luther. This approach "prefers works to suffering, glory to the cross, strength to weakness, wisdom to folly, and . . . good to evil" (*Heidelberg Disputation*, 21). A theologian of glory focuses on what God has revealed in creation, human reason, and personal insight while giving little weight to the cross, shunning suffering, and minimizing evil. For Luther, this approach is wrong because it belittles what God has done to rescue the world in its actual fallenness. *See also* Lutheranism / Martin Luther; theology of the cross (*theologia crucis*).

THEOLOGY OF HOPE A theological method beginning with and grounded on eschatology that sees all doctrine in light of the theme of hope. Associated with Jürgen Moltmann (*Theology of Hope*, 1967), its tenets include (1) eschatology exerts a significant influence on all earthly existence; (2) Christianity is eschatology, and thus is hope that transforms present reality; (3) eschatology centers on the future of Jesus, so theology addresses not only who Christ was and is but who he will be; and (4) the promise of hope upsets the status quo and becomes the condition of new reality, not just a dream of a utopia. *See also* eschatology; hope; theological method.

THEOLOGY OF THE CROSS (*THEOLOGIA CRUCIS*) One of two ways of doing theology (the other being a theology of glory), as expressed by Martin Luther. According to this approach, the cross of Christ leads to theology and is its proper and only starting point. As seen in the cross, God works contrary to human expectations, acting in humiliation and suffering rather than glory. Indeed, the cross appears as foolishness and confounds the world (1 Cor. 1:18, 23). A theologian, then, must rely on grace, forsake human effort, depend on divine revelation rather than human reason, suffer, and wrestle with paradox. *See also* Lutheranism / Martin Luther; theology of glory (*theologia gloriae*).

THEOPNEUSTOS *See* inspiration of Scripture.

THEOSIS   *See* deification.

THEOTOKOS   A title for Mary that conveys an affirmation about Jesus in relation to her as his mother. From the Greek (*theos*, "god"; *tokos*, "childbirth"), *theotokos* means literally, with reference to Mary, "the one who bore God": her son is the Son of God and fully divine. The Council of Ephesus (431) was the first to proclaim Mary as *theotokos*, and its declaration was in the context of its condemnation of Nestorianism, an early heresy about Christ. Accordingly, Mary is *theotokos* as the mother of *the one who is God*. She is not *theotokos* as the *Mother* of God in terms of exalted status, as Catholicism holds. *See also* Council of Ephesus; Mariology; Mary; Nestorianism; virgin birth / virginal conception.

THIRD WAVE EVANGELICALISM   A contemporary type of evangelicalism featuring both similarities to and differences from Pentecostal theology (first wave) and the charismatic movement (second wave). Originating with John Wimber in the 1980s, third wave proponents include Wayne Grudem, Sam Storms, the early Vineyard churches, and the Sovereign Grace network. Similar to Pentecostal and charismatic theology, third wave evangelicalism is continuationist, believing that all the spiritual gifts, including the sign or miraculous gifts, continue in the church today. It differs from Pentecostal and charismatic theology in its position that the baptism with the Holy Spirit occurs at salvation, not subsequent to it. *See also* baptism with/in/by the Holy Spirit; cessationism; charismatic movement; continuationism; Pentecostalism.

THIRTY-NINE ARTICLES   The doctrinal standard for the Church of England. Known also as the *Articles of Religion*, they originated with the strongly Reformed Forty-Two Articles written by Thomas Cranmer. After a few modifications (1563), the Thirty-Nine Articles were published in 1571. Not a complete statement of faith, they articulate the Anglican Church's beliefs in continuity with the historical church and in opposition to Catholic theology and other Protestant positions. Key doctrines: God, Jesus Christ, the Holy

Spirit, Scripture, original sin, free will, good works, predestination, salvation, the church, purgatory, the sacraments (baptism, the Lord's Supper), church ministry, and state-church relationships. *See also* Anglicanism.

THOMISM / THOMAS AQUINAS   One of the church's most significant scholars (1225–74), Thomas Aquinas is a "doctor" in the Catholic Church and a major source for the Reformation. Born in Aquino, Italy, he was a Dominican monk and scholastic theologian best known for integrating Christian theology and Aristotelian philosophy. His most important writing is the *Summa Theologica*, whose topics include: the nature of doctrine and Scripture's multiple senses; arguments for God's existence; the Trinity; angels and demons; human nature; Christology; the sacraments, including Aquinas's philosophical foundation for transubstantiation; and eschatology. His philosophical theology, which Catholicism considers to be eternally true, is called Thomism. *See also* Aristotelianism; *Summa Theologica*; systematic theology; theological method.

THREE FORMS OF UNITY   The doctrinal standards of Reformed churches in the Netherlands. The Belgic Confession (1561), written by de Brey, demonstrated the legitimacy of Reformed doctrine as it was attacked by Catholicism. The Heidelberg Catechism (1563), written by Ursinus and Olevianus, defended Reformed doctrine after the Peace of Augsburg. The Canons of Dordt, composed by the Synod of Dordt (1619), established Reformed theology over Arminianism through the five points of Calvinism. The synod also established the Belgic Confession and the Heidelberg Catechism, and its canons, as the doctrinal positions of Dutch churches. *See also* Calvinism / John Calvin; Reformed theology.

TIME/TIMELESSNESS   Time is that which is measured in terms of the succession of moments, and timelessness is that which has no succession of moments. With regard to the doctrine of God, a debated question is how God relates to time, with several proposals: (1) God, in creating the universe, created space and time;

he is outside time. (2) God, being eternal, is never in time; he is atemporal, or timeless. (3) God, being temporal, is in time; he is everlasting rather than timeless. (4) God, "before" creating the universe, was timeless, but when he brought the spatial-temporal creation into existence, he became temporal. *See also* eternity.

TOTAL DEPRAVITY   With respect to the Reformed doctrine of sin, the view that every element of human nature is thoroughly infected with sin. Such utter depravity does not mean that sinful people are as evil as they possibly could be, do not possess a will or lack all moral sense, and cannot do any good whatsoever. Rather, total depravity means that every aspect—intellect, mind, reason; emotions, feelings, sentiments; will and volition; motivations and purposing; body—experiences the devastating corruption of sin. No personal element—for example, rationality, free will—escapes sin's dreadful impact. Both Pelagianism and semi-Pelagianism reject total depravity. *See also* corruption; original sin; Reformed theology; sin; total inability.

TOTAL INABILITY   With respect to the Reformed doctrine of sin, the view that sinful people cannot do anything to initiate salvation and cannot change their nature to please God. It does not mean that sinful people are as evil as they possibly could be, do not possess a will or lack all moral sense, and cannot do any good whatsoever. Rather, total inability means that sinners lack the ability to desire salvation, to do good that merits God's favor, and to reorient themselves from sinfulness and selfishness to righteousness and God-centeredness. Pelagianism and semi-Pelagianism reject total inability. *See also* corruption; original sin; Reformed theology; sin; total depravity.

TRADITION   According to Catholic theology, Tradition is one mode of divine revelation, along with Scripture, the written Word of God. It consists of the teachings of Jesus that he communicated orally to his disciples, who did not write them down but transmitted them orally to their successors, the bishops, who retain them in the Catholic Church. The pope can proclaim this Tradition to be official doctrine, like the immaculate conception of Mary (1854) and her bodily assumption (1950). In another sense, tradition is the accumulated wisdom of the church passed down as correct interpretations of Scripture and sound theological formulations. *See also* bodily assumption of Mary; immaculate conception; Scripture; *solas* of Protestantism.

TRADUCIANISM   With regard to theological anthropology, the view that both the soul and the body of a person come into existence—they are generated or transmitted—through pro-creation by parents. Traducianism (from Lat. *tradux*, referring to "propagation") was first formulated by Tertullian in the early church. Support includes the similarities between parents and their children, and reasoning from death, the separation of the soul and the body, to the conclusion that life must be the combination of the two at conception. The opposing view, creationism, holds that while parents generate the body of their children, God creates their soul. *See also* creationism; preexistence of the soul; soul.

TRANSCENDENCE   God's infinite exaltedness over creation. As Creator of and Lord over creation, the supreme, independent, sovereign God is "the One who is high and lifted up" (Isa. 57:15), "enthroned in the heavens" (Ps. 123:1). The Son is called "the first-born of all creation," referring to his preeminence over all that was created "through him and for him" (Col. 1:15–16). Transcendence underscores the Creator-creature distinction: there is an infinite gap between God and people. At the same time, it must be balanced with God's immanence: he dwells "also with him who is of a contrite and lowly spirit" (Isa. 57:15). *See also* holiness; immanence.

TRANSUBSTANTIATION   With respect to Catholic theology of the Eucharist, the view of the presence of Christ, "whose body and blood are truly contained in the sacrament . . . under the forms of bread and wine. The bread is transubstantiated [changed] into the body and the wine into the blood by the power of God" (Fourth Lateran

213

Council). Aquinas explained this conversion of one substance (bread, wine) into another (body, blood), while naturally impossible, takes place by divine power. The accidents—the smell, taste, feel, and appearance of bread and wine—remain the same; their nature changes. Protestantism rejects transubstantiation. *See also* Eucharist; Fourth Lateran Council; real presence of Christ; substance.

TRIBULATION *See* Great Tribulation; suffering.

TRICHOTOMY In regard to the doctrine of humanity, the view that complex human nature consists of three elements: one material aspect, or body, and two immaterial aspects, soul and spirit. Commonly, the soul is the intellect, emotions, and will, and the spirit is the capacity to relate to God. Support includes biblical descriptions of human nature as spirit, soul, and body (1 Thess. 5:23; cf. Heb. 4:12). Trichotomy is opposed by dichotomy, the view that complex human nature consists of two elements: one material aspect, or body, and one immaterial aspect, soul or spirit (which are interchangeable terms). Both views reject monism. *See also* dichotomy; dualism; embodiment; human nature; monism; soul.

TRINITY The doctrine that the one true God eternally exists as three persons: the Father, the Son, and the Holy Spirit. Each of the three persons is fully God: the Father is fully God, the Son is fully God, and the Holy Spirit is fully God. Yet there is only one God. The three persons are equal in nature, power, will, and glory, sharing in the one divine essence. They are distinguished by different eternal relationships (paternity, generation, procession) and different roles in creation, redemption, and consummation. This orthodox view stands opposed to Arianism (which denies the deity of the Son), Pneumatomachianism (which denies the deity of the Holy Spirit), Unitarianism (which denies the tri-personality of God), modalism (which denies the distinctions between the three persons), and polytheism (which denies there is only one God). *See also* economic Trinity; eternal generation; eternal procession; ontological Trinity; social Trinity; tritheism.

TRITHEISM   The heresy that there are three (Gk. *tri-*) gods (*theoi*). Tritheism results from a wrong view of the doctrine of the Trinity, misunderstanding its affirmation—the Father is fully God, the Son is fully God, and the Holy Spirit is fully God—to mean that there are three gods. But the doctrine of the Trinity affirms instead that the Father, the Son, and the Spirit are three persons in the one Godhead, trinity in unity, and unity in trinity. The three persons are coeternal and coequal, one in essence, equal in glory and majesty, and not three gods. *See also* theism; Trinity.

TRUTH   A property of sentences whose content corresponds to reality. According to the correspondence theory of truth, "This book is a dictionary" is a true statement. With respect to theology, truthfulness is a divine attribute signifying that God never lies but always tells the truth (Num. 23:19; Heb. 6:18). This means that Scripture, which is the Word of the truth-telling God, is inerrant (without error) and always affirms the truth (John 17:17). In a secondary sense, it is a human attribute reflective of divine truthfulness, in which people tell the truth, avoid gossip, maintain confidentiality, and love what is true. *See also* inerrancy.

TULIP   *See* Reformed theology.

TWO NATURES OF CHRIST   *See* hypostatic union.

TYPOLOGY   In regard to biblical interpretation, the method of noting the correspondence between what went on previously in the Old Testament (the type) and something later in the New Testament (the antitype). This intentional relationship between an earlier person (e.g., Moses), place or institution (e.g., the temple), or event (e.g., the lifting up of the bronze serpent) and a later person (e.g., Christ), place or institution (e.g., the church), or event (e.g., Christ's crucifixion on a cross) underscores the divinely purposed unity of Scripture. Typology also highlights the promise-fulfillment theme, that earlier Scripture anticipates later Scripture, which presents its realization. *See also* Antiochene School; hermeneutics.

U

UBIQUITY   *See* omnipresence.

UNCONDITIONAL ELECTION   The position that God's choice of people for salvation is based on his sovereign will and good pleasure to save them. Key tenets: (1) God is sovereign, and so is election; (2) in eternity past, and from his grace in Christ, God chose certain people to be saved; (3) in time, God grants saving grace and faith to the elect alone; (4) election precedes and results in justification, regeneration, conversion, sanctification, good works, and glorification. This view contrasts with conditional election: God's choice is dependent on his foreknowledge of people's faith in the gospel and continuation in salvation. *See also* conditional election; decree; election; foreknowledge; Reformed theology; saving grace.

UNION WITH CHRIST   In regard to the application of salvation, the mighty work of God to join his people in eternal covenant with the Son, who accomplished their salvation. Through union, believers are identified with Christ's death, burial, resurrection, and ascension (Rom. 6:1–11; Eph. 2:6), and God communicates all his blessings of salvation: grace, regeneration, redemption, eternal life, justification, sanctification, and glorification. Christ dwells in those with whom he is united, and they in turn dwell in him (John 15:1–5; Gal. 2:20). Union with Christ is vividly expressed and confirmed in baptism, and celebrated and fostered through the Lord's Supper. *See also* salvation.

UNITARIANISM   The theological position and movement that God is only one person, not three, and thus a rejection of the Trinity. Having roots in Arianism's denial of the deity of Christ, Unitarianism was condemned by the early church. Contemporary expressions are influenced by Socinianism and the Enlightenment and thus reject miracles like the virgin birth, the authority and inerrancy of Scripture, original sin, the substitutionary atonement of Christ, and more. For Unitarians, Jesus is a great moral teacher; human beings are essentially good and worthy of affirmation; and Christianity is inclusivistic, creedless, and one of many religions that help people. *See also* Arianism; Enlightenment, the; monotheism; Socinianism; Trinity.

UNITY   With respect to ecclesiology, one of the four traditional attributes of the church (the others being holiness, catholicity, and apostolicity). This attribute signifies that the church is united in oneness. For the Catholic Church, its visible unity is centered on a common profession of faith (the Apostles' Creed), a common liturgy involving the sacraments, and apostolic succession (from the apostles to its bishops today). For Protestants, unity comes from the two marks of the church: "it is sufficient to agree concerning the doctrine of the gospel and the administration of the sacraments [baptism and the Lord's Supper]" (Augsburg Confession, 7). *See also* Apostles' Creed; apostolicity; catholicity; holiness of the church.

UNIVERSALISM   The position that if not in life, then after death, all people will ultimately embrace salvation. Support includes the affirmations that in and through Christ, all will be justified and live (Rom. 5:18; 1 Cor. 15:22), and that one day all things will be subjected to Christ "that God may be all in all" (1 Cor. 15:28). Universalism fails to respect death as the point at which human destiny, based on one's faith in Christ during one's lifetime, is fixed (Heb. 9:27). The church's historic position, that only believers will be saved, has always included a denunciation of universalism. *See also* death; Origen; postmortem evangelism.

UNLIMITED ATONEMENT   The position that Christ died with the intent that his death be the payment for sin for everyone, making it possible for any and all to be saved. Biblical support includes

217

affirmations that Christ died for "the whole world" (1 John 2:2; cf. 2 Cor. 5:17–21). Theological support includes (1) an argument from God's universal love and desire that everyone be saved (2 Pet. 3:9), which makes it impossible that Christ died only for some; and (2) an argument from prevenient grace, which restores to everyone the ability to embrace salvation. Unlimited atonement stands opposed to limited atonement and the multiple-intentions view. *See also* atonement; limited atonement; multiple-intentions view of the atonement.

UNPARDONABLE SIN Blasphemy against the Holy Spirit, which cannot be forgiven (Matt. 12:22–32). When denounced by his critics for casting out demons by Satan, Jesus pointed out the absurdity of their charge and claimed that he exorcises them by the Holy Spirit. Maliciously and irrationally attributing the Spirit's work in Jesus to Satan is blasphemy against the Spirit, and Jesus underscored, "Whoever speaks against the Holy Spirit will not be forgiven, either in this age or in the age to come" (12:32). Other views consider the unpardonable sin to be persistent unbelief (1 John 5:16) or apostasy (Heb. 6:6). *See also* Holy Spirit, work of the; Satan.

V

VATICAN COUNCIL I The twentieth general council of the Roman Catholic Church (1869–70), held three centuries after the Council of Trent. Convened by Pope Pius IX to treat the disturbing movements of rationalism, materialism, and atheism, it is most known for its proclamation of the dogma of papal infallibility

(*Pastor aeternus*, July 18, 1870). Other matters addressed: God and creation *ex nihilo*; the knowledge of God through the light of reason and divine revelation, which consists of both Scripture and Tradition; faith, as both reasonable and supernatural; and faith and its connection to reason. Opposing views were condemned with anathemas. *See also* council, general; Council of Trent; infallibility, papal; Roman Catholicism.

VATICAN COUNCIL II The twenty-first general council of the Roman Catholic Church (1962–65). Convened by Pope John XXIII and brought to completion by Pope Paul VI, it was an *aggiornamento* (updating) of the Church in the modern world. The main issues (addressed in the constitutions) treated were divine revelation, the nature of the church, the mission of the church, and the liturgy. The other topics addressed: missionary activity; the training, life, and ministry of priests; the renewal of the religious life; ecumenical relationships with other Christians such as the Orthodox and Protestants; religious liberty; Christian education; and the Church's relationship with non-Christian religions. *See also* council, general; Roman Catholicism.

VENERATION Respect and reverence that is rendered to an excellent superior. In regard to Catholic theology's view of Mary, a distinction is made between three acts of devotion: (1) *latria* is worship or adoration that belongs to God alone; (2) *dulia* is veneration that is given to all the saints; and (3) *hyperdulia* is superveneration that is reserved for Mary. The veneration accorded to the saints is expressed through invoking their prayers, help, and blessings. The superveneration that is reserved for Mary is manifested by acknowledging her as Advocate, Helper, Benefactress, and Mediatrix; imploring her intercession; and following her example. *See also* Mariology; Mary; saints.

VENIAL SIN According to Catholic theology, one of two types of sin, the other being mortal sin. Venial sin involves a less serious matter than does mortal sin, in several ways. The law is disobeyed in a less grave matter, or it is disobeyed in a serious matter but without full knowledge or complete consent. Venial sin wounds love but does not destroy it, and it impedes progress in doing good. It does not result in the loss of grace but merits temporal punishment in purgatory. Confession and repentance, rather than the sacrament of penance, is needed to repair grace. *See also* mortal sin; purgatory; sin.

VERBAL INSPIRATION   *See* inspiration of Scripture.

VESTIGES OF THE TRINITY (*VESTIGIA TRINITATIS*)   The idea that there are traces of the triune God in certain threefold structures in creation. It is commonly associated with Augustine (*On the Trinity*), who found specific vestiges in the human soul, which is the image of God, who is the Trinity: (1) the one who loves, the one who is loved, and love; (2) memory, understanding, and will; (3) mind, knowledge, and love; (4) remembering, understanding, and love. Common analogies include water as ice, liquid, and steam. As Augustine admitted, all analogies fail, so caution is warranted in appealing to trinitarian vestiges. *See also* Augustinian theology; Trinity.

VICARIOUS   Done or experienced by one person acting in the place of another or for the sake of another. With respect to Christology, the death that Christ underwent was a vicarious sacrifice, an act of atonement substituting for the death people deserved to pay for their sins. Scripture employs the language of vicariousness: God "did not spare his own Son but gave him up for us all" (Rom. 8:32), making Christ "who knew no sin to be sin on our behalf" (2 Cor. 5:21 NASB). The vicarious nature of the atonement is part of the forensic, or legal, framework of salvation. *See also* atonement; penal substitution theory.

VIRGIN BIRTH / VIRGINAL CONCEPTION   With regard to Christology, the doctrine that Mary was a virgin who conceived Jesus supernaturally by the Holy Spirit and not by sexual intercourse. Because of this miracle, the incarnate Son was fully human yet did not have a sinful nature like all other human beings. Biblical support for this work of the Holy Spirit is Luke 1:34–35 and Matthew 1:18–25, and the early church included its belief in the virgin birth in its earliest creeds. Protestant liberalism dismissed the virgin birth because of its miraculous nature, but the church has historically considered it a major doctrine. *See also* Christology; Mary.

VIRGIN MARY *See* Mary.

VIRTUE A disposition, trait, or habit to do the good. Theological discussions of virtue often distinguish between human and theological virtues. Human virtues are habits that promote individual and societal flourishing and include justice (giving others their due), determination or courage (perseverance through difficulty), judgment (applied reason), wisdom (applied knowledge), and moderation (restraint in pleasures). Theological virtues are rooted in and flow from salvation. The dispositions emphasized are faith, hope, and love (1 Cor. 13:13), but joy, peace, patience, kindness, goodness, gentleness, and self-control (Gal. 5:22–23) may be added. Virtues are contrasted with vices, the dispositions to do the evil.

VOCATION A person's work or occupation, as well as a calling to a profession. In his mandate to human beings created in his image, God commissioned them with the responsibility to exercise dominion, and thus originated vocation (Gen. 1:28). Initial vocations included shepherding and farming, building cities, tending livestock, making music, and fashioning tools (Gen. 4). Contemporary vocations include politics, education, medicine, athletics, science and technology, and more. Vocation is also a calling. Often this is limited to pastoral ministry or missionary service, but wrongly so, as God charges all human beings with the task of building civilization through vocation. *See also* humanity / human being; ordination; person/personhood; stewardship; work.

VOLUNTARISM The position that emphasizes the role of the will. Voluntarism (from Lat. *voluntas,* "will") contrasts with rationalism's focus on the intellect. Theological voluntarism maintains that the will of God is supreme: God does not command something because it is right, but his command makes it right. When applied to people, voluntarism holds that what is most decisive is not the mind that thinks but the will that acts. Immanuel Kant's categorical imperative—"act only according to that maxim by which you can at the same time will that it will become a universal law" *—is an example of ethical voluntarism. *See also* Kant, Immanuel; mind; rationalism; will.

VOLUNTARY SOCIETY In regard to ecclesiology, the view that the church consists of members who willfully associate themselves with others for worship, discipleship, and mission. More precisely, because God first calls people into a new covenant relationship with himself, those Christians make a willful choice to covenant together as a voluntary society. This voluntarism is at the heart of the free-church movement (e.g., Baptists), which broke from the historic state-church relationship. According to that tradition, church membership is by natural citizenship (being European makes one Christian) or church rite (being baptized as an infant makes one a church member). *See also* Baptistic theology; church; free-church movement; magisterial Reformation; radical Reformation.

VULGATE, THE LATIN The important translation of the Bible by Jerome. In 382 the bishop of Rome commissioned Jerome to make a Latin translation, and Jerome began his work on the Old Testament from a Hebrew original. Augustine pressed him to include translations of the Old Testament apocryphal writings, which Jerome did. This Latin translation, with an expanded Old Testament and the New Testament, was the Vulgate (or "common") version. Whereas the Reformers went back to a Hebrew original for their

---

* Immanuel Kant, *Grounding for the Metaphysics of Morals*, in *Ethical Philosophy*, trans. James W. Ellington, 2nd ed. (1785; Indianapolis: Hackett, 1994), 30.

Old Testament, the Catholic Church proclaimed the Vulgate to be its official version at the Council of Trent (1546). *See also* Apocrypha; canon of Scripture; Council of Trent.

W

WESLEYAN QUADRILATERAL   The theological method developed by John Wesley. It embraces four sources for theology: Scripture, tradition, reason, and experience. Though affirming these norms, Wesley emphasized the supremacy of Scripture: it alone is necessary for salvation, and from it everything else must be proved. Tradition refers to the accumulated wisdom of the past that helps shape contemporary theology. Reason, not on its own but assisted by the Holy Spirit, is necessary for understanding the truth of Scripture and, as logical coherence, aids in formulating doctrine. The experience of doctrine through vital faith furnishes proof of doctrine and contributes to theology. *See also* Scripture; theological method; Wesleyanism / John Wesley.

WESLEYANISM / JOHN WESLEY   John Wesley (1703–91) was a pastor, missionary, theologian, and evangelist whose open-air preaching and Arminian-influenced doctrine contributed to the Evangelical Revival in Great Britain and became the foundation of the Methodist Church. Wesley was a devoted Anglican and missionary in America who was later converted (May 24, 1738) through the influence of Moravian missionaries and the writings of Martin Luther. Wesley rejected the Reformed doctrine of predestination, affirmed conditional election, emphasized prevenient grace for all, considered justification to include the impartation of new life, and encouraged Christians to pursue entire sanctification. These and other doctrines constitute Wesleyanism or, more accurately, Wesleyan-Arminian theology. *See also* Arminian theology; conditional election; perfectionism; prevenient grace.

WESTMINSTER STANDARDS Three doctrinal formulations written in 1646–47 by leading Reformed theologians in England and Scotland and still used by many Presbyterian and Reformed churches worldwide. The Westminster Confession of Faith sets forth doctrinal matters in the form of a confession of faith. The Westminster Larger Catechism and Westminster Shorter Catechism are catechisms in question-and-answer format, the larger with 196 entries and the shorter with 107. The doctrines treated are Scripture, God, the decree, creation, providence, the fall, covenants, Christ, salvation, the law and conscience, the church, the state, the sacraments, and eschatology. *See also* catechism/catechesis; confession; Reformed theology.

WILL The capacity for volition, or decision making. Along with mind and emotions, it is one aspect of divine, angelic, and human nature. Willing involves desiring, choosing, and determining. The divine will is God's eternal purpose and the revelation of his moral standard. Angelic will is distinguished between the settled holy will of angels and the settled evil will of demons. Human will before the fall was able not to sin and able to sin. Fallen human will is not able not to sin. A redeemed will renders people able not to sin, moving toward not able to sin in the intermediate state and in the age to come. *See also* human nature; humanity / human being; mind; *posse peccare* (and related phrases); soul; voluntarism.

WILL OF GOD An aspect of divine sovereignty, the eternal purpose of God and the expression of his moral demands (commands and prohibitions) for his creatures. Two aspects: (1) God's secret will, which is his decree or plan for everything that exists and comes to pass. Although people cannot know this secretive will, it becomes manifested in the events of this world. (2) God's revealed will, which is his moral requirements and is communicated generally through the human conscience and specifically through Scripture. People are responsible for knowing and obeying God's revealed will and are held morally accountable for doing so. *See also* authority; decree; sovereignty; will.

WISDOM   A divine attribute signifying that God always wills the greatest goals, and the best means to achieve those goals, for his own glory and his people's blessing. Yet, wisdom is not mere efficiency, a calculated and streamlined process designed solely for greater productivity. God employed wisdom in creating the world (Ps. 104:24–25) and in designing salvation, though his wisdom appears as foolishness (1 Cor. 1:18–31). Through the church God reveals his wisdom to heavenly beings (Eph. 3:10). In a secondary sense, it is a human attribute reflective of divine wisdom, obtained through prayer (James 1:5) and Scripture (Ps. 119:99).

WORD OF GOD   Jesus Christ, divine speech, and Scripture. (1) The eternal second person of the Trinity took on human nature to become the incarnate Word of God, Jesus Christ. He renders visible the invisible God (John 1:1, 14, 17). (2) Divine speech ("Thus says the LORD") is the spoken Word of God that creates (Ps. 33:6), addresses his people (e.g., the Ten Commandments; Exod. 20), and blesses them (Deut. 28:10–14). (3) Scripture, written by human authors through the superintending work of the Holy Spirit, is the inspired Word of God. It is truthful, authoritative, sufficient, necessary, clear, and powerful. *See also* incarnation; inspiration of Scripture; Jesus Christ, deity of; Jesus Christ, humanity of; Scripture.

WORK   The divinely designed activity in which human beings are engaged. Work is purposeful, reflecting the divine intentionality in creation. It is divinely given: to his image bearers, God entrusted the cultural mandate, one part of which is vocation ("subdue [the earth] and have dominion"; Gen. 1:28). The first examples of work were shepherding, farming, city building, tending livestock, making music, and tool making (Gen. 4). Contemporary examples include politics, education, business, construction, and technology. Because of sin, work is cursed: workers engage in hard labor while meeting resistance to productivity. The gospel changes people from consumers to contributors, thus redeeming work. *See also* humanity / human being; person/personhood; vocation.

WORSHIP An act of acknowledging and acclaiming the majestic greatness of God in ways that he prescribes. Though daily expressions of praise and thanksgiving by individual believers constitute worship, Christians gather regularly for a service of worship. This corporate act consists in ascribing honor to God through praise of his nature and mighty works by singing and praying; reading, preaching, and hearing the Word of God, with responses of obedience and faithfulness to covenantal responsibilities (e.g., giving money, confessing sin, edifying one another, sending missionaries); and the administration of the new covenant ordinances of baptism and the Lord's Supper. *See also* liturgy / liturgical theology; normative principle; regulative principle.

WRATH The divine attribute by which God intensely hates sin and is poised to punish it fully. For forgiveness leading to salvation from God's wrath to occur, his anger must be assuaged. On the Day of Atonement, the high priest sprinkled the blood of the sacrificed animal on the mercy seat, appeasing God's wrath (Lev. 16). This was a foretaste of the sacrificial death of Christ as a propitiation for sin, which once for all accomplished satisfaction (1 John 2:2). Accordingly, Christians will never face the wrath of God (Rom. 5:9–10), but nonbelievers will experience God's fury in eternal punishment. *See also* atonement; condemnation; eternal conscious punishment; forgiveness; mercy; propitiation; sin.

X–Z

ZWINGLI, HULDRYCH Swiss Reformer (1484–1531) who developed the principles of justification by faith and of Scripture independently of, but in parallel with, Martin Luther. He served as pastor of the Great Church in Zurich, from which he attacked Catholic theology. As a theologian, he had much in common with Luther but also clashed with him, especially on the nature of the presence of Christ in the Lord's Supper. Against Luther's consubstantiation, Zwingli offered a memorial view, focusing on Christ's instructions to celebrate the Supper in remembrance of him. Zwingli also denounced the Anabaptists, especially their practice of withholding baptism from infants. *See also* Anabaptism; consubstantiation; infant baptism; justification; memorial view; Reformed theology.

Appendix

of French, German, and Korean Terms

Grammatical abbreviations: adj. (adjective), n.f. (noun, feminine), n.m. (noun, masculine), n.n. (noun, neuter), pl. (plural)

English Term	French Translation	German Translation	Korean Translation and Transliteration
accommodation	*accommodation* (n.f.)	*Akkomodation* (n.f.)	조정/맞추심, *jojeong/majchusim*
adoption	*adoption* (n.f.)	*Sohnschaft* (n.f.)	양자됨, *yangjadoem*
adoptionism	*adoptianisme* (n.m.)	*Adoptianismus* (n.m.)	양자설, *yangjaseol*
advent	*avent* (n.m.)	*Advent* (n.m.)	강림, *ganglim*
agnosticism	*agnosticisme* (n.m.)	*Agnostizismus* (n.m.)	불가지론, *bulgajilon*
amillennialism	*amillénarisme* (n.m.)	*Amillennialismus* (n.m.)	무천년설, *mucheonnyeonseol*
annihilationism	*annihilationisme* (n.m.)	*Annihilationismus* (n.m.)	영혼 멸절설, *yeonghon myeoljeolseol*
anthropology, theological	*anthropologie théologique* (n.f.)	*Anthropologie, theologische* (n.f.)	신학적 인간론, *sinhagjeog inganlon*
antinomianism	*antinomisme* (n.m.)	*Antinomianismus* (n.m.)	반율법주의, *banyulbeobjuui*
apologetics	*apologétique* (n.f.)	*Apologetik* (n.f.)	변증학, *byeonjeunghag*
apophatic theology	*théologie apophatique* (n.f.) / *théologie négative* (n.f.)	*apophatische Theologie* (n.f.)	부정 신학, *bujeongsinhag*
apostasy	*apostasie* (n.f.)	*Apostasie* (n.f.)	배교, *baegyo*
apostle	*apôtre* (n.m.)	*Apostel* (n.m.)	사도, *sado*
apostleship	*apostolat* (n.m.)	*Apostolat* (n.n.)	사도직, *sadojig*

English Term	French Translation	German Translation	Korean Translation and Transliteration
apostolicity	apostolicité (n.f.)	Apostolozität (n.f.)	사도성, sadoseong
ascension	ascension (n.f.)	Himmelfahrt (n.f.)	승천, seungcheon
asceticism	ascétisme (n.m.)	Askese (n.f.)	금욕주의, geumyogjuui
assurance of salvation	assurance du salut (n.f.)	Heilsgewißheit (n.f.)	구원의 확신, guwonui hwagsin
atheism	athéisme (n.m.)	Atheismus (n.m.)	무신론, musinlon
atonement	expiation (n.f.)	Sühne (n.f.)	속죄, sogjoe
authority	autorité (n.f.)	Autorität (n.f.)	권위, wonwi
baptism	baptême (n.m.)	Taufe (n.f.)	세례/침례, selye/chimlye
baptismal regeneration	régénération baptismale (n.f.)	Taufwiedergeburt (n.f.)	세례 중생론, selye jungsaenglon
bibliology	bibliologie (n.f.)	Bibliologie (n.f.)	성경론, seonggyeonglon
bishop	évêque (n.m.)	Bischof (n.m.)	감독, gamdog
blasphemy	blasphème (n.m.)	Blasphemie (n.f.)	신성모독, sinseongmodog
body of Christ	corps du Christ (n.m.)	Leib Christi (n.m.)	그리스도의 몸, Geuliseudoui mom
canon of Scripture	canon de l'écriture (n.m.)	Kanon (n.m.) der Schrift (n.f.)	정경, jeonggyeong

English Term	French Translation	German Translation	Korean Translation and Transliteration
catholicity	catholicité (n.f.)	Katholizität (n.f.)	보편성, bopyeonseong
celibacy	célibat (n.m.)	Zölibat (n.n.)	독신, dogsin
cessationism	cessationisme (n.m.)	Lehre (n.f.) vom Ende (n.n.) der Wundergaben (n.f.pl.)	은사중단론, eunsajungdanlon
charismatic movement	mouvement charismatique (n.m.)	charismatische Bewegung (n.f.)	은사주의 운동, eunsajuui undong
Christian	chrétien (n.m.; adj.)	Christ (n.m.); christlich (adj.)	기독교인, Gidoggyoin
church	église (n.f.)	Kirche (n.f.)	교회, gyohoe
church discipline	discipline dans église / discipline écclésiastique (n.f.)	Gemeindezucht/Kirchenzucht (n.f.)	권징, gwonjing
circumcision	circoncision (n.f.)	Beschneidung (n.f.)	할례, hallye
clergy	clergé (n.m.)	Klerus (n.m.)	성직자, seongjigja
common grace	grâce commune (n.f.)	allgemeine Gnade (n.f.)	일반 은총 / 은혜, ilban eunchong / eunhye
communicable attributes	attributs communicables (n.m.)	äquivoke Eigenschaften (n.f.pl.)	공유적 속성, gongyujeog sogseong
compatibilism	compatibilisme (n.m.)	Kompatibilismus (n.m.)	양립가능론, yanglibganeunglon

English Term	French Translation	German Translation	Korean Translation and Transliteration
complementarianism	*complementarisme* (n.m.)	*Ergänzungstheorie* (n.f.)	남녀상보주의, *namnyeosangbojuui*
concupiscence	*concupiscence* (n.f.)	*Konkupiszenz* (n.f.)	정욕, *jeongyog*
condemnation	*condamnation* (n.f.)	*Verdammnis* (n.f.)	정죄, *jeongjoe*
conditional election	*élection conditionnelle* (n.f.)	*bedingte Erwählung* (n.f.)	조건적 선택, *jogeonjeog seontaeg*
conditional immortality	*immortalité conditionnelle* (n.f.)	*bedingte Unsterblichkeit* (n.f.)	조건적 불멸설, *jogeonjeog bulmyeolseol*
confession	*confession* (n.f.)	*Bekenntnis* (n.n.)	고백, *gobaeg*
congregationalism	*congrégationalisme* (n.m.)	*Kongregationalismus* (n.m.)	회중정치, *hoejungjeongchi*
conscience	*conscience* (n.f.)	*Gewissen* (n.n.)	양심, *yangsim*
consubstantiation	*consubstantiation* (n.f.)	*Konsubstantiation* (n.f.)	공재설, *gongjaeseol*
consummation	*consommation* (n.f.)	*Vollendung* (n.f.)	종말적 완성, *jongmaljeog wanseong*
continuationism	*continuationisme* (n.m.)	*Lehre* (n.f.) *von der kontinuierlichen Dauer* (n.f.) *der Wundergaben* (n.f.pl.)	은사지속론, *eunsajisoglon*
conversion	*conversion* (n.f.)	*Bekehrung* (n.f.)	회심, *hoesim*
corruption	*depravation* (n.f.)	*Korruption* (n.f.)	타락/부패, *talag/bupae*

English Term	French Translation	German Translation	Korean Translation and Transliteration
cosmological arguments	arguments cosmologiques (n.m.)	kosmologische Argumente (n.n.pl.)	우주론적 증명, ujulonjeog jeungmyeong
covenant	alliance (n.f.)	Bund (n.m.)	언약, eonyag
creation ex nihilo	création ex nihilo (n.f.)	Schöpfung (n.f.) aus dem Nichts (n.n.)	무로부터의 창조, mulobuteoui changjo
creationism	créationnisme (n.m.)	Kreationismus (n.m.)	창조론, changjolon
creed	credo (n.m.)	Bekenntnis (n.n.)	신경, singyeong
cross	croix (n.f.)	Kreuz (n.n.)	십자가, sibjaga
deacon/deaconess (see also "diaconate")	diacre (n.m.) / diaconesse (n.f.)	Diakon (n.m.) / Diakonin (n.f.)	집사(남)/집사(여), jibsa(nam)/jibsa(yeo)
death	mort (n.f.)	Tod (n.m.)	죽음, jugeum
decree	décret (n.m.)	Dekret (n.n.)	작정, jagjeong
demon, demons	démon (n.m.) / les démons	Dämon (n.m.), Dämonen (n.m.pl.)	귀신/귀신들, gwisin/gwisindeul,
determinism	déterminisme (n.m.)	Determinismus (n.m.)	결정주의, gyeoljeongjuui
diaconate	diaconat (n.m.)	Diakonat (n.n.)	집사직, jibsajig
dichotomy	dichotomie (n.f.)	Dichotomie (n.f.)	이분설, ibunseol

English Term	French Translation	German Translation	Korean Translation and Transliteration
dictation theory	théorie de la dictée (n.f.)	Diktationstheorie (n.f.)	축자영감설, chugjayeonggamseol
disciple	disciple (n.m.)	Jünger (n.m.)	제자, jeja
discipleship	discipulat (n.m.)	Jüngerschaft (n.f.)	제자도, jejado
dispensationalism	dispensationalisme (n.m.)	Dispensationalismus (n.m.)	세대주의, sedaejuui
divorce	divorce (n.m.)	Scheidung (n.f.)	이혼, ihon
doctrine	doctrine (n.f.)	Lehre (n.f.)	교리, gyoli
dualism	dualisme (n.m.)	Dualismus (n.m.)	이원론, iwonlon
ecclesiology	ecclésiologie (n.f.)	Ekklesiologie (n.f.)	교회론, gyohoelon
economic Trinity	trinité économique (n.f.)	ökonomische Trinität (n.f.)	경륜적 삼위일체, gyeongtyunjeog Samwiilche
effective/effectual call	appel efficace (n.m.)	effektiver Ruf (n.m.)	효과적/유효한 부르심, hyogwajeog/yuhyohan buleusim
egalitarianism	égalitarisme (n.m.)	Egalitarismus (n.m.)	남녀 평등주의, namnyeo pyeongdeungjuui
elder	ancien (n.m.)	Ältester, der Älteste (n.m.)	장로, janglo
eldership	anciennat (n.m.)	das Amt (n.n.) des Ältesten (n.m.)	장로직, janglojig

English Term	French Translation	German Translation	Korean Translation and Transliteration
embodiment	incarnation (n.f.)	Verkörperung (n.f.)	체현, chehyeon
episcopalianism	épiscopalianisme (n.m.)	Episkopalismus (n.m.)	감독정치, gamdogjeongchi
epistemology	épistémologie (n.f.)	Epistemologie (n.f.)	인식론, insiglon
eschatology	eschatologie (n.f.)	Eschatologie (n.f.)	종말론, jongmallon
eternal conscious punishment	punition éternelle consciente (n.f.)	ewige bewußte Verdammnnis (n.f.)	의식적 영원한 형 벌, uisigjeog yeongwonhan hyeongbeol
eternal generation	génération éternelle (n.f.)	ewige Schöpfung (n.f.)	영 원 출생 설, yeongwonchulsaengseol
eternal life	vie éternelle (n.f.)	ewiges Leben (n.n.)	영 생, yeongsaeng
eternal procession	procession éternelle (n.f.)	ewiges Hervorgehen (n.n.)	영 원 발출 설, yeongwonbalchulseol
eternity	éternité (n.f.)	Ewigkeit (n.f.)	영 원 성, yeongwonseong
evangelicalism	mouvement évangélique (n.m.)	Evangelikalismus (n.m.)	복 음주 의, bogeumjuui
evangelism	évangélisation (n.f.)	Evangelisation (n.f.)	복 음 전 도, bogeumjeondo
evil	mal (n.m.)	das Böse (n.n.)	악, ag
exaltation of Christ	exaltation de Christ (n.f.)	Erhöhung (n.f.) Christi (n.m.)	그리스도의 승귀, Geuliseudoui seunggwi
exclusivism	exclusivisme (n.m.)	Exklusivismus (n.m.)	배타주의, baetajuui

English Term	French Translation	German Translation	Korean Translation and Transliteration
excommunication	excommunication (n.f.)	Exkommunikation (n.f.)	출교/출회, chulgyo/chulhoe
exorcism	exorcisme (n.m.)	Exorzismus (n.m.)	축귀, chuggwi
expiation	expiation (n.f.)	Sühnung (n.f.)	보상(속죄), bosang(sogjoe)
external call	appel externe (n.m.)	äußerlicher Ruf (n.m.)	외적 부르심, oejeog buleusim
faith	foi (n.f.)	Glaube (n.m.)	믿음, mideum
fall	chute (n.f.)	Fall (n.m.)	타락, talag
fear of God	crainte de Dieu (n.f.)	Furcht (n.f.) Gottes (n.m.)	하나님을 경외함, Hananimeul gyeongoeham
federal headship	tête fédérale (n.f.)	Föderalismus (n.m.)	언약적 머리됨, eonyagjeog meolidoem
filled with the Holy Spirit	rempli du Saint-Esprit	mit dem Heiligen Geist gefüllt	성령충만, Seonglyeongchungman
flesh	chair (n.f.)	Fleisch (n.n.)	육/육체, yug/yugche
foreknowledge	prescience (n.f.)	Vorkenntnis (n.f.)	예지, yeji
forensic	forensique (adj.)	forensisch (adj.)	법정적, beobjeongjeog
forgiveness	pardon (n.m.)	Vergebung (n.f.)	용서, yongseo

English Term	French Translation	German Translation	Korean Translation and Transliteration
free will	*libre arbitre* (n.m.)	*der freie Wille* (n.m.) or *Willensfreiheit* (n.f.)	자유 의지, *jayuuiji*
general revelation	*révélation générale /* *révélation naturelle* (n.f.)	*allgemeine Offenbarung* (n.f.)	일반계시, *ilbangyesi*
glorification	*glorification* (n.f.)	*Verherrlichung* (n.f.)	영화, *yeonghwa*
glory	*gloire* (n.f.)	*Herrlichkeit* (n.f.)	영광, *yeonggwang*
God	*Dieu* (n.m.)	*Gott* (n.m.)	하나님, *Hananim*
God-breathed	*expiré par Dieu*	*Gott-gehaucht*	하나님의 감동으로 된, *Hananimui gamdongeulo doen*
good works	*bonnes oeuvres* (n.f.)	*gute Werke* (n.n.pl.)	선행, *seonhaeng*
goodness	*bonté* (n.f.)	*das Gute* (n.n.)	선함/좋음, *seonham/joheum*
gospel	*évangile* (n.m.)	*Evangelium* (n.n.)	복음, *bogeum*
grace	*grâce* (n.f.)	*Gnade* (n.f.)	은혜, *eunhye*
Great Commandment	*grand commandement* (n.m.)	*das größte Gebot* (n.n.)	큰 계명, *keun gyemyeong*
Great Commission	*grand mandat* (France) / *grande commission* (Quebec) (n.f.)	*Missionsbefehl* (n.m.)	지상 대위임령, *jisang daewiimlyeong*

English Term	French Translation	German Translation	Korean Translation and Transliteration
guilt	culpabilité (n.f.)	Schuld (n.f.)	죄책, joechaeg
hamartiology	hamartiologie (n.f.)	Hamartiologie (n.f.)	죄론, joelon
healing	guérison (n.f.)	Heilung (n.f.)	치유, chiyu
heaven	ciel (n.m.)	Himmel (n.m.)	천국, cheongug
hell	enfer (n.m.)	Hölle (n.f.)	지옥, jiog
heresy	hérésie (n.f.)	Ketzerei (n.f.)	이단, idan
historic premillennialism	prémillénarisme historique (n.m.)	historischer Prämilleniarismus (n.m.)	역사적 전천년설, yeogsajeog jeoncheonmyeonseol
holiness	sainteté (n.f.)	Heiligkeit (n.f.)	거룩성, geolugseong
Holy Spirit	Saint-Esprit / Esprit saint (n.m.)	Heiliger Geist (n.m.)	성령, Seonglyeong
hope	espoir / espérance (n.f.)	Hoffnung (n.f.)	소망/희망, somang/huimang
human nature	la nature humaine (n.f.)	die menschliche Natur (n.f.)	인간본성, inganbonseong
humanity / human being	humanité (n.f.) / être humain (n.m.)	die Menschheit (n.f.) / der Mensch (n.m.)	인류/인간, inlyu/ingan
humiliation of Christ	humiliation de Christ (n.f.)	Erniedrigung (n.f.) Christi (n.m.)	그리스도의 비하, Geuliseudoui biha
hypostatic union	union hypostatique (n.f.)	hypostatische Einheit (n.f.)	위격적 연합, wigyeogjeog yeonhab

English Term	French Translation	German Translation	Korean Translation and Transliteration
illumination	illumination (n.f.)	Erleuchtung (n.f.)	조명, jomyeong
image of God / imago Dei	image de Dieu (n.f.)	Ebenbild (n.n.) Gottes (n.m.) / imago Dei	하나님의 형상, Hananimui hyeongsang
immanence	immanence (n.f.)	Immanenz (n.f.)	내재성, naejaeseong
immersion	immersion (n.f.)	Eintauchen (n.n.)	침수, chimsu
imminence	imminence (n.f.)	nahes Bevorstehen (n.n.)	임박성, imbagseong
immortality	immortalité (n.f.)	Unsterblichkeit (n.f.)	불사성, bulsaseong
immutability	immuabilité (n.f.)	Unveränderlichkeit (n.f.)	불변성, bulbyeonseong
impassibility	impassibilité (n.f.)	Leiden(schaft)slosigkeit (n.f.)	무감각성, mugamgagseong
impeccability	impeccabilité (n.f.)	Sündlosigkeit (n.f.)	범죄 불능성, beomjoe bulheungseong
imputation	imputation (n.f.)	Imputation/Zurechnung (n.f.)	전가, jeonga
incarnation	incarnation (n.f.)	Inkarnation (n.f.) / Fleischwerdung (n.f.)	성육신/강생, seongyugsin/gangsaeng
inclusivism	inclusivisme (n.m.)	Inklusivismus (n.m.)	포괄주의, pogwaljuui
incommunicable attributes	attributs incommunicables (n.m.)	univoke Eigenschaften (n.f.pl.)	비공유적 속성, bigongyujeog sogseong
incompatibilism	incompatibilisme (n.m.)	Inkompatibilismus (n.m.)	양립불가론, yanglibbulgalon

English Term	French Translation	German Translation	Korean Translation and Transliteration
incomprehensible	incompréhensible (adj.)	unverständlich (adj.)	불가해한, bulgahaehan
independence	indépendance (n.f.)	Unabhängigkeit (n.f.)	독립성/자존성, doglibseong/jajonseong
inerrancy	inerrance (n.f.)	Irrtumslosigkeit (n.f.)	무오성, muoseong
infallibility	infaillibilité (n.f.)	Unfehlbarkeit (n.f.)	불오성, buloseong
infant baptism	baptême des enfants (n.m.)	Säuglingstaufe (n.f.) or Kindertaufe (n.f.)	유아세례, yuaselye
infinite	infini (adj.)	unendlich (adj.)	무한한, muhanhan
infusion	infusion (n.f.)	Infusion/Einhauchen (n.n.)	주입, juib
inspiration of Scripture	inspiration des Écritures (n.f.)	Inspiration (n.f.) / Eingebung (n.f.) der Schrift (n.f.)	성경 영감설, Seonggyeong yeonggamseol
intercession	intercession (n.f.)	Fürbitte (n.f.)	중보기도, jungbogido
intermediate state	état intermédiaire (n.m.)	Zwischenstadium (n.n.)	중간기 상태, junggangi sangtae
irresistible grace	grâce irrésistible (n.f.)	unwiderstehliche Gnade (n.f.)	불가항력적 은혜, bulgahanglyeogjeog eunhye
jealousy	jalousie (n.f.)	Eifersucht (n.f.)	질투, jiltu
Jesus Christ	Jésus-Christ (n.)	Jesus Christus (n.m.)	예수 그리스도, Yesu Geuliseudo
justice	justice (n.f.)	Gerechtigkeit (n.f.)	정의/공의, jeongui/gongui

English Term	French Translation	German Translation	Korean Translation and Transliteration
justification	justification (n.f.)	Rechtfertigung (n.f.)	칭의, chingui
kenosis	kénose (n.f.)	Kenosis (n.f.)	자기비움, jagibium
kerygma	kérygme (n.m.) / proclamation (n.f.)	Kerygma (n.n.) / Botschaft (n.f.)	복음선포, bogeumseonpo
kingdom	royaume (n.m.)	Königreich (n.n.)	왕국, wanggug
knowledge	connaissance (n.f.)	Wissen (n.n.)	지식, jisig
laity	laïcité (n.f.)	Laie (n.m.)	평신도, pyeongsindo
law	loi (n.f.)	Gesetz (n.n.)	율법, yulbeob
legalism	légalisme (n.m.)	Gesetzlichkeit (n.f.)	율법주의, yulbeobjuui
limited atonement	expiation limitée (n.f.)	begrenzte Sühne (n.f.)	제한적 속죄, jehanjeog sogjoe
Lord's Supper	repas du Seigneur (n.m.) / sainte cène (n.f.)	Abendmahl (n.n.)	성찬/성찬식, seongchan/seongchansig
love	amour (n.m.)	Liebe (n.f.)	사랑, salang
magisterial Reformation	réforme magistérielle (n.f.)	—	관료적 종교개혁, gwanlyojeog jonggyogaehyeog
marriage	mariage (n.m.)	Ehe (n.f.)	결혼, gyeolhon

English Term	French Translation	German Translation	Korean Translation and Transliteration
means of grace	moyens de grâces	Gnadenmittel (n.n.)	은혜의 수단(방편), *eunhyeui sudan*(*bangpyeon*)
mediator	médiateur (n.m.)	Vermittler (n.m.)	중보자, *jungboja*
memorial view	approche mémorialiste (n.f.)	Erinnerungsmahl (n.n.)	기념설, *ginyeomseol*
mercy	miséricorde (n.f.)	Barmherzigkeit (n.f.)	자비/긍휼, *jabi/geunghyul*
merit	mérite (n.m.)	Verdienst (n.n.)	공로, *gonglo*
Messiah	Messie (n.m.)	Messias (n.n.)	메시아 / 기름부음 받은 자, *Mesia* / *gileumbueum badeun Ja*
middle knowledge	connaissance du milieu (n.f.)	Mittelwissen (n.n.) / *Molinismus* (n.m.)	중간지식, *junggganjisig*
millennium	millenium (n.m.)	tausendjähriges Reich (n.n.)	천년왕국, *cheonnyeonwanggug*
mind	esprit (n.f.) / intelligence (n.f.)	Verstand (n.m.)	지성, *jiseong*
ministry	ministère (n.m.)	Dienst (n.m.)	사역, *sayeog*
miracle	miracle (n.m.)	Wunder (n.n.)	기적, *gijeog*
mission	mission (n.f.)	Mission (n.f.)	선교, *seongyo*
modalism	modalisme (n.m.)	Modalismus (n.m.)	양태론, *yangtaelon*

English Term	French Translation	German Translation	Korean Translation and Transliteration
monasticism	monachisme (n.m.)	Mönchstum (n.n.)	수도원주의, sudowonjuui
monergism	monergisme (n.m.)	Monergismus (n.m.)	단동설, dandongseol
monism	monisme (n.m.)	Monismus (n.m.)	일원론, ilwonlon
monophysitism	monophysisme (n.m.)	Monophysitismus (n.m.)	단성론, danseonglon
monotheism	monothéisme (n.m.)	Monotheismus (n.m.)	유일신론, yuilsinlon
monothelitism	monothélisme (n.m.)	Monotheletismus (n.m.)	단일의지론, daniluijilon
moral arguments	arguments moraux (n.m.)	moralische Argumente (n.n.pl.)	도덕론적 증명, dodeoglonjeog jeungmyeong
mortal sin	péché mortel (n.m.)	Todsünde (n.f.)	대죄/죽음에 이르는 죄, daejoe/jugeume ileuneun joe
mortification	mortification (n.f.)	Demütigung (n.f.)	죄 죽임, joe jugim
mystery	mystère (n.m.)	Geheimnis (n.n.)	신비/비밀, sinbi/bimil
natural headship of Adam	position naturelle d'Adam comme tête fédérale	naturhaftes Erbe (n.n.) des Adam (n.m.)	아담의 자연적 머리됨, Adamui jayeonjeog meolidoem
natural law	loi naturelle (n.f.)	Naturgesetz (n.n.)	자연법, jayeonbeob
necessity of Scripture	nécessité des écritures (n.f.)	Notwendigkeit (n.f.) der Schrift (n.f.)	성경의 필요성, Seonggyeongui pilyoseong

English Term	French Translation	German Translation	Korean Translation and Transliteration
new covenant	nouvelle alliance (n.f.)	neuer Bund (n.m.)	새 언약, sae eonyag
new heaven and new earth	nouveaux cieux et nouvelle terre	neuer Himmel (n.m.) und neue Erde (n.f.)	새 하늘과 새 땅, sae haneulgwa sae ttang
noetic effect	effet noétique (n.m.)	noetischer Effekt (n.m.)	(죄의) 인지적 영향, (joeui) injijeog yeonghyang
obedience	obéissance (n.f.)	Gehorsam (n.m.)	순종, sunjong
offices of the church	offices de l'église (n.m.)	Ämter (n.n.pl.) der Gemeinde (n.f.)	교회의 직분, gyohoeui jigbun
old covenant	ancienne alliance (n.f.)	alter Bund (n.m.)	옛 언약, yet eonyag
omnipotence	omnipotence (n.f.)	Allmacht (n.f.)	전능성, jeonneungseong
omnipresence	omniprésence (n.f.)	Allgegenwart (n.f.)	편재성, pyeonjaeseong
omniscience	omniscience (n.f.)	Allwissenheit (n.f.)	전지성, jeonjiseong
ontological arguments	arguments ontologiques (n.m.)	ontologische Argumente (n.n.pl.)	존재론적 증명, jonjaeronjeog jeungmyeong
ontological Trinity	trinité ontologique (n.f.)	ontologische Trinität (n.f.)	존재론적 삼위일체, jonjaeronjeog Samwiilche
open theism	théisme ouvert (n.m.)	offener Theismus (n.m.)	개방적 유신론, gaebangjeog yusinlon

English Term	French Translation	German Translation	Korean Translation and Transliteration
ordinance	ordonnance (n.f.)	Verordnung (n.f.)	예식, yesig
original righteousness	justice originelle (n.f.)	Ur-Gerechtigkeit (n.f.)	원의 / 원래적 의, wonui / wonlaejeog ui
original sin	péché originel (n.m.)	Ursünde (n.f.)	원죄, wonjoe
patience	patience (n.f.)	Geduld (n.f.)	인내/오래참음, inrae/olaechameum
peace	paix (n.f.)	Friede (n.m.)	평화/화평, pyeonghwa/hwapyeong
penal substitution theory	théorie de la substitution pénale (n.f.)	forensische Rechtfertigungslehre (n.f.)	형벌대속론, hyeongbeoldaesoglon
perfectionism	perfectionnisme (n.m.)	Perfektionismus (n.m.)	완전주의, wanjeonjuui
perseverance	persévérance (n.f.)	Ausharren (n.n.)	견인, gyeonin
person	personne (n.f.)	Person (n.f.)	인격/위격, ingyeog/wigyeog
perspicuity of Scripture	perspicuité de l'Écriture (n.f.)	Klarheit (n.f.) der Schrift (n.f.)	성경의 명료성, Seonggyeongui myeonglyoseong
pluralism	pluralisme (n.m.)	Pluralismus (n.m.)	다원주의, dawonjuui
pneumatology	pneumatologie (n.f.)	Pneumatologie (n.f.)	성령론, seonglyeonglon
postmillennialism	postmillénarisme (n.m.)	Postmillenniarismus (n.m.)	후천년설, hucheonnyeonseol
praise	louange (n.f.)	Anbetung (n.f.)	찬양, chanyang

English Term	French Translation	German Translation	Korean Translation and Transliteration
prayer	prière (n.f.)	Gebet (n.n.)	기도, gido
preaching	prédication (n.f.)	Predigt (n.f.)	설교, seolgyo
predestination	prédestination (n.f.)	Prädestination (n.f.)	예정, yejeong
presbyterianism	presbytérianisme (n.m.)	Presbyterianismus (n.m.) or reformierter Glaube	장로정치, janglojeongchi
prevenient grace	grâce prévenante (n.f.)	allgemeine Gnade (n.f.)	선제적 은혜, seonjaejeog eunhye
priest	prêtre (n.m.)	Priester (n.m.)	성직자/사제, seongjigja/saje
priesthood	prêtrise (n.f.)	Priestertum (n.n.)	성직자/사제직, seongjig/sajejig
profession of faith	profession de foi (n.f.)	Glaubensbekenntnis (n.n.)	신앙고백, sinanggobaeg
progressive revelation	révélation progressive (n.f.)	progressive Offenbarung (n.f.)	점진적 계시, jeomjinjeog gyesi
promise	promesse (n.f.)	Versprechen (n.n.)	약속, yagsog
prophecy	prophétie (n.f.)	Prophetie (n.f.)	예언, yeeon
prophet	prophète (n.m.)	Prophet (n.m.)	선지자, seonjija
propitiation	propitiation (n.f.)	Versöhnung (n.f.)	유화(속죄), yuhwa(sogjoe)
providence	providence (n.f.)	Vorsehung (n.f.)	섭리, seobli
purgatory	purgatoire (n.m.)	Fegefeuer (n.n.)	연옥, yeonog

English Term	French Translation	German Translation	Korean Translation and Transliteration
radical Reformation	réforme radicale (n.f.)	radikale Reformation (n.f.)	급진적 종교개혁, geubjinjeog jonggyogaehyeog
rapture	enlèvement (n.m.)	Entrückung (n.f.)	휴거, hyugeo
real presence of Christ	présence réelle du Christ (n.f.)	Realpräsenz (n.f.) Christi (n.m.)	실제적 임재설, siljaejeog imjaeseol
reason	raison (n.f.)	Vernunft (n.f.)	이성, iseong
reconciliation	réconciliation (n.f.)	Versöhnung (n.f.)	화목/화해, hwamog/hwahae
redemption	rédemption (n.f.)	Erlösung (n.f.)	구속, gusog
regeneration	régénération (n.f.)	Wiederherstellung (n.f.)	중생, jungsaeng
repentance	repentance (n.f.)	Buße (n.f.)	회개, hoegae
representative headship of Adam	Adam comme représentant en sa qualité de tête fédérale	repräsentatives Erbe (n.n.) des Adam (n.m.)	아담의 대표적 머리 됨, Adamui daepyojeog meolidoem
reprobation	réprobation (n.f.)	Verwerfung (n.f.)	유기, yugi
resurrection	résurrection (n.f.)	Auferstehung (n.f.)	부활, buhwal
righteousness	justice (n.f.)	Gerechtigkeit (n.f.)	의/의로움, ui/uiloum
sacrament	sacrement (n.m.)	Sakrament (n.n.)	성례, seonglye
saints	saints (n.m.)	Heilige (n.m.pl.)	성도, seongdo

English Term	French Translation	German Translation	Korean Translation and Transliteration
salvation	salut (n.m.)	Errettung (n.f.)	구원, guwon
sanctification	sanctification (n.f.)	Heiligung (n.f.)	성화, seonghwa
saving faith	foi qui sauve / foi salvatrice (n.f.)	rettender Glaube (n.m.)	구원하는 믿음, guwonhaneun mideum
saving grace	grâce salvatrice (n.f.)	rettende Gnade (n.f.)	구원하는 은혜, guwonhaneun eunhye
Scripture	écriture (n.f.)	Schrift (n.f.)	성경/성서, Seonggyeong/Seongseo
second coming	seconde venue (n.f.)	das zweite Kommen (n.n.)	재림, jaelim
servant	serviteur (n.m.)	Diener (n.m.)	종, jong
service	service (n.m.)	Dienst (n.m.)	섬김, seomgim
session of Christ	intronisation du Christ	Sitzung (n.f.) Christi (n.m.)	보좌에 앉으신 그리스도, bojwae anjeusin Geuliseudo
shame	honte (n.f.)	Schande (n.f.)	부끄러움/수치, bukkeuleoum/suchi
sin	péché (n.m.)	Sünde (n.f.)	죄, joe
sin nature	nature pécheresse (n.f.)	Sündennatur (n.f.)	죄성, joeseong
social Trinity	relations intratrinitaires	soziale Trinität (n.f.)	사회적 삼위일체, sahoejeog Samwiilche

English Term	French Translation	German Translation	Korean Translation and Transliteration
soteriology	sotériologie (n.f.)	Soteriologie (n.f.)	구원론, guwonlon
soul	âme (n.f.)	Seele (n.f.)	혼, hon
sovereignty	souveraineté (n.f.)	Souveränität (n.f.)	주권, jugwon
special revelation	révélation spéciale (n.f.)	besondere Offenbarung (n.f.)	특별계시, teugbyeolgaesi
spirit	esprit (n.m.)	Geist (n.m.)	영, yeong
spiritual presence	présence spirituelle (n.f.)	geistliche Gegenwart (n.f.)	영적 임재설, yeongjeogimjaeseol
stewardship	intendance (n.f.)	Haushalten (n.n.)	청지기직, cheongjigijig
submission	soumission (n.f.)	Unterwerfung (n.f.)	복종, bogjong
subordinationism	subordinatianisme (n.m.)	Subordinatianismus (n.m.)	종속설, jongsogseol
substance	substance (n.f.)	Substanz (n.f.)	실체, silche
suffering	souffrance (n.f.)	Leiden (n.n.)	고통/고난, gotong/gonan
sufficiency of Scripture	suffisance des Écritures (n.f.)	Genügsamkeit (n.f.) der Schrift (n.f.)	성경의 충분성, Seonggyeongui chungbunseong
systematic theology	théologie systématique (n.f.)	systematische Theologie (n.f.)	조직신학, jojigsinhag
teaching	enseignement / instruction (n.m.)	Lehre (n.f.)	교육, gyoyug

English Term	French Translation	German Translation	Korean Translation and Transliteration
teleological arguments	arguments téléologiques (n.m.)	teleologische Argumente (n.n.pl.)	목적론적 증명, mogjeoglonjeog jeungmyeong
thanksgiving	actions de grâces (n.f.)	Dank (n.m.), Dankbarkeit (gratitude) (n.f.)	감사, gamsa
theodicy	théodicée (n.f.)	Theodizee (n.f.)	신정론, sinjeonglon
total depravity	dépravation totale (n.f.)	völlige Verderbtheit (n.f.)	전적 타락, jeonjeog talag
total inability	incapacité totale (n.f.)	völlige Unfähigkeit (n.f.)	전적 무능, jeonjeog muneung
tradition	tradition (n.f.)	Tradition (n.f.)	전통, jeontong
traducianism	traducianisme (n.m.)	Traduzianismus (n.m.)	영혼 유전설, yeonghon yujeonseol
transcendence	transcendance (n.f.)	Transzendenz (n.f.)	초월성, chowolseong
trichotomy	trichotomie (n.f.)	Trichotomie (n.f.)	삼분설, sambunseol
truth	vérité (n.f.)	Wahrheit (n.f.)	진리, jinli
unconditional election	élection inconditionnelle (n.f.)	bedingungslose Erwählung (n.f.)	무조건적 선택, mujogeonjeog seontaeg
unity	unité (n.f.)	Einheit (n.f.)	통일성, tongilseong
universalism	universalisme (n.m.)	Universalismus (n.m.)	만인 구원설, manin guwonseol
unlimited atonement	expiation illimitée (n.f.)	begrenzte Sühne (n.f.)	무제한적 속죄, mujehanjeog sojoe

English Term	French Translation	German Translation	Korean Translation and Transliteration
venial sin	péché véniel (n.m.)	lässliche Sünde (n.f.)	소죄 / 용서받을 수 있는 죄, sojoe / yongseobadeul su inneun joe
vicarious substitution	vicaire/remplacement	stellvertretend	대리적/대속적, daelijeog/daesogjeog
virgin birth / virginal conception	naissance virginale (n.f.) / conception virginale (n.f.)	Jungfrauengeburt (n.f.)	동정녀 탄생 / 동정녀 잉태, dongjeongnyeo tansaeng / dongjeongnyeo ingtae
vocation	vocation (n.f.)	Berufung (n.f.)	소명/부르심, somyeong/buleusim
will	volonté (n.f.)	Wille (n.m.)	뜻/의지, tteus/uiji
wisdom	sagesse (n.f.)	Weisheit (n.f.)	지혜, jihye
Word of God	Parole de Dieu (n.f.)	Wort (n.n.) Gottes (n.m.)	하나님의 말씀, Hananimui Malsseum
work	travail (n.m.)	Arbeit (n.f.)	일/행위, il/haengwi
worship	adoration (n.f.)	Anbetung (n.f.)	예배, yebae
wrath	colère (n.f.)	Zorn (n.m.)	진노, jinno

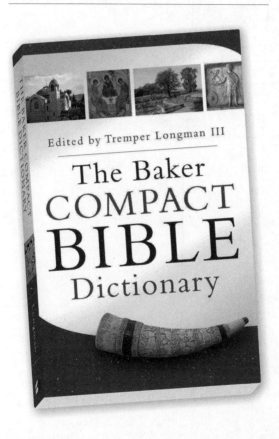

Bring the Bible to life with these **full-color resources**

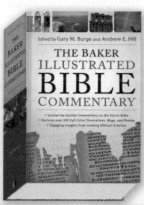

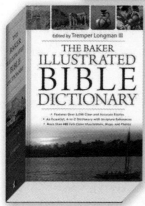

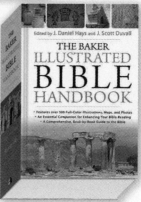